LOGICAL ABILITIES IN CHILDREN

VOLUME 3

**Reasoning in Adolescence:
Deductive Inference**

CHILD PSYCHOLOGY

A series of volumes edited by **David S. Palermo**

Logical Abilities in Children

BY DANIEL N. OSHERSON

University of Pennsylvania

VOLUME 3

REASONING IN ADOLESCENCE: DEDUCTIVE INFERENCE

 LAWRENCE ERLBAUM ASSOCIATES, PUBLISHERS

1975   Hillsdale, New Jersey

DISTRIBUTED BY THE HALSTED PRESS DIVISION OF

JOHN WILEY & SONS

New York   Toronto   London   Sydney

Lawrence Erlbaum Associates, Inc., Publishers
62 Maria Drive
Hillsdale, New Jersey 07642

Distributed solely by Halsted Press Division
John Wiley & Sons, Inc., New York

Library of Congress Cataloging in Publication Data
Osherson, Daniel H
    Reasoning in adolescence.

    (His Logical abilities in children; v. 3)
(Child psychology)
    Bibliography: p.
    Includes indexes.
    1. Reasoning (Child psychology)   2. Adolescent
psychology.   I. Title.   II. Series: Child psychology.
LB1134.084 vol.3 [BF724.3.R4] 370.15'2s[155.5]
ISBN 0-470-65730-8   75-25623

Printed in the United States of America

Contents

Preface

Volume 2 of this series presented a model for certain deductive abilities in children and adults. A partial explanation of the growth of these abilities was also suggested. In this volume the model is much expanded with regard to both propositional logic and the logic of class inclusion. For this purpose a new methodology is employed. Several chapters of the book are devoted to the effect of content in deductive reasoning. Developmental questions are formulated differently than before. Only data from adolescent subjects are presented, but the stage is set in this volume for potentially illuminating developmental comparisons. This comes in Volume 4.

A number of people provided helpful comments on the manuscript, including Janet Davis, Ellen Markman, Rochel Gelman, D. Paul Snyder, Edward E. Smith, and Ewart Thomas. Janet Davis also ran the laboratory from which the experiments originated; she accomplished this with a combination of care and imagination that has left its imprint on the finished work. The research was supported by grant number GB 44078 from the National Science Foundation.

The model developed in this book is innocent of concerns that I now consider central to the study of deductive reasoning. Discussion of these matters begins in Sections 21.2 and 21.3 and resumes in Volume 4.

LOGICAL ABILITIES IN CHILDREN

VOLUME 3

**Reasoning in Adolescence:
Deductive Inference**

Part I

INTRODUCTION

1

Developmental Issues

1.1 AN OLD QUESTION REEXAMINED

Children think differently than adults. This much is undeniable. Disputes arise when developmental psychologists attempt to characterize this difference, account for it, and explain why the difference decreases as the child matures. These three questions are related and appear also to be ordered. Explaining how the gap between children's and adults' reasoning diminishes with maturity presupposes an explanation for the differences at any given age, and the latter explanation requires elucidation of what those differences are. So the question "What is the difference between children's and adults' thinking?" is basic.

Yet this basic question harbors subquestions. One of these is: "Are children's thought processes qualitatively different than those of adults, that is, are there discontinuities in the development of reasoning, or are the differences only of degree in the scope and power of a common intellectual faculty?"[1] Clarification of the ideas of discontinuity and differences of degree would be helpful here (see Pinard & Laurendeau, 1969; Toulmin, 1971). We shall return to the matter in Section 1.4, but the question in general outline is clear.

Many developmental psychologists would answer this question on the basis of Piaget's work. To these psychologists, it is evident that Piaget has demonstrated qualitative disparities between adult and juvenile thought

---

[1] The question is limited to thought processes and excludes the ideas that may result from them. The latter could be judged qualitatively different in children and adults without the former being so judged. For example, a small difference in memory span could result in a large difference in the conclusions one would be willing to draw from a long list of premises (cf. Trabasso, Riley, & Wilson, 1975).

processes as well as between the thinking of children at different stages of development. While stressing the continuity of the transition between developmental stages, Piaget's theory is based squarely on the claim that these stages are qualitatively distinct (see Flavell, 1963, pp. 19–24; Piaget, 1973, pp. 49–50).

Other psychologists believe that positing such stages to account for the peculiarities of children's reasoning is unnecessary, that more continuous differences in memory capacity or other information-processing parameters are sufficient to explain children's performance in Piagetian-type reasoning tasks (e.g., Pascual-Leone, 1970; Trabasso, Riley, & Wilson, 1975). Basic cognitive functioning is the same.[2] Fodor (1972) formulates one version of this position this way:

> One thus considers the possibility of viewing the mental life of children in a way that is quite alien to the Vygotskyian (or the Piagetian) tradition. Classical developmental psychology invites us to think of the child as a realization of an algebra which can be applied, relatively indifferently, to a wide variety of types of cognitive integrations, but which differs in essential respects from the mathematics underlying adult mentation. The alternative picture is that the child is a bundle of relatively special purpose computational systems which are formally analogous to those involved in adult cognition but which are quite restricted in their range of application, each being more or less tightly tied to the computation of a specific sort of data, more or less rigidly endogenously paced, and relatively inaccessible to purposes and influences other than those which conditioned its evolution. Cognitive development, on this view, is the maturation of the processes such systems subserve, and the gradual broadening of the kinds of computations to which they can apply [pp. 92–93].

Fodor's view of cognitive development is contrary to Piaget's, and it is no less plausible on first examination.[3] Deciding between these two positions would help us construct a revealing description of the difference between children's and adults' thinking. Such a characterization, moreover, would inform one's theory of developmental change. These issues concern this book.

1.2 THE ADOLESCENT BOUNDARY: PIAGET'S HYPOTHESIS

Having formulated the problem in general terms, we now focus and narrow it (not beyond recognition, hopefully). If cognitive functioning changes qualitatively during development, the transition from childhood to adoles-

---

[2] This view was also advanced in Volume 2 (Osherson, 1974b; hereafter referred to as Volume 2), Chapter 7, and Section 11.4. In this Volume we examine the issue afresh.

[3] Sinclair (1972), however, accuses Fodor of some misrepresentation of Piaget's theory.

cence will likely mark one such transformation. Adolescence brings physical and emotional changes. It is plausible that intellectual reorganization accompanies them. There is already support for the idea that efficient language learning strategies are available only through childhood (Lenneberg, 1967). In this book we begin to investigate whether adolescence brings a reorganization of the mental operations underlying logical competence.[4]

Piaget's theory offers an affirmative answer to the question of whether there are qualitative changes in the reasoning of children and adolescents. From age 7 or 8 (roughly) to puberty, children are said to be *concrete operational*. During adolescence they become *formal operational*. These are different stages. Stages are discontinuous, providing a qualitative change in the mental operations governing logical reasoning. According to Genevan theory, mental operations exist only interdependently, within systems called *structures*. Different mental structures flourish in different stages of development; in fact they are one defining characteristic for stages. The difference between concrete and formal operational thought thus resides in the different structures underlying each. The structure proper to concrete operations is called the *grouping*. The structures for formal operations involve a lattice of Boolean functions, as well as a group of transformations that operate on these functions (viz., the "INRC" group, consisting of identity, negative, reciprocal, and correlative transformations of Boolean functions). The difference in structures for these two stages suggest a dramatic change in reasoning at adolescence.

However, Piaget's theoretical account of the differences he finds in adolescent and childhood reasoning must be questioned. One difficulty is that the structures Piaget postulates for the different stages enjoy only tenuous connections to the experiments Piaget has performed. Moreover, these structures are incoherent in certain respects. Regarding the first point, consider the conservation paradigms (Piaget, 1965). Piaget claims that success in these problems rests on the presence of groupings. But it is unclear how the laws of groupings given by Piaget (1942, 1949) allow the deduction that a quantity of liquid is invariant through changes in the shape of its container, but escape the deduction that the surface area of the liquid (including the area contiguous to the sides of the container) is also conserved. To see the difficulty, consider the three kinds of conservation explanations that Piagetians accept, i.e., reversibility, no addition or subtraction,

---

[4] Only logical abilities in the "strict sense" of Volume 2, Chapter 1 are directly investigated. The distinction drawn in Volume 2 between logical abilities in the strict sense and broader senses was not designed to separate standard extensional logic from the study of other kinds of logical truth. We agree with Katz (1972) that such a separation would be an arbitrary division among necessary inferences. We argued only that it is worthwhile to know what kind of inferential reasoning is being studied at a given moment.

and compensation. A similar question arises for other properties of things that are variant or invariant through different transformations.[5] Equally important, at the level of generality at which Piaget discusses the relationship between groupings and conservation (e.g., Piaget & Inhelder, 1969, pp. 95–99), no hint is given why the grouping rather than some other algebra is invoked for explanation. At the analogical level with which Piaget is content, many alternative systems will embody the key Piagetian concepts of "reversibility," "identity," "associativity," etc. The same problems beset Piaget's treatment of concrete operational classificatory skills, number skills, etc. See Flavell (1963, Chapter 5) for a review of the kinds of abilities relevant to groupings.

The evidence supporting the formal operational structures is no more convincing. Bynum, Thomas, and Weitz (1972), for example, find little in Inhelder and Piaget's (1958) data to support the claim that adolescents possess the lattice of all binary truth-functional operations.

In addition to the lack of empirical grounding, the structures that Piaget posits are suspect for internal reasons. In *The Psychology of Intelligence* (1950; see also Flavell, 1963), Piaget describes a grouping as a group with the additional condition he calls "tautology": for all elements, x, of the grouping, $x \circ x = x$, where "$\circ$" is the grouping operation.[6] In other places (e.g., Piaget, 1942, 1957, 1970a) a further law is given, called "resorption," stating that some elements, presumably not themselves the identity element, can operate on at least one other element and leave it unchanged. In other words, there is an element $y \neq e$, such that $x \circ y = x$ for at least one x.[7] But a group restricted by the tautology law is mathematically trivial in the sense of having no more than one member. This is because (a) the identity element of a group is unique, and (b) the only idempotent element of a group, that is, the only element for which Piaget's "tautology" law holds, is the identity element. The proof of this last statement is as follows: Assume $x \circ x = x$. Then, by the inverse and composition laws of groups, $(x \circ x) \circ x^{-1} = x \circ x^{-1}$. By associativity, $x \circ (x \circ x^{-1}) = x \circ x^{-1}$. This yields $x \circ e = e$ by the inverse law, giving $x = e$ by the identity law. So, every element for which the tautology property, $x \circ x = x$, is true is identical to e. But in groupings all elements enjoy the tautology property. Therefore, groupings

[5] This difficulty is compounded by the claim that the conservations become necessary truths for the concrete operational child. See Hall and Kingsely (1968), and Volume 2, Chapter 1.

[6] For a more detailed exposition of the abstract grouping laws as well as their interpretation into more concrete settings, see Volume 1 (Osherson, 1974a; hereafter referred to as Volume 1), Chapter 1, or Flavell (1963).

[7] It is not clear whether this law is meant to be: $\forall x \, \exists y(x \circ y = x \cdot \& \cdot y \neq e)$, or: $\exists x \, \exists y(x \circ y = x \cdot \& \cdot y \neq e)$. The distinctness of y from e seems not to be explicitly stated, but without it, either version of the resorption law is deducible from the identity law for groups.

have one element at most. This fact condemns groupings as systematizations of classificatory skills since classification involves more than one classified item. If we add the resorption property to groupings, with its stipulation of an element distinct from e, then the grouping is self-contradictory.

The demonstration that groupings are trivial (and perhaps contradictory) will not go through unless associativity and composition are unrestricted. In some places (Piaget, 1949, 1970a; Piaget & Inhelder, 1969) limitations on these properties are indicated. In other sources, including *The Psychology of Intelligence,* such limitations are not stated. Hence, at best, the grouping structure is not formulated clearly enough for serious examination.[8]

According to Genevans, formal operational thought includes mastery, in an implicit sense, of the truths of (standard) propositional logic (Inhelder & Piaget, 1958). Piaget employs lattices of n-place Boolean operations and INRC groups of transformations to represent the adolescent's logical competence.[9] As indicated above, one difficulty with this representation is that it is grossly underdetermined by Inhelder and Piaget's (1958) data. The truths of propositional logic can be captured in a variety of formal schemes. Little reason is provided for preferring Piaget's. It is true that many representations of propositional logic will not meet the criteria for true structures, as stated by Piaget (1970b). This might appear to be one reason for favoring Piaget's system. But imposing such preconditions on the representation of logical competence begs the ostensibly empirical question of whether Piaget's kind of structures are appropriate for the job. The claim that intellect is structured in the Piagetian fashion is supposed to be an empirically demonstrable claim based on data. But, in the case of lattices at least, the data of Inhelder and Piaget (1958) do not seem to demand this representation over others that also yield propositional logic.

In addition, there are internal problems with the formal schemes that Inhelder and Piaget (1958) present. Parsons (1960) has treated these thoroughly.[10] We give one illustration from Parsons' review. On Piaget's interpretation of propositional logic, two formulas based on the same propositions can both be true only if the formulas are logically equivalent. Thus, in Piaget's system, if p & q is true, then p ∨ q must be false; if p ↔ q is true, then $p \rightarrow q$ must be false, etc. These strange results are not a feature of propo-

[8] Rigorous axiomatizations of the grouping have been devised, however, especially by J. B. Grize (1960). See Volume 1 for discussion.

[9] But see Wason and Johnson-Laird (1972), who question whether adults honor the truths of propositional logic. See Bynum *et al.* (1972) for a convincing argument that not even Inhelder and Piaget's (1958) subjects demonstrate an implicit grasp of all 16 binary propositional operations.

[10] Papert (1963) replies.

sitional logic as commonly understood, nor are they likely to correspond to adolescents' intuitions about implication. (On the other hand, Piaget's system has some plausibility as an account of mature inductive reasoning in the experimental situations described in Inhelder & Piaget, 1958.)

There is, of course, more to Piaget's theory of concrete and formal operational thought than the formalisms he invokes. According to Piaget, a major difference between the stages is that the adolescent can reason with the hypothetical, rather than being restricted, like the child, to the actual (see Flavell, 1963, pp. 202–211). Connected to this difference, only the adolescent can combinatorily construct a set of possibilities that exhaust the potential hypotheses relevant to a given phenomenon.

The claim that children cannot reason hypothetically, however, seems to be contradicted by studies showing that children do have a modest ability to deduce conclusions from arbitrary premises (e.g., Suppes, 1965). On the other hand, Shapiro and O'Brien (1970) have shown that this task is more difficult for 6-, 7-, and 8-year-olds when they are given the option of responding "not enough clues" to an argument, rather than deciding simply whether it is the conclusion of an argument or its negation that follows from the argument's premises. Further research can clarify this issue. Similarly, further work is required to determine the causes and extent of the difference in hypothesis generation between children and adolescents. Certainly the child can generate some hypotheses. Equally clearly, the adolescent cannot generate all the hypotheses that could account for a given phenomenon. On even a mild interpretation of "possible," the set of possible explanations for anything is infinite.[11] The more restricted claim that children cannot produce all possible combinations of a small set of two-valued dimensions has not yet been subjected to much empirical testing.

We conclude that the issue of qualitative discontinuities between children and adolescents in logical reasoning is still open, despite the obviously important work of Piaget.

1.3   THE IDEA OF A QUALITATIVE DIFFERENCE

We have asked whether there is a qualitative change in logical competence between childhood and adolescence. It is not evident, however, what to count as such a change. Much of the present book is devoted to this problem. Appealing to the continuity or discontinuity of the transition from one level to the next is no help. Whether a change looks continuous or

[11] In particular, the adolescents who solve the problem of "colored and colorless chemical bodies" in Chapter 7 of Inhelder and Piaget (1958) do not generate all of the possible causes of the appearance of yellow coloring in the test fluid.

discontinuous depends as much on the precision of measurement as on the phenomenon itself.

Sheer observation and cataloging of childhood and adolescent abilities, no matter how carefully and sympathetically done, will also not suffice for deciding whether the change is qualitative. This is a point to which we shall return many times. Surface differences can hide deeper similarities. Compare the sound pattern of Jamaican English and New York English. Speakers of the two dialects are virtually unintelligible to each other. Yet at a deeper level the languages are similar. Even clearer cases of this type involve "Pig Latin" versions of natural languages (see Keyser & Halle, 1968).[12] In the same way, it is possible that distinct patterns of logical abilities in children and adolescents result from similar reasoning processes.[13] Conversely, there is the danger that superficially similar abilities may mask genuine differences in the mental structures mediating them. As a simple example, different algorithms for finding square roots of numbers can result in identical performance on a test of this ability.

The question of qualitative differences is best answered in light of well-supported theories of the phenomena in question. Jamaican and New York English are considered dialects of the same language because the difference between them can be largely predicted by small variations in the phonological component of their grammars. In the same way, regardless of the superficial similarities or dissimilarities between adolescent and childhood logical abilities, we should judge the underlying thought processes governing these abilities to be similar if and only if the theories accounting for the abilities at the two ages are similar.

Such an emphasis on theory may seem to shift the problem of qualitative differences rather than solve it. Whereas before we had to decide on the basis of the data alone, now we have to decide on the basis of theories that explain the data. But when are two theoretical accounts qualitatively different and when are they the same? Conceivably, criteria could be supplied that would do justice to the notion of qualitatively similar theoretical explanations. But such criteria are not necessary, since some vagueness at this level is innocuous. For equivocal cases, a detailed comparison of two theories for different age levels deprives of interest the question of whether the theories "genuinely" differ qualitatively. It is also true of the present conception that whether two phenomena are considered alike or unalike depends on the state of current theorizing. Moreover, proponents of different theories may answer the question differently. This, too, is as it should be.

[12] For a general statement regarding the underlying reality of language, as distinct from its surface manifestations, see Katz (1971).

[13] More is said about this possibility in Chapter 13, after a model for inferential abilities is presented.

1.4   PLAN OF THIS WORK

In sum, to determine the nature of cognitive development between child-hood and adolescence, with particular concern for logical reasoning, it will be necessary to construct viable theories of reasoning for both children and adolescents separately. The resulting theories may then be compared.[14] We believe that information-processing models are a suitable kind of theory for this purpose.

In Volume 2 (Osherson, 1974b; hereafter referred to as Volume 2) a fragment of a process-model logic was proposed. It was based on data from adults and 10- and 11-year-olds. The present volume focuses on adolescents. The previous model is expanded to account for a wider range of inferential abilities. Our aim is to provide a theory of adolescent logical inference that is sufficiently general and empirically well-enough supported to justify a comparison with a similar model for childhood logical inference (if one can be constructed). The remainder of the present work largely ignores children and developmental issues in general. But the narrowness of our present concerns represents no more than a strategic retreat. The developmental question posed in Section 1.1 is our ultimate concern.

This book is organized as follows: The research question is presented and discussed in Chapter 2. Chapter 3 describes some broad theoretical alternatives. Chapter 4 illustrates one of these alternatives. Chapter 5 concerns criteria of adequacy for models like ours. Chapter 6 discusses methodological issues. The overall method for all the experiments reported in the book is presented in Chapter 7. Chapters 8–12 develop the model and test it against data from five experiments. Chapters 13–19 attempt to extend the model to problems with more familiar causal contexts, and to problems dealing with class inclusion.

---

[14] The latter comparison would obviously not be necessary should the data for the two theories be identical, that is, if there is no discernible difference in the logical performance of children and adolescents on every logic task. It is certain, however, that such differences exist.

2

The Research Question Sharpened

2.1 ARGUMENTS

The logical abilities to be investigated in adolescents pertain to *arguments,* in the logical sense of this term. An argument is a finite list of statements, one being designated as the *conclusion,* the rest as *premises,* as in the following schema:

$$P_1$$
$$P_2$$
$$.$$
$$.$$
$$.$$
$$\frac{P_n}{C}$$

Four things are worth knowing about an argument. These are (*a*) whether the conclusion is true; (*b*) whether the premises are true; (*c*) whether the argument is inductively strong; and (*d*) whether the argument is deductively valid. Logic has no interest in (*a*) and (*b*) for their own sake. Rather, logic concerns the relation between the truth of the premises and the truth of the conclusion. *Inductive logic* bears on (*c*). *Deductive logic* bears on (*d*). According to Skyrms (1966), "an argument is *deductively valid* if and only if it is *impossible* that its conclusion is false while its premises are true [p. 7]."[1] On the other hand, "an argument is *inductively*

---

[1] Important problems attend this use of the word "impossible." We rely on our subjects' intuitions about when conclusions are "necessarily true," given certain premises. Whether this kind of procedure provides clarification of ideas like "possibility" and related notions is currently controversial. See Katz (1967) and Quine (1972b). See also Section 5.3, below.

strong if and only if it is *improbable* that its conclusion is false [given that] its premises are true, and it is not deductively valid." The following is an example of a deductively valid (or, more briefly, *valid*) argument:

Premise: All millionaires live in Brooklyn.
Premise: The Rockefellers do not live in Brooklyn.
Conclusion: The Rockefellers are not millionaires.

Notice that the argument is valid despite the falsity of both its first premise and its conclusion. An example of an inductively strong argument is the following:

Premise: Fish exist on Mars.
Premise: Turtles exist on Mars.
Premise: Lizards exist on Mars.
Premise: Salamanders exist on Mars.
Conclusion: Frogs exist on Mars.

Notice that the argument is not deductively valid. (See Skyrms, 1966, for an introduction to inductive logic.)

We are concerned in this book with the validity of simple arguments. Inductive strength is not at issue. A person cannot have memorized all the arguments that he recognizes as valid. There are too many such arguments.[2] Instead, he must be constructing them in some manner. We hope to shed light on that process.

A psychological literature exists on how adults decide whether arguments are valid. We shall appeal to these studies in subsequent chapters. Most of the experiments in previous studies involve Aristotelian syllogisms (also known as *categorical syllogisms*). In contrast, most of the arguments that we shall employ come from propositional logic. The logic of simple class relations is also treated. Categorical syllogisms are discussed in Wason and Johnson-Laird (1972), and in Revlis (1975). These authors also provide excellent literature reviews.

We shall say that a subject *accepts* or *honors* an argument if he thinks that it is valid. A subject *rejects* an argument that he thinks is invalid.

2.2   TWO WAYS TO DECIDE THE VALIDITY
OF AN ARGUMENT

This book bears on *deductive inference,* or, in other words, on the use of a deductively valid argument to infer the truth of a conclusion from given premises. These sorts of inferences are of two kinds: one kind in-

---

[2] Our intuitions about valid arguments have, in fact, a surprisingly broad range. Section 21.4 provides a sample of the kind of arguments about which we automatically and implicitly generate intuitions.

volves *proofs* or *derivations,* the other kind concerns our more immediate logical judgment or intuition.

When we construct a proof, we infer the last line of the proof from the given premises. Normally, one or more intermediate steps fill the gap between premises and conclusion. The logical connection between each successive step should be intuitively obvious if the proof is to serve as a convincing demonstration of the truth of the conclusion. But until the proof is devised, the logical connection between the premises and conclusion may not be obvious at all. Indeed, the proof is necessary only because we cannot grasp such logical relationships all in one intuitive step. The ability to assemble a desired proof will be called *proof-finding ability.* In contrast, the ability to recognize the validity of simple arguments (including successive steps in a proof) will be said to require logical judgment or intuition. Psychologically, logical judgments are not themselves felt to require proof, but are rather themselves the stuff out of which proofs are made.[3] An example was given in Section 2.1 of a deductive argument requiring (for most people) only logical judgment.

The present research involves logical judgment, not proof-finding ability. Subjects in the experiments to be reported were not asked to construct derivations of conclusions from premises. Judging from their introspective reports neither did they construct a conscious derivation spontaneously. Rather, in postexperimental interviews, subjects often report that they repeat the premises and conclusion to themselves a number of times until they "figure it out." Insight typically comes suddenly, although the problem might require some minutes of study.

The following arguments illustrate the kind of deduction germane to the present work:

(a)   Premise: If either Steve runs the store or Jane runs the store, then the profits are high.
      Premise: Steve runs the store.
      ———————————————————————————————
      Conclusion: The profits are high.

(b)   Premise: Pam is in school and either she is learning physics or she is learning math.
      ———————————————————————————————
      Conclusion: Either Pam is in school and she is learning physics, or Pam is in school and she is learning math.

(c)   Premise: If the test is either multiple choice or true–false, then Kate gets a good grade.
      Premise: Kate does not get a good grade.
      ———————————————————————————————
      Conclusion: The test is not multiple choice.

[3] This is not to say that further justification of logical intuition is impossible, but only that most people do not typically desire further justification.

Evaluating the validity of these arguments does not seem to involve conscious proof construction. The problems used in the experiments reported here were of a similar nature.

In contrast to logical intuition, Newell and Simon (1963a) have provided insight into the psychology of proof finding. Their work on adult problem-solving strategies, however, including the simulation known as the Logic Theorist, is not directly relevant to the present work. Their work relates to the explicit, verbal introspections of college students asked to convert abstract formulas of symbolic logic into other formulas by means of given conversion rules. Newell and Simon (1963b) stress their interest in conscious, step-by-step reasoning:

> The first thing we have learned—and the evidence is by now quite substantial—is that we can explain many of the processes of human thinking without postulating mechanisms at subconscious levels which are different from those that are partly conscious and partly verbalized. The processes of problem solving, it is turning out, are the familiar processes of noticing, searching, modifying the search direction on the basis of clues, and so on [p. 402].

Our research question, by comparison, has to do with a more intuitive and unconscious variety of problem solving. Our problems provoke a more sudden apprehension than those employed by Newell and Simon.

Another difference is that subjects in the Newell and Simon task do not decide whether an argument is valid but are asked only to find the abstract derivation that shows it to be so. Our subjects are asked to decide whether each argument presented to them is logically valid.

A third, more important, difference is that our experiments concern intuitions about necessary truth, namely, the logical connection of premises and conclusions. To facilitate this, in our experiments the arguments are formulated in natural language. The Newell and Simon task, in contrast, seems not to pertain to such intuitions, since subjects work within an uninterpreted formal system whose rules are, from their point of view, arbitrary. Newell and Simon (1972, p. 405) comment on their task of "solving problems in a simple system of symbolic logic." They say: "In a sense this label for the task is misleading, since the subjects whose behavior will be examined were not told that they were concerned with symbolic logic, but instead that they were to 'recode' certain strings of symbols into other, specified, strings, using a given set of rules to transform the strings."[4] From the point of view of the subject, the strings employed in the Newell and Simon task are meaningless. The subject treats them "entirely in terms of their syntactic properties and without reference to semantic meaning

---

[4] Naturally, one could convert the arguments used here into formulas of symbolic logic and use these formulas in the Newell and Simon task. The point is that these problems, at least for our subjects, do not require that kind of treatment.

[p. 407]." Although standard symbols for propositional logic are used, the subjects do not know their intended interpretation; nor are they told.

We shall make use of the Newell and Simon (1972) idea of searching for and eliminating differences between premises and conclusions of arguments. Moreover, the formal structure of the theory to be developed in this book puts it within the broad class of automata that Newell and Simon (1972, Chapter 2) call *production systems*. Nevertheless, the previous discussion shows that the present research problem is distinct from that of Newell and Simon.

It might be asked whether the boundary between proof finding and logical judgment is a sharp one. Perhaps proof finding grades continuously into logical intuition rather than being qualitatively distinct from it. In line with the discussion of Section 1.3, this question of continuity—discontinuity is best answered in light of theories for each kind of paradigm. Newell and Simon have devised a theory for proof finding. We shall propose a fragment of a theory for logical intuition. Comparison of the theories may or may not reveal interesting similarities. In any event, the possibility that proof finding and logical intuition are only quantitatively different does not jeopardize the distinction urged in this section. Logical abilities at the opposite poles of a common continuum are nonetheless distinct. We may attempt to study one in isolation from the other.

3

Three Kinds of Models for
Logical Judgment

This chapter concerns three classes of models for logical judgment. It may be omitted without loss of continuity.

3.1 RECOURSE TO FORMAL LOGIC

Logicians have devised techniques to sort valid from invalid arguments. These techniques may be considered competence models for selected areas of logical judgment. Like any competence model, they can be evaluated with respect to the fidelity with which they match actual judgment, among other criteria.[1] Such techniques might provide a clue to the mechanisms used by ordinary people to evaluate arguments.[2]

Three broad classes of methods for determining the validity of arguments exist. They may be called *logistic, semantic,* and *natural deductive.* We examine them in turn, asking which, if any, approximate actual human processes. Our discussion is limited to propositional logic since most of the experimental arguments fit propositional notation. Propositional logic serves as a simple example from which general lessons may be learned.

[1] But see Section 5.3. For illuminating discussion of classical logic as a competence model of human judgment, see Wason and Johnson-Laird (1972) and Katz (1972, Preface). J. D. Fodor (1970) compares formal logic with the transformational kind of competence model for natural language; see also Volume 2, Section 5.4. For some further remarks, see Osherson (1975), although we shall reach somewhat different conclusions here.

[2] Naturally, there is no guarantee that such competence models will resemble the real-time mental steps involved in the logical judgment of untutored subjects. This general point about competence models was made forcefully in the domain of language (see Fodor & Garrett, 1966).

3.2 LOGISTIC SYSTEMS

A logistic system is a formal axiomatization of a logic. The axioms and rules of inference of a successful logistic system allow the deduction of all the truths of the logic being axiomatized. In more detail, following Copi (1967, pp. 190–194), a logistic system is comprised of (*a*) a list of primitive symbols, (*b*) a syntactic criterion for labeling any sequence of these primitive symbols as either a *well-formed* or ill-formed formula (but not both), (*c*) a list of well-formed formulas to serve as axioms of the system,[3] and (*d*) a syntactic criterion for deciding whether a list of well-formed formulas $f_1, \ldots, f_n$ is a *demonstration* of f_n.

The notion of a demonstration relies on the presence of *inference rules* that characterize the admissible transformations of formulas $f_1, \ldots, f_m$ into a new formula f_n of the demonstration. These inference rules are not themselves well-formed formulas, or even expressible in terms of the system's primitive symbols. Rather, the inference rules of a logistic system are stated in the *metalanguage* of the system. The metalanguage contrasts with the system's *object language*. The latter consists of all well-formed formulas of the system.

From the idea of a demonstration, *logical theorem* may be defined. A formula f_n is a logical theorem if and only if it is the last formula in some demonstration $f_1, \ldots, f_n$. We shall provide sample derivations shortly.

The validity of arguments can be determined within a logistic system as follows (Copi, 1967, p. 214): "We define a *demonstration* of the validity of an argument having as premises the formulas $P_1, P_2, \ldots, P_n$ and as conclusion the formula Q, to be a sequence of well-formed formulas $S_1, S_2, \ldots, S_k$ such that: every S_i is either one of the premises $P_1, P_2, \ldots, P_n$, or is one of the axioms of [the logistic system], or follows from two preceding S's by one of the inference rules of the system; and such that S_k is Q . . . an argument is to be regarded as valid if and only if there exists a *demonstration* of its validity." Alternatively, we could attempt to deduce the conditional $(P_1 \,\&\, P_2 \,\&\, \cdots \,\&\, P_n) \rightarrow Q$ solely from the axioms and rules of inference of the system, using no premises. If such a demonstration exists, the conditional is a logical theorem, and consequently the argument having $P_1, P_2, \ldots, P_n$ as premises and Q as conclusion is valid.

A variety of logistic systems are sketched in Copi (1967), Quine (1972a), and Stoll (1963). A classic example is that set forth in Whitehead and Russell (1970). Following Hughes and Cresswell (1968, Ch. 1), we may describe the object language of the system this way. Our primitives are a set of letters

---

[3] More precisely, since the list of axioms may be infinite, the logistic system must provide a decision procedure for determining whether a well-formed formula is an axiom.

$p, q, r, \ldots$ that stand as elementary propositions. By means of numerical subscripts we allow as many such letters as needed. The following four symbols are also taken as primitive: $-, \lor, ($ and $)$. The well-formed formulas are specified by three rules:

> (*a*) A letter by itself is a well-formed formula;
> (*b*) If the formula α is a well-formed formula, then $-\alpha$ is also;
> (*c*) If the formulas α and β are well-formed formulas, then $(\alpha \lor \beta)$ is also.

The other logical connectives may be defined from the primitive symbols. For two formulas α and β,

> $(\alpha \,\&\, \beta) = \text{def} - (-\alpha \lor -\beta)$
> $(\alpha \rightarrow \beta) = \text{def}\,(-\alpha \lor \beta)$
> $(\alpha \equiv \beta) = \text{def}\,((\alpha \rightarrow \beta) \,\&\, (\beta \rightarrow \alpha))$

Whitehead and Russell provide five axioms for propositional logic[4]:

> 1. $(p \lor p) \rightarrow p$
> 2. $q \rightarrow (p \lor q)$
> 3. $(p \lor q) \rightarrow (q \lor p)$
> 4. $(p \lor (q \lor r)) \rightarrow (q \lor (p \lor r))$
> 5. $(q \rightarrow r) \rightarrow ((p \lor q) \rightarrow (p \lor r))$

There are two rules of inference:

> *Modus Ponens:* If α and $(\alpha \rightarrow \beta)$ are theorems of the axioms, then β is also;
> *Substitution:* Uniformly replacing any proposition letter in a theorem by any well-formed formula yields a new theorem.

Two demonstrations provided by Whitehead and Russell (1970, p. 100) are as follows:

$(p \rightarrow -p) \rightarrow -p$

> Demonstration:
> 1. $(p \lor p) \rightarrow p$ (Axiom 1)
> 2. $(-p \lor -p) \rightarrow -p$ (substitution of $-p$ for p in Step 1)
> 3. $(p \rightarrow -p) \rightarrow -p$ (definition of $\alpha \rightarrow \beta$ applied to Step 2)

$(p \rightarrow (q \rightarrow r)) \rightarrow (q \rightarrow (p \rightarrow r))$

---

[4] One of these axioms proved to be redundant.

Demonstration:

1. $(p \vee (q \vee r)) \rightarrow (q \vee (p \vee r))$
(Axiom 4)
2. $(-p \vee (-q \vee r)) \rightarrow (-q \vee (-p \vee r))$
(substitution of $-p$ for p and $-q$ for q in Step 1)
3. $(p \rightarrow (-q \vee r)) \rightarrow (q \rightarrow (-p \vee r))$
(definition of $\alpha \rightarrow \beta$, applied to Step 2)
4. $(p \rightarrow (q \rightarrow r)) \rightarrow (q \rightarrow (p \rightarrow r))$
(definition of $\alpha \rightarrow \beta$, applied to Step 3)

An indefinite number of such theorems are forthcoming from the White-head and Russell axioms, including those formulas representing valid arguments. It can be proved that the system is *complete* for propositional logic in the sense that every theorem of propositional logic is derivable from the Whitehead and Russell axioms. One method for antecedently specifying the truths of propositional logic is given in Section 3.3. For completeness proofs and different kinds of completeness, see Stoll (1963).

Do logistic systems resemble the procedures subjects implicitly use when asked to judge the validity of simple arguments? These systems have been described in some detail because we wish now to dismiss them as plausible psychological models. We shall not rely on experimental evidence.

One difficulty in assuming that subjects derive logical theorems in the logistic way is that such demonstrations are difficult to find. Even relying on previously proved theorems (if any), the demonstration of a desired theorem can be long and elusive.[5] That subjects perform such demonstrations implicitly, even though they experience difficulty in finding them at the explicit level, is doubtful.

Even if a set of psychologically plausible axioms were proposed, it would still be necessary to devise a method for finding demonstrations of desired theorems. If this method did not guarantee a unique demonstration for a given theorem, some means of amalgamating the complexity of different demonstrations for the same theorem would be necessary before predictions of inference difficulty could be derived. These additions to the theory are not trivial.[6] For attempts to program computers to find demonstrations, see Nilsson (1971).

[5] At the level of explicit demonstrations, even Quine (1972a) does not recommend the axiomatic method for deciding validity within propositional logic. He remarks that it is of "dubious value" in light of simpler and more reliable methods. He also says: "Lukasiewicz swore by axiomatic truth-functional logic as a training ground for axiomatic method in more demanding domains. I swear rather by the sufficiency, unto the day, of the evil thereof [p. 75]."

[6] We ran into this difficulty in Volume 1 in our attempt to use Grize's (1960) axiomatization of classes and lengths as a psychological model of children's understanding of these concepts. See Sections 6.5 and 11.5 of that volume.

3.3 SEMANTIC TECHNIQUES

Logistic systems rely on the form or syntax of a formula whose validity is in question. Semantic techniques rely on the formula's meaning, or intended interpretation. The most important feature of the semantics of propositional logic is its *truth-functionality*. Propositional logic is truth-functional because the truth-value of a formula (for our purposes, either truth or falsity) can be computed from the truth-values of its constituent propositions, that is, given any logical connective, $*$, in propositional logic, we can determine the truth of the formula $*(p_1, \ldots, p_n)$ on the basis of the truth-values of the propositions $p_1, \ldots, p_n$.[7]

Truth-functionality yields simple definitions for the logical connectives, &, $\vee$, $\rightarrow$, $-$, and so forth. Since only the truth and falsity of constituent propositions are relevant to the truth of a formula, the meaning of these connectives can be given in terms of *truth tables* as follows:

$-p$	$p \mathbin{\&} q$	$p \vee q$	$p \rightarrow q$
f t	t t t	t t t	t t t
t f	t f f	t t f	t f f
	f f t	f t t	f t t
	f f f	f f f	f t f

Consider $p \mathbin{\&} q$ as an illustration of these tables. The statement $p \mathbin{\&} q$ is true if both p is true and q is true, and false otherwise.

The customary English renditions of the connectives ("and" for &; "or" for $\vee$; "if . . . then . . ." for $\rightarrow$; and "not" for $-$) are unnatural and often misleading (see Quine, 1972a, Ch. 8). We return to this matter in Section 5.3.

The truth-value of a complicated formula may be computed stepwise from the truth-values of smaller subformulas. This is best explained by example. Consider the formula $-(p \rightarrow (p \mathbin{\&} (q \vee r)))$. By examining the formula's parentheses, we see that it is a negation; the stroke, $-$, on the left is therefore called the *main connective* of the formula. The formula being negated is $p \rightarrow (p \mathbin{\&} (q \vee r))$. This latter formula is a conditional, having the $\rightarrow$ as its main connective. The antecedent of this conditional is p. The consequent is the conjunction $p \mathbin{\&} (q \vee r)$. The conjuncts of this conjunction are p and the disjunction $q \vee r$. The disjuncts of the latter are q and r. Suppose that p and r

---

[7] Many contexts for propositions do not enjoy truth-functionality, for example, belief contexts. Thus, although the statements "animals respire" and "tomatoes are fruits" have the same truth-value (namely, both are true), they may result in opposite truth-values when placed in the context "John believes that. . . ." Much work has gone into the development of logics for such epistemic contexts (see Hintikka, 1962). Propositional logic, by itself, cannot elucidate such interesting notions as belief, knowledge, and doubt.

stand for false propositions and that q stands for a true one. Then, by the truth table definitions of the logical connectives, the disjunction $(q \vee r)$ is true. But since p is false, the conjunction $p \& (q \vee r)$ is false. But since p is false, the falsity of both the antecedent and consequent of $p \rightarrow (p \& (q \vee r))$ makes that conditional true. Hence, the negation of that true conditional, viz., $-(p \rightarrow (p \& (q \vee r)))$, is false. Consequently the whole formula is false. The following schema summarizes these steps:

$$-(p \rightarrow (p \& (q \vee r)))$$

```
        f     f   t  f
                     t
               f
          t
  f
```

Writing all the truth-values on the same line gives

$$-(p \rightarrow (p \& (q \vee r)))$$

```
  f  ft  ff  ttf
```

The formula represents a falsehood because its main connective, $-$, is marked with an f. Here is another example. Suppose p and q are true and r is false. Then the formula $(p \& -q) \rightarrow (r \vee p)$ is marked true because the main connective, $\rightarrow$, is labeled "t" in the following schema:

$$(p \& -q) \rightarrow (r \vee p)$$

```
  t f ft   t   ftt
```

In propositional logic, a formula is a logical truth (i.e., a *tautology*) if and only if the formula is true regardless of how truth and falsity are assigned to its constituent propositions.[8] If there are n elementary propositions in a formula, then, since each can be either true or false, there are 2^n possible assignments of truth and falsity to them. A truth table can be used to enumerate the possibilities as well as to calculate their consequences for the truth of the entire formula. As an example, consider the formula $p \vee (-q \& p)$. Its truth table is as follows:

$$p \vee (-q \& p)$$

```
  t t  ft  f t
  t t  tf  t t
  f f  ft  f f
  f f  tf  f f
```

8 Naturally, this assignment must be consistent, that is, two occurrences of the same proposition must receive the same truth-value, both t or both f.

The main connective of the formula is $\vee$, and since some rows result in an f for the column dominated by $\vee$, the formula is not a tautology. The following truth table, on the other hand, shows that $(p \mathbin{\&} q) \vee (-p \vee -q)$ is a tautology[9]:

$(p \mathbin{\&} q) \vee (-p \vee -q)$

```
t t t t   f t f f t
t f f t   f t t t f
f f t t   t f t f t
f f f t   t f t t f
```

Returning to the problem of evaluating arguments with premises $P_1, \ldots,$ P_n, and conclusion Q, one test is to construct a truth table for the formula $(P_1 \mathbin{\&} \ldots \mathbin{\&} P_n) \to Q$. For example, to show that the premise $p \to (q \mathbin{\&} r)$ implies the conclusion $-p \vee q$, we form the conditional $(p \to (q \mathbin{\&} r)) \to (-p \vee q)$ and test it by a truth table:

$(p \to (q \mathbin{\&} r)) \to (-p \vee q)$

```
t t t t t   t   f t t t
t f t f f   t   f t t t
t f f f t   t   f t f f
t f f f f   t   f t f f
f t t t t   t   t f t t
f t t f f   t   t f t t
f t f f t   t   t f t f
f t f f f   t   t f t f
```

The main connective is the right-hand $\to$. Since it dominates a column of t's, the formula is a tautology and the inference from antecedent to consequent is valid.

Do ordinary people decide the validity of arguments by means of such truth tables? This hypothesis runs into a major difficulty. Were people using truth tables, the difficulty of an argument would be a function of the difficulty of constructing the required table. In turn, this is likely to be related to its size in terms of the number of t's and f's placed within it.[10] The effect of truth table size is enhanced by the mental nature of the experimental problems. No pencil and paper are available nor do subjects desire

---

[9] The completeness of various logistic systems, mentioned in the last section, refers to the fact that all of the truth table tautologies may be derived from each of these systems' sets of axioms, given their inference rules. What is more, formulas that are not tautologies cannot be derived.

[10] Here and elsewhere we abide by standard process-model assumptions regarding the relationship between the number and nature of the mental steps assumed to underlie the completion of a task, on the one hand, and various measures of task difficulty, such as latency and error rate, on the other. For examples of studies based on such assumptions, see Hunter (1957) and Clark and Chase (1972).

them, given the intuitiveness of the arguments. However, the size of the truth table associated with an argument is only marginally related to its difficulty. This is true for problems used in the experiments of Volume 2 (see Sections 4.1 and 8.4). It is true also for experimental arguments in this Volume (see Section 20.3).

This blow to the truth table hypothesis is not fatal. There are a variety of methods for constructing slightly different truth tables than those illustrated above. Each kind results in somewhat different numbers of entries for the same arguments. It is possible, although unlikely, that one of these alternative versions affords a more substantial relation between inference difficulty and table size. It is also conceivable that appropriately weighting certain kinds of truth table entries will increase predictive power.

There are a variety of other semantic techniques for deciding the validity of inferences, including methods for finding falsifying truth-value assignments (see Jeffrey, 1967), and reduction to canonical form (Quine, 1972a). These methods also rely on the truth functionality of propositional logic but constitute different kinds of procedures for determining validity compared to truth tables. One of these procedures may correctly predict argument difficulty on the basis of the number of steps required for a decision. We have attempted to base psychological models on some of these techniques, but without success. Problem difficulty is occasionally predicted, but only by means of post hoc and arbitrary decisions in the formulation of the model. Many possible models based on semantic techniques remain unexplored.

We tentatively reject the hypothesis that people engage in truth-functional analysis to decide whether arguments are valid. Efforts to build a model in line with this hypothesis have failed, whereas a different kind of model has met with some success. Still, the question remains open.

3.4 NATURAL DEDUCTION

With natural deduction we return to syntactic techniques. Deriving conclusions from premises is the central concern of natural deduction systems, as opposed to the determination of logical truth per se. Whereas logistic and semantic techniques treat the validity of arguments as a special case of logical truth (namely, truth of conditionals with conjunctions of premises as antecedents and conclusions as consequents), in natural deduction the reverse is true: logical truth is a special case of valid inference, a formula being counted logically true if it can be derived from no premises at all (see Mates, 1972).[11]

---

[11] Despite the difference in emphasis, standard logistic and natural deduction systems yield the same results. See Copi (1967, Section 9.4).

Logistic systems include both a set of axioms and a set of rules of inference. Typically there are few inference rules and a moderate number of axioms.[12] The paucity of inference rules is reasonable in view of the goal of logistic systems to axiomatize logic itself: the more logic left in the metalanguage as rules of inference, the fewer the logical truths there are left to derive from the axioms.

Natural deduction systems, rather than axiomatizing logic itself, attempt to formulate rules for correct inference from contingent premises to contingent conclusions (Anderson & Johnstone, 1962, p. 16). Accordingly, natural deduction dispenses with axioms in exchange for more inference rules.[13] These inference rules legitimate adding lines to derivations on the basis of previous lines in the derivation. For example, the rule

$$\frac{A \ \& \ B}{A}$$

asserts that formula A may be written as a line of a derivation if formula $A \ \& \ B$ occurred as a previous line. The rule

$$\frac{A \to B, A}{B}$$

asserts that B may be written as a line of a derivation if both formulas $A \to B$ and A occurred as previous lines. Natural deduction systems consist of a number of such inference rules. Their statement and use becomes more complex in accounting for the introduction and elimination of premises not given in the original argument.

We believe that natural deduction is the kind of procedure subjects use implicitly to decide whether an argument is valid.[14] Indeed, natural deduction is of interest to logicians partly because of its correspondence to informal reasoning.[15] It must now be decided which of the many possible natural deduction systems formalizes in detail the processes underlying subjects' logical intuitions. Again, we may turn to professional logicians for help.

[12] There is, however, an axiomatization of propositional logic that consists of just a single axiom and two rules of inference. See Quine (1972a, Ch. 13).

[13] Anderson and Johnstone (1962) say: "In general, there seems to be a choice between a plurality of rules but no axioms or a plurality of axioms but a small number of rules. . . . When the motive for formulating PL [propositional logic] is that of analyzing deductions in axiom systems, it is somewhat unsatisfactory to present PL as itself an axiom system. The question of the nature of deductive reasoning seems to be postponed rather than answered when this is done [p. 74]."

[14] In a thoughtful paper, Johnson-Laird (1975) has independently made a comparable proposal. He also suggests a psychologically plausible set of inference rules.

[15] Gentzen (1955, p. 4), one of the inventors of natural deduction, writes: "J'ai voulu d'abord construire un formalisme qui soit le plus près possible du raisonement réel."

Natural deduction systems adequate for propositional logic (in particular, ones yielding the same results as the method of truth tables) are presented by Anderson and Johnstone (1962), Copi (1967), Quine (1972a), and Suppes (1957), among others. In attempting to devise a psychologically faithful model, we have had constant recourse to these established systems. However, they do not, by themselves, constitute a psychological theory. The reason is that these systems do little to indicate the order of application of the inference rules they specify. Although they allow an unambiguous answer to the question of whether a given derivation is sound, they provide no guaranteed method for constructing a derivation that connects a given conclusion with given premises that imply it. Consequently, these systems do not provide unambiguous hypotheses about the processes mediating logical judgment.

This defect is not an oversight. Providing simple algorithms for generating desired derivations is a recalcitrant problem (see Nilsson, 1971, for a survey of attempts). This suggests that finding derivations is idiosyncratic, that there is little discoverable regularity among subjects.

But it must be remembered that we are concerned with logical intuition, not proof finding (see Section 2.2). Whereas finding a simple algorithm for deriving arbitrarily complex arguments is difficult, finding one for the smaller class of intuitively valid arguments is likely to be easier. In addition it is more likely that the processes mediating logical judgment (as opposed to proof finding) are uniform.

Established natural deduction systems, then, do not constitute the desired model of logical judgment, although they are of heuristic value due to their relevance to proof finding. Rather than recapitulate one of these established systems for propositional logic, we shall elaborate one of our own design. It will not have the deductive power of standard systems, but it will, we believe, be closer to the actual processes mediating logical judgment.

4

Deduction Models: General Considerations and an Exemplification

In this chapter we present the formal outlines of the model developed in this book. A version of the system of Volume 2 is used for illustration. Henceforth, models for logical judgment that have the form of natural deduction systems (cf. Section 3.4) will be called *deduction models*.

4.1 OPERATIONS AND EXECUTIVE

Pursuant to the discussion in Section 3.4, a deduction model consists of a set of inference rules together with instructions that determine the use of the rules in derivations. The inference rules will be called *operations*. The ordered n-tuple $\langle o_1, \ldots, o_n \rangle$ denotes a model's set of them. The set of instructions that determines the use of the rules will be called the *executive* of the theory. The operations and executive determine the derivations of a deduction model. These represent hypotheses about the mental steps involved in evaluating arguments.

With a minor qualification, the arguments to which the model of this book applies have one premise. Furthermore, there is no "branching" within a derivation. Hence, there are no lemma-structure proofs, that is, there are no derivations in which a previously proved result is brought to bear within another derivation. Rather, the derivations proceed in linear and "markovian" fashion. The first line in a derivation is always the argument's premise. Each succeeding line in the derivation stems from the preceding line by means of one operation.[1] The lines in a derivation consist of formulas in the notation of propositional logic; no assumptions or indices

[1] In some experiments there will be a minor exception to this generality.

are carried along. In these derivations assumptions are never "discharged," as is often the case in standard natural deduction systems. Each operation of the theory may be considered a simple rewrite rule. It takes one kind of formula as input, and outputs another formula in its place. The input formula may comprise an entire line of a derivation, or only be a proper subformula of the formula comprising that line.[2] The output formula will be an entire line of a derivation whenever the input formula is an entire line; otherwise, it will be a proper subformula.

These restrictions on derivations and operations simplify the model, but only in exchange for a loss of deductive power, that is, deduction models with these restrictions probably cannot handle arguments that are correctly evaluated by standard systems. This is not necessarily a defect. As pointed out earlier, limitations on deductive power are essential in modeling logical judgment, as opposed to proof finding. More importantly, we have constructed the model within these constraints because we think that adolescents evaluate an interesting class of arguments in just this way.

The foregoing restrictions on derivations give them a property congenial with testing their psychological fidelity. Given a derivation consisting of lines $l_1, \ldots, l_p$, there is an argument with premise $P = l_1$ and conclusion $C = l_p$ that is validated by the derivation. Moreover, given any sequence of lines within $l_1, \ldots, l_p$, say, $l_i, \ldots, l_{i+k}$, there is a corresponding argument with premise $P = l_i$ and conclusion $C = l_{i+k}$ that is validated by the derivation $l_i, \ldots, l_{i+k}$, that is, every "piece" of a derivation is itself a derivation, provided that the piece has no internal "gaps" (i.e., provided that there are no lines $l_i, l_j, l_k, i < j < k$ of the original derivation such that the piece has premise $P = l_i$, conclusion $C = l_k$, but line l_j does not occur within it). We shall thus be able to test for each step in a proposed derivation by assessing subjects' performance on other arguments based on subderivations of the derivation (see Chapter 5).[3]

Judgments of nonvalidity have the same status as in Volume 2. An argument is judged invalid if the model provides no complete derivation for it. There is one qualification, however. For the model to predict that an argument will be judged invalid, the model must exhaust its possibilities for constructing a derivation before the number of lines in the derivation exceeds processing limitations of the subject. Otherwise, the argument is

---

[2] A subformula of a formula F is any formula that occurs within F. Conjunctions, disjunctions, and conditionals should all be parenthesized when determining whether a string of symbols from a formula is a subformula. For example, $(p \,\&\, q)$, $-(p \,\&\, q)$, and r are subformulas of $-(r \lor -(p \,\&\, q))$, whereas $s \lor t$, $-(p$, and $\& \, q$ are not. Note that $(p \,\&\, q)$ is not a subformula of $(-p \,\&\, q)$. A proper subformula of a formula F is a subformula of F other than F itself. (In the text, outermost parentheses of formulas are often dropped for convenience.)

[3] For further remarks on the empirical consequences of these kinds of derivations, see Volume 2, Section 5.4.

judged by the subject not to be invalid, but to lie beyond the bounds of his logical intuition; proof finding is seen to be necessary. The same considerations apply to valid arguments. For the model to predict that an argument will be labeled valid the system must produce a derivation, but the derivation must remain below complexity limitations. The distinction between judgments of validity, invalidity, and "processing overload" will concern us again in later chapters. For more on the distinction, see Volume 2, Chapters 6, 7, and 11.

4.2   A SIMPLE EXAMPLE

To illustrate the preceding considerations we present a modified version of the system discussed in Volume 2, Chapter 5. This preliminary model shares the essential properties of the enlarged model of Chapters 8–12. The illustrative model will be referred to as the *initial model*.

The operations are as follows[4]:

1. $\dfrac{A \to (B \,\&\, C)}{A \to B}$

2. $\dfrac{(A \lor B) \to C}{A \to C}$

3. $\dfrac{A \to B}{-B \to -A}$

4. $\dfrac{A \to B}{(A \,\&\, C) \to (B \,\&\, C)}$

5. $\dfrac{A \to B}{(A \lor C) \to (B \lor C)}$

6. $\dfrac{A \to B}{(A \,\&\, C) \to B}$

7. $\dfrac{A \to B}{A \to (B \lor C)}$

The following four remarks about the operations are required:

1. The letters A, B, and C in the operations stand for formulas of arbitrary complexity, not only for "prime" (or "atomic") propositions. Thus, the

---

[4] Operations and arguments will sometimes be written on one line, with the use of a slash. For example, Operation (1) may be written $A \to (B \,\&\, C)/A \to B$. In either arrangement, the *upper formula* of, for example, Operation (1), is $A \to (B \,\&\, C)$. The *lower formula* is $A \to B$.

letter A in Operation (1) could represent the simple formula "p," or the disjunction "p v $-q$," etc. Naturally, the same formula, whatever it may be, is represented by both occurrences of A in Operation (1); similarly for the other letters. In general, an operation is relevant to any *substitution instance* of the formula written above its line. Formula F_1 is a substitution instance of a formula F_2 if F_1 can be converted into F_2 by relabeling subformulas of F_1 with single letters, never giving different subformulas the same letter. Taking Operation (3) as an example, $-p \rightarrow (r$ v $s)$ is a substitution instance of $A \rightarrow B$. The theoretical consequences of substitution instances will concern us in Chapter 9. (For further discussion see Volume 2, Section 5.4.)

2. We have reversed the notation used in Volume 2. In Volume 2, capital letters from the beginning of the alphabet represented prime propositions (those like "Today is sunny," for which no further logical analysis is given). Small letters from the middle of the alphabet figured in the operations and represented formulas of arbitrary complexity. In this book the letters p, q, r, s, t, etc. stand for prime propositions. The letters A, B, C, D, etc. stand for formulas of arbitrary complexity.

3. Two operations from Volume 2 have been omitted from the initial model. They are

$$\frac{A \text{ v } B}{-(-A \text{ \& } -B)}$$

and

$$\frac{A \text{ \& } B}{-(-A \text{ v } -B)}$$

These operations, concerning "De Morgan" principles, appear in modified form later.

4. The operations are ordered by their corresponding numbers. The order is total, not partial as in Volume 2. This total ordering insures that a derivation provided by the model for a given argument is unique if that derivation exists. The ordering constitutes part of the executive, to which we now turn.[5]

The operations are instructions to rewrite a line in a derivation as the bottom formula of the operation, given that certain conditions are met. For each operation these conditions amount to a description of the circumstances under which application of that operation in a derivation will "help" in reaching the conclusion. Let l_i stand for the latest line written in an ongoing derivation, and let "the conclusion" stand for the conclusion of the argument under evaluation. We shall say that an operation is *legal* at line i in the derivation if l_i is a substitution instance of the upper formula of the

---

[5] For further observations about these operations, see Volume 2, Section 5.4.

operation. Given that an operation is legal, the result of its application is line l_{i+1}. The conditions for each operation being *helpful* at line i may now be stated:

Operation (1): $A \to (B \& C)/A \to B$. No subformula of C occurs in the conclusion.

Operation (2): $(A \lor B) \to C/A \to C$. No subformula of B occurs in the conclusion.

Operation (3): $A \to B/-B \to -A$. A subformula of A and a subformula of B occur in the conclusion, each having a different sign than they had in l_i.[6]

Operation (4): $A \to B/(A \& C) \to (B \& C)$. $A \& F$ and $B \& F$ occur in the conclusion, for some formula, F. Then C equals F in line l_{i+1}.

Operation (5): $A \to B/(A \lor C) \to (B \lor C)$. $A \lor F$ and $B \lor F$ occur in the conclusion, for some formula, F. Then C equals F in line l_{i+1}.

Operation (6): $A \to B/(A \& C) \to B$. $A \& F$ occurs in the conclusion for some formula, F. Then C equals F in line l_{i+1}.

Operation (7): $A \to B/A \to (B \lor C)$. $A \lor F$ occurs in the conclusion for some formula, F. Then C equals F in line l_{i+1}.

The helping condition for Operation (6) is to be understood this way: Given that line l_i has been parsed as a conditional with antecedent A and consequent B, then for Operation (6) to apply, A must occur in the conclusion, conjoined with some other formula. We call that latter formula, F. Line l_{i+1} is then written as $(A \& C) \to B$, where $C = F$. Operations (4), (5), and (7) are understood similarly.[7] The other operations do not insert new propositions into line l_{i+1}. Their helping conditions are straightforward.

Construction of the desired derivation $l_1, \ldots, l_p$ is achieved by the following steps:

1. Set l_1 equal to the premise of the argument to be evaluated.

2. Given l_i, the latest line of the derivation to be constructed, check to see if l_i matches the desired conclusion. If it does, exit with the decision "valid." If l_i does not match the conclusion, proceed to Step 3.

---

[6] Two formulas have different signs if one has a negation as its main connective and the other one does not. In the helping condition for Operation (3), if p occurred in l_i, then it occurs with a changed sign in the conclusion if $-p$ occurs in the conclusion; similarly for the pairs $-p, p$; $p \& q$, $-(p \& q)$; $-(r \lor s)$, $r \lor s$; etc.

[7] These helping conditions are adequate for present purposes but fail for certain complex arguments. A more complete version of the helping conditions is given in the Appendix.

3. Going down the list of operations in order, starting with Operation (1), find the first operation that is legal and helpful. If there are no such operations, exit with the decision "invalid." Otherwise, apply the specified operation to l_i, deriving l_{i+1}, and return to Step 2. (The newly derived line l_{i+1} now counts as line l_i in Step 2, the latest line of the derivation to be constructed.)

To make the intended meaning of the operations and executive clear, some sample derivations are presented.[8] Subsequently, we make some observations about the model.

Given the argument

If either the Orioles won or the Yankees lost, then the Tigers were eliminated.

If the Tigers were not eliminated and the fans were hostile, then the Orioles did not win.

which goes into symbols as

$$\frac{(p \lor q) \to r}{(-r \ \& \ s) \to -p}$$

the system produces the following derivation:

(a) $(p \lor q) \to r$
(b) $p \to r$
(c) $-r \to -p$
(d) $(-r \ \& \ s) \to -p$

Since line (d) matches the conclusion of the argument, the argument is judged to be valid. The executive constructs the derivation as follows. Pursuant to Step 1, line (a) is the argument's premise. Line l_i of Step 2 of the executive at this point is line (a). Since line (a) is not identical to the conclusion, we proceed through Step 2 to Step 3. Operation (1) is not legal. Operation (2) is legal, and since q does not occur in the argument's conclusion, Operation (2) is also helpful. Hence it is applied to line (a), yielding line (b). Line (b) now counts as line l_i. Since line (b) does not yet match the conclusion, we look through the operations again. Neither Operation (1) nor Operation (2) is legal. Operation (3) is legal, and it is helpful because p and r occur with changed signs in the conclusion. The resulting line is (c), which is the current l_i for the executive's Step 2. Since line (c) does not match the conclusion,

---

[8] Naturally, the question of alternative derivations resulting from a different executive or set of operations is best considered in light of empirical constraints on these derivations. These constraints are the topic of Chapter 5.

we again search through the operations. Operations (1) and (2) are not legal. Operation (3) is legal but no longer helpful. Operations (4) and (5) are legal but are also not helpful. Operation (6) is legal and it is helpful because $-r \& s$ occurs in the conclusion. The result is line (d), which is the current l_i for Step 2. Since line (d) does match the desired conclusion, the Step 2–Step 3 "loop" of the executive is exited with a decision of *valid*.

Suppose that the conclusion was the invalid $(-r \lor s) \to -p$ instead of the valid $(-r \& s) \to -p$. In that case, after line (c) had been written, no operations would be both legal and helpful, and the Step 2–Step 3 loop would be exited in Step 3 with a decision of not valid.

Following are two more derivations with operation numbers written beside each step:

Argument: $\dfrac{p \to (q \& r)}{(p \lor s) \to (q \lor s)}$

Derivation:

(a) $p \to (q \& r)$ (Premise)
(b) $p \to q$ (Operation 1)
(c) $(p \lor s) \to (q \lor s)$ (Operation 5)

Argument: $\dfrac{p \to (q \& r)}{-q \to (-p \lor s)}$

Derivation:

(a) $p \to (q \& r)$ (Premise)
(b) $p \to q$ (Operation 1)
(c) $-q \to -p$ (Operation 3)
(d) $-q \to (-p \lor s)$ (Operation 7)

4.3   A DOZEN REMARKS ABOUT THE MODEL

The following remarks apply to the expanded model of Part 2 as well as to the initial model:

1. In Volume 2 (Section 5.2), the "helping conditions" for each operation were called "context restrictions."[9] Terminology has changed because the research question is formulated differently in the present study. The functions of context restrictions and helping conditions are the same. Nonetheless, here we have differed slightly from Volume 2 in the conditions

---

[9] Arguments in Volume 2 were written in the form $P \to C$, where P was the premise and C the conclusion. The operations were applied to the antecedent of that conditional, converting it by stages into the consequent, much as done here. The conditions for an operation's use were called context restrictions because they hinged on the context in which the premise P occurred, namely, the consequent of the conditional $P \to C$.

for some of the operations. The change is motivated by our decision to focus attention on valid arguments and ignore, for the most part, invalid arguments (see Section 6.4).

2. The Operations (1)–(7) in the sample derivations rewrite whole formulas as other whole formulas. They do not apply to proper subformulas. For the simple arguments of concern to us, this policy is convenient, since otherwise restrictions on the use of operations are needed to prevent invalid arguments from being labeled valid. The underlying factor is that, with the exception of Operation (3), the upper formulas of operations are not implied by the lower formulas.

In subsequent chapters, operations are posited that may apply to proper subformulas. For example, in Chapter 10 a double-negation operation

$$\frac{--A}{A}$$

is introduced that allows the line $p \rightarrow --q$ to be rewritten as $p \rightarrow q$. In this case, the operation applies to the proper subformula $--q$ of the formula $p \rightarrow --q$, changing it to q, and thereby changing the whole formula to $p \rightarrow q$.

3. The order of the operations is consequential. Suppose Operation (3) were placed first on the list. The sample argument

$$\frac{(p \vee q) \rightarrow r}{(-r \ \& \ s) \rightarrow -p}$$

would then be labeled invalid. The first line of the derivation would be the premise, $(p \vee q) \rightarrow r$. The second line would be $-r \rightarrow -(p \vee q)$. Operation (6) would then be legal and helpful, giving $(-r \ \& \ s) \rightarrow -(p \vee q)$. But then no further operations are helpful. Since this second line does not match the conclusion, the argument is labeled invalid, unlike before. This defect can be remedied by adding the operation (applicable to subformulas)

$$\frac{-(A \vee B)}{-A \ \& \ -B}$$

with the helping condition that either $-A$ or $-B$ occurs in the conclusion. If we place this operation second on the list, just after the lead-off Operation (3) (or else, place the new operation first on the list), we get the following derivation:

(a) $(p \vee q) \rightarrow r$ (Premise)
(b) $-r \rightarrow -(p \vee q)$ (former Operation 3)
(c) $-r \rightarrow -p \ \& \ -q$ (new operation)
(d) $-r \rightarrow -p$ (former Operation 1)
(e) $(-r \ \& \ s) \rightarrow -p$ (former Operation 6)

The argument would thus be labeled valid, as before. But changing the system in this way is still consequential. We have produced a derivation different than that used before for the same argument. The new derivation is one line longer and involves different operations. A different derivation is a different hypothesis about the implicit mental steps people use to judge the validity of an argument. The two derivations result in testably different predictions, as will be seen in the next chapter.[10]

Other changes in the ordering of the operations have effects on derivations. On the other hand, some of the ordering is rather arbitrary. Reversing Operations (1) and (2) has only a slight effect. Evaluating the argument

$$\frac{(p \vee q) \to (r \ \& \ s)}{p \to r}$$

with the present order gives the derivation

(a) $(p \vee q) \to (r \ \& \ s)$
(b) $(p \vee q) \to r$
(c) $p \to r$

whereas reversing the order of Operations (1) and (2) gives the derivation

(a) $(p \vee q) \to (r \ \& \ s)$
(b) $p \to (r \ \& \ s)$
(c) $p \to r$

In principle, there is a way of deciding which, if either, of these derivations is closer to the psychological truth (see Chapter 9).[11] In practice, the difference is not discernible. We have chosen the present order of Operations (1) and (2), (4) and (5), and (6) and (7) in view of the findings that disjunction is more difficult to work with than conjunction (see Bruner, Goodnow, & Austin, 1956; Neimark, 1970; Neimark & Slotnick, 1970; and references cited in Bourne, 1966). The idea is that in a derivation subjects tend to use more wieldy operations before less wieldy operations.

4. After an operation is applied, the executive returns to the top of the list and again looks for the first legal and helpful operation. This procedure is more powerful than that proposed in Volume 2, Section 5.1, where only one "pass" through the operations was countenanced. The new procedure provides the solution to problems raised in Section 11.1 of Volume 2. With

---

[10] In Section 12.5 we argue that the original derivation provided for the argument considered here is the correct one.

[11] It is possible that the operations are not applied serially in this case at all, but that, rather, they apply simultaneously to the premise. We shall be forced to leave this question unanswered.

only one pass allowed, any ordering of the operations prevents proper evaluation of some of the following arguments:

(1) $p \rightarrow q/((p \vee r) \& s) \rightarrow ((q \vee r) \& s)$
(2) $p \rightarrow q/((p \& r) \vee s) \rightarrow ((q \& r) \vee s)$
(3) $p \rightarrow q/((p \vee r) \& s) \rightarrow (q \vee r)$
(4) $p \rightarrow q/(p \& s) \rightarrow ((q \& s) \vee r)$
(5) $p \rightarrow q/((p \& s) \vee r) \rightarrow (q \vee r)$
(6) $p \rightarrow q/(p \& s) \rightarrow ((q \vee r) \& s)$

With the present executive, all of the arguments are labeled valid. Consider Argument (1). The first line of its derivation is $p \rightarrow q$. At this point, Operation (4) is not helpful. In Operation (4) $A = p$, and $B = q$. C would equal s.[12] The helping condition for Operation (4) is not fulfilled because neither $p \& s (= A \& C)$ nor $q \& s (= B \& C)$ is present in the conclusion. On the other hand, Operation (5) is helpful. For Operation (5), $A = p$, $B = q$, and $C = r$.[13] Operation (5) is helpful because both $p \vee r (= A \vee C)$ and $q \vee r$ $(= B \vee C)$ occur in the conclusion. The application of Operation (5) gives the derived line $(p \vee r) \rightarrow (q \vee r)$. Next time around, it is Operation (4) that is helpful rather than Operation (5). In this case, $A = p \vee r$, $B = q \vee r$, and $C = s$. Since both $(p \vee r) \& s (= A \& C)$ and $(q \vee r) \& s (= B \& C)$ occur in the conclusion, Operation (4) is helpful. Its application yields the desired conclusion. Argument (2) triggers the operations in the other order. First Operation (4) is helpful because both $p \& r (= A \& C)$ and $q \& r (= B \& C)$ occur in the conclusion, yielding $(p \& r) \rightarrow (q \& r)$. Then Operation (6) is helpful because both $(p \& r) \vee s (= A \vee C$, for $A = p \& r)$ and $(q \& r) \vee s$ $(= B \vee C$, for $B = q \& r)$ occur in the conclusion. The other arguments are derived similarly.

It is possible to reformulate the initial model as well as the expanded system of Part 2 in such a way that derivations are constructed "upside down." In this version, the upper and lower formulas of operations are interchanged, the order of operations is reversed, the helping conditions are restated to deal with the premise rather than the conclusion, and derivations begin with the conclusion and work backward to the premise (cf. Volume 2, Section 5.4). It is also possible that a combination of these two directions is involved when a subject evaluates an argument. Nothing in the data to be examined seems capable of resolving this issue.

5. In Section 4.1 a criterion was given for separating valid from invalid arguments. Below some level of derivation complexity (beyond which proof finding rather than logical judgment is necessary), an argument

[12] Note that s is the only candidate for C because only s occurs twice as a conjunct in the conclusion. See Remark 9 on substitution instances below.

[13] Note that r is C because r occurs disjoined in the conclusion to both p $(= A)$ and q $(= B)$.

judged to be valid is one for which the system provides a derivation; invalid arguments are provided no such derivation.[14] In the latter case, the executive procedure halts before the desired conclusion is reached. This halt occurs in Step 3 of the executive routine (see Section 4.2). In this step, it is decided whether there are any legal and helpful operations to be applied to the current line of the derivation. If there are none, the executive exits with a decision of "not valid."

For any given argument, is our executive guaranteed either to reach the conclusion or to exit with a "not valid" decision? Is it possible for the Step 2–Step 3 loop of the executive to cycle indefinitely without ever reaching the conclusion? Suppose the condition for Operation (3) were: Either A or B occurs in the conclusion with changed sign. Suppose also that the theory contains a double-negation operation $--A/A$ that applies to subformulas of lines. In that case, for the invalid argument $p \rightarrow (q \& s)/-p \rightarrow q$, Operation (3) is repeatedly legal and helpful past the second line in the derivation. This derivation spins endlessly on as follows:

    (a) $p \rightarrow (q \& s)$ (Premise)
    (b) $p \rightarrow q$ (Operation 1)
    (c) $-q \rightarrow -p$ (Operation 3)
    (d) $--p \rightarrow --q$ (Operation 3)
    (e) $p \rightarrow q$ (double negation applied twice)
    (f) $-q \rightarrow -p$ (Operation 3)
    (g) $--p \rightarrow --q$ (Operation 3)
       etc.

It is desirable that every derivation either ends with the conclusion or exits in some pass through Step 3. We shall attempt to formulate our operations and executive so as to meet this condition. However, we do not know how to prove that any of the systems we propose do in fact meet it.

6. The helping conditions make no reference to the antecedent or consequent of a conditional in the conclusion. This is true despite the fact that all the conclusions in our examples are conditionals. Not mentioning the antecedent and consequent of the conclusion-conditional in the helping conditions is a change from Volume 2 (see Section 5.2 of Volume 2).

The reason for the change is that further operations will be added, some of which convert conditionals into formulas with different main connectives. One such operation is as follows:

$$\frac{A \rightarrow B}{-(A \& -B)}$$

[14] Similarly, in a transformational grammar, a sentence is classified as ungrammatical if there exists no derivation that produces it (Katz & Bever, 1974).

This operation figures in the following derivation:

(a) $(p \lor q) \to r$ (Premise)
(b) $p \to r$ (Operation 2)
(c) $-(p \,\&\, -r)$ (new operation)

The application of Operation (2) would be blocked in this derivation if its helping condition hinged on the conclusion being a conditional. As the helping condition is now written, Operation (2) will be applied to line (a) because no subformula of q occurs in the conclusion. There is no reference to a conditional.

7. However, for a different reason, the helping conditions for Operations (1) and (2) are not adequate as now written. They do not legitimate the following arguments, which seem intuitively valid:

(1) $p \to (q \,\&\, r)/p \to (q \lor r)$
(2) $(p \lor q) \to r/(p \,\&\, q) \to r$

Consider Argument (1). We would like to construct the following derivation:

(a) $p \to (q \,\&\, r)$ (Premise)
(b) $p \to q$ (Operation 1)
(c) $p \to (q \lor r)$ (Operation 7)

But the step from line (a) to line (b) is blocked because the helping condition for Operation (1) is not fulfilled. The reason is that r (which is a subformula of itself, and thus of C) occurs in the conclusion. This problem is remedied by reformulating the helping condition for Operation (1) as follows: No subformula of C occurs in the conclusion conjoined to B. Since r does not occur in the conclusion conjoined to q, the operation will apply to line (a).

The same considerations apply to Argument (2). The desired derivation

(a) $(p \lor q) \to r$ (Premise)
(b) $p \to r$ (Operation 2)
(c) $(p \,\&\, q) \to r$ (Operation 6)

is blocked because q (a subformula of itself, and thus of B) occurs in the conclusion. The operation may be rewritten as follows: No subformula of B occurs in the conclusion disjoined to A.

For present purposes it is not crucial that the helping conditions for Operations (1) and (2) be reformulated in this way. We shall not consider arguments in which the same proposition is both added and deleted. (This is in sharp contrast to Volume 2; see Sections 5.4 and 11.3 of Volume

2 for discussion.) We have raised this issue here mainly to indicate the kind of considerations that arise in attempting to construct deduction models.[15]

8. In giving helping conditions, a concept that will be useful in later chapters is *scope of a negation*. A formula is in the scope of a negation if it is a subformula of a formula whose main connective is a negation.[16] Consider a formula, F, occurring in the conclusion of an argument and in line l_i of the argument's derivation. We shall say that in l_i, F occurs in the conclusion under the scope of a changed sign if either (*a*) F is under the scope of a negation in l_i but not under the scope of a negation in the conclusion, or (*b*) F is under the scope of a negation in the conclusion, but not under the scope of a negation in line l_i.

Now the helping condition for Operation (3) refers to a change in sign of the formulas A and B. Suppose we replaced that helping condition with: A subformula of A and a subformula of B occur in the conclusion, each under the scope of a changed sign. All the derivations presented so far will go through with this new helping condition. However, later we shall introduce the operation $A \rightarrow B/-(A \& -B)$, with the helping condition: A and $-B$ occur conjoined to each other in the conclusion, the conjunction occurring under the scope of a negation. Suppose that this new operation is placed after Operation (3) in the ordering of operations. Now consider the argument $p \rightarrow q/-(p \& -q)$. The premise for its derivation is $p \rightarrow q$. The first legal operation is Operation (3). But we do not wish it to apply. With our new helping condition, however, it will apply, since p and q both occur in the conclusion under the scope of a changed sign. The new line is $-q \rightarrow -p$. This line does not allow the new operation to apply, so the derivation cannot be constructed.

To avoid this problem, we may either (*a*) change the ordering of the operations, placing our new operation before Operation (3), or (*b*) restore the helping condition of Operation (3) to its former simplicity. Either option allows proper derivation of $p \rightarrow q/-(p \& -q)$. As will be seen later (cf. Table 11.1), we have chosen option (*b*). The purpose of this remark is to stress the interconnectedness of the decisions that go into constructing a deduction model.

9. Neither the initial model, nor the expanded one of Part 2 is entirely explicit, for no procedure is given for ascertaining whether line l_i is a substitution instance of an operation's upper formula, nor is it specified how to parse the conclusion in order to determine whether an operation's helping

---

[15] We have let certain minor problems, less serious than this last one, go unresolved in formulating a more complete system. Likely as not, we have unwittingly allowed more important errors to slip by as well.

[16] Thus, in the following formulas p is within the scope of a negation: $-p$, $-(p \& q)$, $-(q \rightarrow p)$, $-(q \vee p)$. In contrast, p is not in the scope of a negation in the following formulas: p, $q \& p$, $p \rightarrow -q$, $-q \vee p$.

condition is satisfied.[17] Potentially, this is a serious deficiency. In some cases, much of the difficulty in recognizing the validity of an argument seems to be due to parsing complexity. Consider an argument of the form Modus Ponens:

$$A \rightarrow B$$
$$\underline{A}$$
$$B$$

It is easier to recognize the validity of simple substitution instances of this argument like

$$p \rightarrow q$$
$$\underline{p}$$
$$q$$

than complex ones, like

$$-(p \ \& \ -q) \rightarrow (r \rightarrow (s \ \& \ t))$$
$$\underline{-(p \ \& \ -q)}$$
$$r \rightarrow (s \ \& \ t)$$

Nothing in our theory, as so far developed, can account for this fact.

The consequences of our theory's inability to deal adequately with the problem of substitution instances is mitigated by the simple arguments with which the theory deals. The difficulty of recognizing one formula as an instance of another is greatest when arguments become complex. Such complexity indicates the use of proof-finding abilities rather than the logical judgments that are the concern of the present work. Chapter 9 returns to the issue of substitution instances. See also Volume 2, Section 5.4.

10. The arguments to which the models in this book apply are administered to subjects in English, not in symbolic notation. We shall not propose, however, a description of the process whereby subjects convert sentences into a representation appropriate for the operations of the model. Translation of natural language into perspicuous logical symbolism is a delicate affair. Standard texts in logic provide no more than helpful hints. (The lack of a theory of translation will be of further concern in Section 5.3; see also Volume 2, Section 1.3.)

11. Operations (1)–(7) are sound, from the point of view of classical logic. Every argument declared valid by our system will be declared valid by standard techniques. All operations added subsequently are likewise sound.[18] The decision to admit only sound operations into our psychological system seems either to court the fallacy of logicism, or to embrace

---

[17] However, both of these questions admit of decision procedures.

[18] We shall take advantage of this fact by letting "valid argument" mean either "valid from the point of view of standard logic" or "valid from the point of view of our model" (or both). Context determines the intended meaning.

the doctrine that people do not make errors in deductive inference (from the point of view of standard logic).[19] We are not guilty of logicism, if logicism refers to an *unconsidered* belief that a given formal system mirrors psychology. Rather, we believe that deductive errors, per se, do not occur (cf. Henle, 1962). Our arguments in behalf of this doctrine are mainly methodological. They are given in Section 5.3. See Revlis (1974) and Chapman and Chapman (1959) for a different view.

The present rules are not complete from the standard logical point of view. There are arguments validated by standard logic that are not validated by our system. We shall bring the system closer to completeness in Part 2, as more operations are added. But it still will not be logically complete. Nor will it be psychologically complete, in the sense that arguments judged to be intuitively valid will not be derivable from our system. While psychological completeness is a virtue for a deduction model, it is not necessary for accomplishing the goal set in Chapter 1. The question of qualitative change in logical abilities from childhood to adolescence is best answered in light of theories for logical abilities in the two periods. It is clear from the discussion in Chapter 1 that even incomplete theories can offer insight into this developmental question.

12. The initial model, as well as the larger system to be elaborated, seems to be a *production system* of the kind discussed and profitably utilized by Newell and Simon (1972). Our helping conditions, in addition, derive from difference-finding and difference-eliminating procedures that flourish in their hands. Despite these similarities at an abstract level, there are great differences in detail between the Newell and Simon (1972) approach and our own. Most importantly, the research questions are distinct. (See Section 2.2, above, for discussion; see also Volume 2, Section 5.4.)

---

[19] Logicism refers to mistaking a purely formal logic with habits of reasoning, without the benefit of psychological experimentation to determine whether the proposed logic is indeed a description of reasoning.

5

Empirical Conditions on Derivations

In this chapter three criteria for the empirical adequacy of deduction models are discussed. The initial model of Chapter 4 is used for illustration.

5.1 THE INVENTORY REQUIREMENT

A deduction model consists of an ordered set of operations $\langle o_1, \ldots, o_n \rangle$ and an executive. Any argument within the deductive range of the theory can be characterized by specifying the operations mediating its solution.[1] Disregarding the order in which operations are applied, an argument requiring operations $o_{\alpha_1}, \ldots, o_{\alpha_m}, m \leq n, 1 \leq \alpha \leq n$, in its derivation may be represented by the unordered set

$$\{o_{\alpha_1}, \ldots, o_{\alpha_m}\}.$$

We shall use this notation only to represent arguments labeled valid by the theory, that is, those for which a derivation is given.

As an example, consider the argument $(p \lor q) \to r/(-r \& s) \to p$. According to the initial model, it has the following derivation:

(a)	$(p \lor q) \to r$	(Premise)
(b)	$p \to r$	(Operation 2)
(c)	$-r \to -p$	(Operation 3)
(d)	$(-r \& s) \to -p$	(Operation 6)

[1] Because of the possibility of different substitution instances of the same operation, there is not a one-to-one mapping between arguments and the sets of operations theoretically underlying them. However, there is a many-to-one function from arguments to the (unordered) set of operations that theoretically underlies them, and this is all we shall need.

This argument is represented by the set

{Operation (2), Operation (3), Operation (6)}

Given the present notation, arguments can be subsets of other arguments. The argument $\{o_i, o_j\}$ is a subset of the argument $\{o_i, o_j, o_k\}$ because every operation involved in the former's derivation is involved in the latter's.

Suppose that a subject rejects argument $\{o_i, o_j\}$. If the theory generating the operational characterization of arguments is correct, then either the subject does not possess at least one of the operations o_i and o_j, or else the subject possesses both operations but succumbs to the complexity of a derivation requiring both of them.[2] We consider each of these alternatives.

If one or both of operations o_i and o_j are not present, the required derivation for the argument $\{o_i, o_j\}$ cannot be constructed. The argument $\{o_i, o_j\}$ therefore appears no more valid to this subject than any other argument for which a derivation cannot be constructed. Recall that the theory classifies an argument as invalid if no derivation with the desired conclusion can be generated (see Section 3.4, and Remark 5 of Section 4.3). Any argument that includes $\{o_i, o_j\}$ will likewise be judged invalid, since its derivation also cannot be constructed for want of o_i, o_j, or both.[3]

The second possible reason for a subject labeling the argument $\{o_i, o_j\}$ invalid is that its derivation exceeds the complexity limit of his logical intuition, that is, the subject implicitly must abandon the derivation before the conclusion is reached, but also before all of the legal and helpful operations have been applied in the derivation, that is, before the exit option is taken in Step 3 of the executive.

We believe that abandoning a mental derivation has different phenomenological consequences than exhausting the legal and helpful operations that may be applied during a derivation. This difference will be discussed shortly. Even without the difference, however, if an argument $\{o_i, o_j\}$ falls beyond a subject's computational limits, then any argument including $\{o_i, o_j\}$ will also fall beyond his computational limits. We discount the possibility that adding operation o_k to a derivation involving o_i and o_j decreases the complexity of that derivation.

Thus, if for either cause a subject rejects an argument that has a derivation within the theory, the same prediction follows: the subject will also reject any

---

[2] Possessing operations need not be an all-or-none matter. See Section 13.1.

[3] This reasoning was employed in Volume 1. See Sections 6.2 and 6.3 of that volume.

It is possible that o_i and o_j function only in the presence of o_k in a derivation. Then the prediction will not be correct, despite the theory's correct identification of the operations in the two arguments. This possibility, however, seems to contradict the idea of an independent operation. If o_i and o_j function only in the presence of o_k we would wish to say that less than three operations are involved here, if we but knew how to individuate them.

argument that includes the first one. More abstractly, considering only arguments for which the theory provides a derivation, rejection of argument $\{\mathbf{o}_{\alpha_1}, \ldots, \mathbf{o}_{\alpha_n}\}$ predicts rejection of the argument $\{\mathbf{o}_{\alpha_1}, \ldots, \mathbf{o}_{\alpha_m}, \ldots, \mathbf{o}_{\alpha_{m+k}}\}$, which includes $\{\mathbf{o}_{\alpha_1}, \ldots, \mathbf{o}_{\alpha_m}\}$. This prediction rests on the assumption that the theory attributes the correct psychologically real operations to arguments. Hence, the prediction tests this assumption. This kind of prediction will be called an *inventory prediction* because its truth depends on the inventory of arguments accepted by the subject. That a viable deduction model make true inventory predictions will be called the *inventory requirement*.

Should we test the theory by predicting that any subject honoring the arguments $\{\mathbf{o}_{\alpha_1}, \ldots, \mathbf{o}_{\alpha_m}\}$ and $\{\mathbf{o}_{\alpha_{m+1}}, \ldots, \mathbf{o}_{\alpha_{m+k}}\}$ will also honor the argument $\{\mathbf{o}_{\alpha_1}, \ldots, \mathbf{o}_{\alpha_m}, \mathbf{o}_{\alpha_{m+1}}, \ldots, \mathbf{o}_{\alpha_{m+k}}\}$? (This is the converse of the last prediction.) The answer is no, because this prediction could be false even though the theory correctly characterizes each argument. For, the argument $\{\mathbf{o}_{\alpha_1}, \ldots, \mathbf{o}_{\alpha_m}, \mathbf{o}_{\alpha_{m+1}}, \ldots, \mathbf{o}_{\alpha_{m+k}}\}$ may be beyond the subject's computational limitations, although $\{\mathbf{o}_{\alpha_1}, \ldots, \mathbf{o}_{\alpha_m}\}$ and $\{\mathbf{o}_{\alpha_{m+1}}, \ldots, \mathbf{o}_{\alpha_{m+k}}\}$ are each, separately, within those bounds.[4]

One sign of mental overload is phenomenological. Overly complex arguments are bewildering, whereas patently invalid arguments are not.[5] This difference is illustrated by the following two arguments, the first being unequivocally invalid, the second, due to Quine (1972a, p. 167), straining the limits of intuitive judgment, even though technically valid:

(1) Harvey won the race.
     _____
     Harvey won the race and Steven won the raffle.

(2) The guard searched all who entered the building except those who
         were accompanied by members of the firm.
     Some of Fiorecchio's men entered the building unaccompanied by
         anyone else.
     The guard searched none of Fiorecchio's men.
     _____
     Some of Fiorecchio's men were members of the firm.

In the experiments to be reported, subjects are given the option of responding that an argument is too complex to be intuitively evaluated. For the simple arguments employed, the option was seldom taken. But in theory,

_____

[4] This problem was of great concern in Volume 1, particularly in Chapters 8 and 9.

[5] The experience is similar to that resulting from multiply embedded sentences such as Miller and Isard's (1964) "The prize that the ring that the jeweler that the man that she liked visited made won was given at the fair."

this precaution reduces the number of false inventory predictions that result from confounding the invalidity of an argument with excessive complexity.[6]

In testing deduction models we shall use a special case of the inventory requirement. It relies on arguments built from one operation. Examples of such arguments from the initial model are: $p \rightarrow q/(p \,\&\, r) \rightarrow q$, and $p \rightarrow q/$ $-q \rightarrow -p$, which are derivable from Operations (7) and (3), respectively. Such arguments will be called *single-operation arguments*, in contrast to *multiple-operation arguments*. The inventory prediction has two parts:

(a) A subject honoring the multiple-operation argument $\{\mathbf{o}_{\alpha_1}, \ldots, \mathbf{o}_{\alpha_m}\}$ will honor each of the single-operation arguments $\{\mathbf{o}_{\alpha_1}\}, \ldots, \{\mathbf{o}_{\alpha_m}\}$.

(b) A subject rejecting the multiple-operation argument $\{\mathbf{o}_{\alpha_1}, \ldots, \mathbf{o}_{\alpha_m}\}$ will reject at least one of the single-operation arguments $\{\mathbf{o}_{\alpha_1}\}, \ldots, \{\mathbf{o}_{\alpha_m}\}$.

Part (b) of the prediction requires the distinction between a judgment of invalidity and a feeling of computational overload. The prediction applies only if the multiple-operation argument $\{\mathbf{o}_{\alpha_1}, \ldots, \mathbf{o}_{\alpha_m}\}$ is definitely rejected.

As an example from the initial model, consider the argument and derivation given at the beginning of this section. The inventory requirement is fulfilled if, first, every subject honoring the multiple-operation argument

(i) $\dfrac{(p \lor q) \rightarrow r}{(-r \,\&\, s) \rightarrow -p}$

also honors each of the single-operation arguments

(ii) $\dfrac{(p \lor q) \rightarrow r}{p \rightarrow r}$

(iii) $\dfrac{p \rightarrow r}{-r \rightarrow -p}$

(iv) $\dfrac{p \rightarrow q}{(p \,\&\, r) \rightarrow q}$

[6] A second index of computation overload refers to subjects' responses to the same argument through multiple presentations. Provided that the argument can be disguised from trial to trial (to prevent response perseveration), and provided that the subject is required to respond either "valid" or "invalid" on every presentation, his replies across presentations should be random rather than systematically "valid" or "invalid." This criterion was employed in Section 11.3 of Volume 2. The two criteria offered for recognizing computational overload should coincide.

In Volume 2 we considered all rejections of inferences validated by our theory to be due to processing limitations. This conclusion was based on data analyses discussed in Volume 2, Chapters 7, 9, and 11. The result was that an inventory analysis like the one proposed here was automatically ruled out on theoretical grounds (see Section 7.3 of Volume 2, Footnote 1). In the present volume, we consider these issues afresh.

which correspond to Operations (2), (3), and (6), respectively; and, second, every subject who deems Argument (i) invalid also deems at least one of Arguments (ii)–(iv) invalid.

5.2 THE ADDITIVITY REQUIREMENT

Let D be a real-valued function defined over arguments based on zero to m operations. For each argument $\{o_{\alpha_1}, \ldots, o_{\alpha_m}\}$ D assigns a difficulty coefficient D $\{o_{\alpha_1}, \ldots, o_{\alpha_m}\}$. This number represents the difficulty experienced by subjects in judging the validity of an argument. The function D should be a psychologically natural measure of difficulty and have interval-scale properties. Time required for a judgment might be one such measure. Other measures are discussed in the next chapter.

When considering the difficulty of arguments, our convention to represent an argument by the set of operations involved in its derivation must be modified. Since two applications of the same operation in a mental derivation can be expected to be more difficult than one alone, we now let each o_i represent an operation application, rather than an operation simply. Thus, for example, the argument $\{o_i, o_j\}$ might involve one application of each of two distinct operations, or two applications of one operation. (Thus, m is no longer restricted to be less than or equal to n.)

A deduction model should reflect the distribution of operations across arguments. The theory would be strongly supported were the following equality to hold:

(1) $D \{o_{\alpha_1}, \ldots, o_{\alpha_m}\} = D \{o_{\alpha_1}\} + \cdots + D \{o_{\alpha_m}\}$

If we use the sample argument of the last section as an illustration, this equation says that the difficulty coefficient for the multiple-operation argument

$$\frac{(p \vee q) \to r}{(-r \,\&\, s) \to -p}$$

equals the sum of the difficulty coefficients for the single operation arguments

$$\frac{(p \vee q) \to r}{p \to r}$$

$$\frac{p \to q}{-q \to -p}$$

$$\frac{p \to q}{(p \,\&\, s) \to q}$$

Although we have expressed Eq. (1) with the use of single-operation arguments, support for the model would accrue from satisfaction of the more general case:

$$D \{o_{\alpha_1}, \ldots, o_{\alpha_j}, o_{\alpha_{j+1}}, \ldots, o_{\alpha_m}\}$$
$$= D \{o_{\alpha_1}, \ldots, o_{\alpha_j}\} + D \{o_{\alpha_{j+1}}, \ldots, o_{\alpha_m}\}$$

In actually evaluating deduction models, however, we shall stick to analyses in which single-operation arguments are summed for comparison with multiple-operation arguments.

It is unlikely that Eq. (1) will hold, regardless of the truth of the theory. One reason is the presence of additive constants for each argument. Such constants reflect the difficulty associated with the general evaluation process, apart from the difficulty of executing operations. Another reason is possible interaction effects between operations. It is possible that some operations are easier to execute in the presence of other operations than alone; or, operation o_i might be more easily executed in a derivation that involves operation o_j than in one that involves o_k. One possibility we shall not countenance, however, is that the addition of an operation renders a derivation easier. Thus, we have the following requirement:

$$(2) \quad D \{o_{\alpha_1}, \ldots, o_{\alpha_m}\} > D \{o_{\alpha_1}, \ldots, o_{\alpha_{m-1}}\}$$

More generally, we might place the following condition on deduction models, assuming that the rank order of operation difficulty does not change as a function of the derivations in which the operations appear:

$$(3) \quad \text{If } D \{o_{\alpha_i}\} > D \{o_{\alpha_{i'}}\}, \text{ then}$$

$$D \{o_{\alpha_1}, \ldots, o_{\alpha_i}, \ldots, o_{\alpha_m}\} > D \{o_{\alpha_1}, \ldots, o_{\alpha_{i'}}, \ldots, o_{\alpha_m}\}$$

Conditions (2) and (3) are acceptable but weak. Fulfillment of these inequalities would not greatly increase our confidence in the models predicting them. Between Requirement 1 and Requirements 2 and 3, there is the family of requirements displayed in (4):

$$(4) \qquad D \{o_i, o_j\} = c_1[D \{o_i\} + D \{o_j\}] + b_1$$
$$D \{o_i, o_j, o_k\} = c_2[D \{o_i\} + D \{o_j\} + D \{o_k\}] + b_2$$
$$\cdot$$
$$\cdot$$
$$\cdot$$
$$D \{o_{\alpha_1}, \ldots, o_{\alpha_m}\} = c_{m-1}[D \{o_{\alpha_1}\} + \cdots + D \{o_{\alpha_m}\}] + b_{m-1}$$

The first equation in (4) says that the difficulty coefficient of a double-operation argument is a linear function of the sum of the difficulty coefficients of the two single-operation arguments that are based on the same operations. The same holds for the other equations. The numbers c_i and b_i are constants for any $(i + 1)$-operation argument. Hopefully, these constants provide the needed flexibility that made Requirement 1 too severe. Flexibility is also achieved by allowing the multiplicative constant c and the additive constant b to vary for arguments involving different numbers of operations.[7]

We have selected a special case of (4) as the empirical condition on deduction models that we shall investigate. This special case is given in Eq. (5):

$$(5) \quad D\{o_{\alpha_1}, \ldots, o_{\alpha_m}\} = c[D\{o_{\alpha_1}\} + \cdots + D\{o_{\alpha_n}\}] + b$$

Equation (5) represents the *additivity requirement*. The sum of the difficulties of single-operation arguments will be used to predict, up to linearity, the difficulty of the relevant multiple-operation argument. We shall not be concerned with the number of operations in the multiple-operation argument. Hence, in any given experiment, the same constants c and b must suffice for multiple-operation arguments based on different numbers of operations. Thus, the c and b in Eq. (5) are not subscripted.[8]

We exemplify the additivity requirement with the initial model. Consider the following multiple-operation arguments:

(i) $p \rightarrow (q \& r)$
$$\overline{-q \rightarrow -p}$$

(ii) $p \rightarrow q$
$$\overline{-q \rightarrow (-p \lor r)}$$

(iii) $(p \lor q) \rightarrow r$
$$\overline{(p \& s) \rightarrow (r \& s)}$$

(iv) $p \rightarrow (q \& r)$
$$\overline{-r \rightarrow (-p \lor s)}$$

Argument (i) is based on Operations (1) and (3) from Section 4.2. Argument (ii) is based on Operations (3) and (7). Argument (iii) is based on Operations (2) and (4). Argument (iv) is based on Operations (1), (3), and (7). We pair the difficulty of Argument (i) with the difficulty of an argument based on Operation (1) plus the difficulty of an argument based on Operation (3). The same applies to the other arguments. The result is summarized in Table 5.1, where o_i is used to represent Operation (i) of the initial model. To determine

---

[7] A more general formulation of Eq. (4), not relying on the use of single-operation arguments, is possible.

[8] In order to reduce the effect of variability due to numbers of operations, we have attempted to subtract some additive constants from each difficulty coefficient of Eq. (5). This was achieved by subtracting the difficulty coefficient of an argument based on virtually no operations from the difficulty coefficients of real arguments (see Section 8.2). Let DØ denote the difficulty of the operationless argument. Then Eq. 5 might be amended to read:

$$D\{o_{\alpha_1}, \ldots, o_{\alpha_m}\} - DØ = C[D\{o_{\alpha_1}\} - DØ + \cdots + D\{o_{\alpha_m}\} - DØ] + b$$

TABLE 5.1

The Additivity Analysis for Four Arguments
Based on the Initial Model

Difficulty coefficients for multiple-operation arguments	Sums of difficulty coefficients for single-operation arguments
(1) $D \{o_1, o_3\}$	$D \{o_1\} + D \{o_3\}$
(2) $D \{o_3, o_7\}$	$D \{o_3\} + D \{o_7\}$
(3) $D \{o_2, o_4\}$	$D \{o_2\} + D \{o_4\}$
(4) $D \{o_1, o_3, o_7\}$	$D \{o_1\} + D \{o_3\} + D \{o_7\}$

whether the left-hand column of Table 5.1 is a linear transformation of the right-hand column we compute a Pearson correlation coefficient. The size of the coefficient indicates the degree of linearity of the relation between the columns.[9]

In the experimental analyses to be reported, more than four pairs of observations are correlated. But the logic of the analysis is the same. The correlation testing the additivity requirement will be called the *additivity correlation*.

We now make seven observations about the inventory and additivity requirements:

1. The additivity requirement (Eq. 5) is formulated in terms of operations. The steps of the executive are not mentioned. The reason is that, according to the present conception, applying an operation requires testing the legality and helpfulness of every operation in the model's list prior to and including the given operation. Hence, any measure of the difficulty of an argument based on operations $o_{\alpha_1}, \ldots, o_{\alpha_m}$ includes not only the difficulty accruing to the transformations of formulas effected by those operations, but also the difficulty of all the tests for legality and helpfulness presupposed by the operations $o_{\alpha_1}, \ldots, o_{\alpha_m}$. The latter difficulty is constant for a given operation, regardless of which other operations accompany it in a mental derivation. This is because the executive specifies a return to the top of the model's list of operations after the application of any operation during a derivation (cf. Section 4.2).

Let us make these points again. A deduction model consists of an ordered set of operations $\langle o_1, \ldots, o_n \rangle$, where each operation has an accompanying helping condition. Given the nature of the executive described in Section 4.2, the difficulty of applying operation o_j results from (a) the difficulty of checking the legality and helpfulness of each operation o_i, $i < j$, and finding each

[9] Only positive correlations are expected.

not applicable, (*b*) the difficulty of checking the legality and helping condition of operation o_j, and finding it both legal and helpful, and (*c*) applying operation o_j to the current line of the derivation in question, converting that line into a new one. The difficulty of an operation o_j in a derivation is independent of whether the operation o_i, $i < j$ has applied first, because after o_i has applied, the executive resumes the search for further applicable operations with o_1, not with o_{i+1} (as described in Section 4.2). In this way, the difficulty of steps in the executive routine are counted into Eq. (5).

2. Although the difficulty of an operation does not depend, theoretically, on which other operations accompany it in a derivation (as just argued), it may depend somewhat on the particular line l_i that has been most recently added to the derivation (particularly, on which substitution instance of the given operation it is). This is because formulas may differ in the difficulty they pose for testing operations' legality and helpfulness. We shall largely ignore this complication. The reason is post hoc. Concern with the operations seems to be all that is required to fulfill the additivity requirement. Improvement may be possible by more refined consideration of the formula being rewritten by an operation, but efforts in this regard have not met with success (see Chapter 9).

3. The order of operations in a derivation is not directly tested by any of the analyses proposed (although such a test based on the additivity requirement is outlined in Chapter 9). Rather, the order of application of operations is indirectly related, via the executive, to the selection of operations that appear in a given derivation.

4. The additivity analysis resembles the prediction of formula difficulty in Voume 2. In Volume 2 some parameter estimation based on prior experimentation by others was employed (see Voume 2, Section 6.3). The present analysis is more self-contained.

5. We desire the most elementary operations possible. There should be no operation o_i deducible from other operations in such a way that an argument based on o_i behaves like a multiple-operation argument with respect to the inventory and additivity requirements. An operation o_i is deducible from operations $o_{\alpha_1}, \ldots, o_{\alpha_m}$ if each application of o_i can be replaced by an application of the sequence of operations $o_{\alpha_1}, \ldots, o_{\alpha_m}$, with the same line in the derivation resulting from o_i as from $o_{\alpha_1}, \ldots, o_{\alpha_m}$. None of the empirical requirements to be proposed can, by themselves, rule out the possibility that the model's operations are not psychologically elementary, for, what is represented as $\{o_i\}$ or D $\{o_i\}$ may actually refer to $\{o_{\alpha_1}, \ldots, o_{\alpha_m}\}$ or D $\{o_{\alpha_1}, \ldots, o_{\alpha_m}\}$. To reveal this, it is necessary to attempt to treat $\{o_i\}$ as the multiple-operation argument $\{o_{\alpha_1}, \ldots, o_{\alpha_m}\}$.

Provided that the natural deduction approach is correct, a theory based on psychologically elementary operations in the sense given would constitute the best account of logical judgment possible without recourse to a reductionist explanation. (See Putnam, 1973, for remarks on reductionism in psychology.)[10]

6. Equation (5) assumes a "city-block" amalgamation of operation difficulties. Euclidean and other amalgamations are possible. The Euclidean version of Eq. (5) is

$$\text{D}\,\{\mathbf{o}_{\alpha_1},\ldots,\mathbf{o}_{\alpha_m}\} = c[(\text{D}\,\{\mathbf{o}_{\alpha_1}\}^2 + \cdots + \text{D}\,\{\mathbf{o}_{\alpha_m}\}^2)^{\frac{1}{2}}] + b$$

In general, this version of the additivity requirement produces worse results. So we stick to Eq. (5).

7. Equation (5) should not be taken to represent any simple model about the details of how argument difficulties are amalgamated. Ewart Thomas (personal communication) has shown that a variety of plausible assumptions about the nature of this amalgamation results in Eq. (5) or in equations that are sufficiently similar to be empirically indistinguishable from it on the basis of the data to be reported.

5.3 SOUNDNESS AND COMPLETENESS REQUIREMENTS

Deduction models should be psychologically complete. A deduction model is psychologically complete if it generates all the inferences that the target population finds logically certain. Thus, assessing psychological completeness presupposes feelings of logical certainty, intuitions of logical necessity. There is room for disagreement about whether intuitions of necessity are absolute or graded, about the status of unclear cases, and even about whether the idea of "necessity" in the intended sense is coherent (see Katz, 1967, 1972; Quine, 1972b, and references cited there for an extended discussion of this point). We find the hypothesis of an absolute dichotomy between analytic (or, necessary) and synthetic (or, contingent) truths to be allied to a set of provocative hypotheses concerning human mental functioning (see Katz & Bever, 1974, for further discussion). Since (a) these hypotheses are not implausible, (b) we have no methodological misgivings about investigating such matters as feelings of logical certainty, and (c) it seems wise to explore more interesting theories before less interesting theories, we shall posit an underlying dichotomy between feelings of logical certainty and other kinds of confidence. As with any empirical hypothesis, this one can be assessed only in light of a predictive theory based on it. Unclear intuitions can be decided by theoretical triangulation on the basis of clearer cases (see Katz, 1972, for elaboration of both of these ideas).

---

[10] It is, of course, possible for the true set of elementary psychological operations to fail to be logically independent. So long as they are psychologically independent, according to the criterion given, the theory is none the worse.

We shall be concerned with a "local" sense of completeness. This sense of completeness rests on a predetermined vocabulary of logical words. A theory is locally complete with respect to a given vocabulary if it can provide derivations for all the intuitively valid arguments expressible with the given vocabulary. A valid argument is expressible with the given vocabulary of logical words only if its validity rests on properties of those words and not on the logical properties of other words in the argument. Uniform-substitution tests can be used to determine which locutions in an argument govern its validity.[11]

The vocabulary for the initial model, and its elaboration in Part 2, consists of the expressions "and," "or," "not," and "if . . . then. . . ."[12] Consequently, an argument like

Some phalaropes are both carnivores and guinea fowls.

Some guinea fowls are phalaropes.

is not within the purview of the theory since its validity hinges partly on logical properties of the word "some."

In addition to completeness, it seems that a deduction model should refrain from providing derivations for arguments that are considered to be invalid. In this sense, the theory should be psychologically sound. In assessing soundness, the distinction drawn in Section 5.1 between arguments firmly rejected as invalid and those rejected for reasons of sheer complexity is important. Unless limitations are built into the executive, derivations of arbitrary length can be generated corresponding to increasingly complex arguments. These arguments may not give rise to an intuition of logical truth. Since they do not produce a conviction of invalidity either, the derivation of such arguments does not count against the theory. We shall not attempt to build into the executive any argument-complexity guidelines. Instead, here as before, when arguments are too complicated to produce intuitions of either validity or invalidity, all bets are off.

The soundness and inventory requirements seem to conflict. According to the latter, a subject's decision to reject an argument for which a derivation is given by the theory is matched by rejection of certain other arguments for which a derivation is also given. But if a subject rejects an argument that is derivable from the theory, then the soundness of the theory is brought into question. So, it seems that only unsound theories allow the inventory requirement to be tested.

---

[11] We are not attempting to distinguish in any fundamental sense between a special class of logical particles and the rest of language. We agree with Katz (1972) that all words have logical properties.

[12] The biconditional concept, expressed as "if and only if," does not appear in experimental arguments.

To avoid this conclusion, soundness may be referred to subjects' *competence,* whereas the inventory and additivity requirements are left at the level of *performance.* Unlike performance, subjects' competence is not directly observable in the array of arguments accepted and rejected. Rejection of arguments can be ascribed to performance factors, and hence not threaten soundness; yet the inventory requirement can still be tested.

This proposal requires that empirical constraints be placed on hypotheses about subjects' logical competence. But formulating such constraints leads to conceptual difficulties. These will be the concern of the seven remarks to follow. Our considerations are tentative. As a result, soundness does not figure prominently in evaluating models proposed in later chapters.

1. One proposal for specifying the logical competence of adolescents is to examine the logical performance of adults. The theory would then be taken to describe adolescent operations as they will be when all have solidified sufficiently in their logical competence to show up in their logical performance. One difficulty with this suggestion is that it is likely to be as true for adults as for adolescents that the inventory requirement will hold but soundness will not. More importantly, the suggestion prejudges the question of whether adult logical abilities have the same organization as that of adolescents (and similarly for other developmental levels). The organization might well be the same and this may be confirmable by independent analyses such as the additivity analysis. But in a book devoted to cognitive development, it is unfortunate to favor this hypothesis so early.

2. Another solution might be to apply the soundness criterion only to the fruits of leisurely reflection. If, after prolonged contemplation, an argument is still considered invalid, then it is a genuine counterexample to the soundness of any theory that generates it. The difficulty with this suggestion is that such contemplation leads the subject into his own kind of theory construction, involving him in explicit rules of inference and proof finding. Subjects' pristine logical intuitions may be smothered by the zeal of system building.

3. We might stipulate that whereas the inventory (and additivity) requirements are to hold for subjects individually, the soundness requirement applies collectively; the theory is justified in generating an argument if at least x percent ($x < 100$) of the population deems it valid. Equally, regarding completeness, the theory is responsible for generating all those arguments honored by at least x percent of the population. By taking the union of the arguments honored by different subjects we hope for a closer look at subjects' competence. As before, the inventory requirement is testable thanks to the presence of performance factors that occasionally block the application of the operations in competence.

A question immediately arises. How can we be sure that taking the union of arguments deemed valid by a given population does not reify a nonexisting common competence? Indeed, by choosing a sufficiently heterogeneous population of subjects for study, we might be forced to include two arguments in competence that are identical except that the conclusion of one is the negation of the conclusion of the other. This would require a set of inconsistent operations. Yet, individually, subjects might seem reasonable enough and deny the validity of at least one of the arguments. Statistical criteria can be imposed to rule out this possibility, but the general problem remains: When are we studying one underlying competence for a population, and when are we unwittingly dealing with the union of two or more competencies distributed throughout the population? It might be suggested that we decide this question on the basis of the homogeneity of the population. A homogeneous population has the same competence. A heterogeneous population need not have the same competence. But what properties shall we use to decide whether a population is homogeneous? Recalling the considerations of Chapter 1, it seems that specifying the properties that count for deciding whether a population is homogeneous is best done in light of a theory of the subjects' logical abilities! It is the empirical criteria for such theories that are now at issue.

4. What kinds of performance factors cause a subject to be unfaithful to his competence? If we knew this, the problem of defining competence would be solved: competence is a subject's ability as it would appear if it were unmarred by performance limitations. Let us not consider such performance factors as distraction and reading errors. These things lead both the inventory and soundness requirements into error and thus do not bear on the present problem. Moreover, that sort of performance factor can be controlled well enough. Another kind of performance factor relates to derivation complexity. Whatever limits our ability to evaluate arguments intuitively (rather than through proof finding) is a kind of performance limitation. Chomsky (1965), similarly, attributes our inability to process very long or nested sentences to performance factors. But this kind of performance factor is also not relevant to our present concern. For purposes of assessing both the inventory and soundness requirements, we have already agreed to ignore arguments that give rise neither to judgments of validity nor invalidity. Although a theory of the limits of allowable derivation complexity would be valuable in its own right, our present concern is how to treat arguments that are honored by some members of the target population but rejected by others. What kind of strange performance factor leads a subject to take a principled stand against the validity of an argument?

5. Perhaps we should concede that a theory of logical judgment is wrong if it provides derivations for arguments that are deemed invalid by a

subject, a subject that the theory nevertheless purports to describe. Subjects who differ in the array of arguments accepted or rejected will simply require different models. The inventory analysis in that case furnishes no new information and should be dropped.

Before reaching this conclusion, one more avenue needs exploration. If two subjects disagree about the validity of an argument (both having firm intuitions), they may not share the same presuppositions about the task. Despite uniform instructions, one subject might be using high inductive strength rather than deductive certainty as the basis for a decision. Or, one of the subjects might have introduced an implicit premise into the argument, contrary to instructions (cf. Henle, 1962). More tellingly, different subjects may understand logical words in the arguments in different ways, again despite instruction. Different interpretations of the word "or" (exclusive versus inclusive) may persist between subjects. This is one explanation for a subject honoring an inference that is invalid by traditional canons: the subject understands key logical words differently than the traditional logician. To the extent that this is true, an erring subject should not be branded illogical, for it is not as if the subject and logician disagree about the validity of an argument. Rather, the subject and logician are evaluating different arguments that happen to have the same orthographic (or phonological) representation.

This is also a possible explanation for a subject failing to honor an argument validated by our theory: he is not using the logical vocabulary in the sense that we intended it, in the sense whose psychology the theory is meant to explicate. Indeed, it is not easy to suppose that a person possesses the same logical concepts we do, yet draws different conclusions about simple intuitive arguments. Rather, the latter fact indicates that the other person was not using the same logical concepts after all. Quine (1970) discusses the present problem in the context of translating languages. He says that "logical truth is guaranteed under translation [p. 83]." "The logics of two cultures will be...incommensurable at worst and never in conflict, since conflict would simply discredit our translation. The same attitude would apply...even to a logical deviant within our linguistic community: we would account his deviation a difference of dialect [p. 96]."[13]

The burden of these considerations is that the soundness requirement is illusory. If a subject fails to honor an argument validated by the theory,

[13] Further, Quine (1970) asks whether a person could "really" be meaning and thinking genuine conjunction in his use of 'and' after all, just as we do, and genuine alternation in his use of 'or,' and merely be disagreeing with us on points of logical doctrine respecting the laws of conjunction and alternation? Clearly this is nonsense. There is no residual essence of conjunction and alternation in addition to the sounds and notations and the laws in conformity with which a man uses those sounds and notations [p. 81]." Except for the last sentence, which unpacks into a full-blown behaviorism, Quine's claim is reasonable.

he is ipso facto understanding key logical words in some operations differently than the way they are explicated by their role in the theory. The deductions involving a logical concept may or may not exhaust its meaning (there may be "surplus meaning" beyond that given within the system of deductions; cf. Section 21.3). But these deductions seem to impose necessary conditions on the meaning of the concepts.

Hence, a deduction model can never be unsound in the present sense. The theory is not necessarily an account of subjects' understanding of "and," "or," "not," etc. Rather, the theory presupposes that understanding. It explains how people draw deductive conclusions from propositions employing particular logical connectives. Whenever the specified connectives are employed by the subject, the operations and executive are as stated. The inventory analysis is possible because performance factors, such as deviations from the concepts involved in the theory, result in a failure to apply particular operations. This opens the door to the inventory analysis of Section 5.1.[14]

In short, it is possible for a proposed deduction model to generate a psychologically incorrect derivation, but it cannot generate a psychologically incorrect argument. The model should generate as many arguments as possible, provided that anyone accepting one of these arguments does so by means of the mental derivation described by the model. The latter proviso is tested by means of the inventory and additivity requirements.

To generate as many arguments as possible, we should not be reluctant to include operations that are invalid from the point of view of classical logic. So long as these operations underlie arguments that some subjects accept, the hypothesized derivations may be tested. The models to be presented in this book do not contain invalid operations, but this is only because few subjects accept invalid arguments once the meaning of certain logical locutions is specified.

6. Against the libertine flavor of these remarks, another consideration must be entered. Theories can be true but uninteresting. It is not enough to specify by means of a set of logical concepts the operations underlying subjects' deductions. Those concepts should have psychological interest.[15] For example, of all the conditional statements possible to express, truth-functional material implication is one of the least interesting. We might hope that a proposed model would not rely on that particular interpretation

[14] Needless to say, lack of a soundness requirement does not rob the theory of empirical content. The inventory and additivity requirements impose two empirical conditions on the truth of proposed deduction models (other criteria can be furnished as well).

[15] Psychological interest is a graded notion, unlike the dichotomous categories of intuitively valid and intuitively invalid. So there is no possibility of reconstructing the soundness requirement on the basis of psychological interest.

of "if. . .then. . ." locutions. In the experiments to be reported, subjects are not instructed to interpret conditionals truth-functionally (see Chapter 7). On the other hand, subjects are instructed to treat "or" inclusively (either. . .or. . .or both), since inclusive disjunction results in a rich set of valid arguments. This cannot be said for exclusive disjunction. The resulting logic gains additional interest from its role in mathematical arguments and other technical contexts.

7. A theory might purport to explicate the logical properties of expressions in unconstrained natural language. Ordinary usage of simple words like "and" is quite complex (Jacobs & Rosenbaum, 1968). An account of the deductions in which such words figure would be of considerable interest. For these systems, there is a clear and nonvacuous criterion of soundness: the system should not generate an argument that is counterintuitive to subjects using their spontaneous vocabulary in a natural way. However, an unsound theory in this sense cannot be criticized for misrepresenting subjects' deductive processes; for, the counterintuitiveness of the unsound argument is best ascribed to the theory's misrepresentation of subjects' spontaneous vocabularies, not the deductions in which those vocabularies appear.

In assessing a deduction model's "linguistic" soundness, a procedure is needed for matching natural-language arguments to the symbolism of the model's derivations. There is more than one way, for example, to translate the notation of propositional logic. However, as mentioned in Section 4.3, Remark 10, we are forced to rely on an intuitive translation procedure. No formal mapping is provided.[16]

Although a complete theory of inferential reasoning will specify the logical properties of natural-language locutions, models for deduction that employ simpler concepts like logical conjunction can also provide insights into the processes of deduction as well as insights into the mechanisms of cognitive development. The present theory is a mixture. It is based on standard logical conjunction, disjunction, and negation, as well as on a less standard conditional locution (the "if. . .then. . ." expression). The latter is left more squarely in the domain of natural language. We emerge, then, with something of a soundness requirement, but not one that applies to deduction per se. Rather, only to the extent that we rely on something akin to the natural-language meaning of "if. . .then. . ." do we want our

[16] The mapping from formulas to natural language, whether intuitive or explicit, also conditions one's choice of operations for the theory. In particular, some mappings will make it unnecessary to include operations that are invalid from the point of view of classical logic (see Remark 5, above). Other mappings will demand such operations if much of the subjects' logical intuitions are to be captured. More to the point, an explicit translation procedure will render the operations mere formal objects to which the characterization of "valid" or "invalid" does not apply.

theory to respect the facts of natural usage (cf. Footnote 9 of Chapter 21).

With these seven remarks the conceptual issue of soundness seems tolerably clear. Few conceptual analyses are empirically innocent, however. In Section 21.1, we return to the question of why subjects reject arguments that are validated by the theory. This time we are armed with data.

6

Methodological Issues

Methodological issues are considered in this chapter, including measures of difficulty and the contents of arguments. The discussion justifies aspects of the methodology presented in the next chapter.

6.1 EXPLAINING THE TASK

Our study deals with deduction. We are not concerned with whether adolescents spontaneously evaluate arguments in terms of validity instead of inductive strength or truth-value of the conclusion. It is important to ensure that subjects use their deductive abilities, and only these, in assessing arguments presented to them. One way to promote the use of deduction is to explain the nature of a valid inference and explain that this is the only basis for evaluating arguments in the experiment. The explanation of validity that we employ is couched in terms of the certainty of the conclusion of an argument given only the truth of the premise.

A second way to promote the use of deduction is to employ premises and conclusions about which the subject is not already committed. As studies by Henle (1962) have shown, an argument like

Water pollution kills millions of fish every year.

Industrialized waste should not be poured into our lakes and rivers.

can seduce subjects away from deduction.

58

6.2 EXPLANATION OF LOGICAL WORDS

An important concept within the logic that we are investigating is inclusive disjunction.[1] To keep the wording of the argument familiar, the natural-language word "or" is employed to represent it.[2] But often the word "or" in English has an exclusive sense. An example is the admonition to a child: "You can have either cake or ice cream." Because of situational factors, "not both" is implicit. We do not wish to determine whether subjects typically interpret "or" inclusively. Commonplace observation indicates that they do not. Instead, the experiment concerns deductive abilities with a few key concepts, among them, inclusive disjunction. It would thus defeat the purpose of the experiments if subjects uniformly interpreted "or" exclusively. The obvious precaution is to explain to subjects that "or" is used inclusively in the experiment, and to explain the inclusive sense.

Related considerations apply to the "if. . .then. . ." expression. Geiss and Zwicky (1971) point out that such conditionals are often taken as biconditionals in ordinary discourse. For example, the sentence "If it is sunny tomorrow then we shall go swimming" is taken to mean "we shall go swimming tomorrow if and only if it is sunny." The psychology of conditional assertions is complex and important. The problem would be trivialized by insisting that subjects understand "if. . .then. . ." locutions truth-functionally. This would render "if. . .then. . ." no more conditional than statements employing "and" and "not."[3] However, so that we have an initial understanding of subjects' use of "if. . .then. . . ," subjects are warned against confusing it with the biconditional.[4]

Our treatment of the two logical concepts is not even-handed. Regarding "or," we impose standard logical usage upon our subjects. Regarding "if. . .then. . . ," we leave subjects more to their own devices, cautioning them only against misconstruing conditionals as biconditionals. We hope to maximize the interest of the logical concepts employed in our model. Inclusive "or" enters into a richer set of deductions than does exclusive "or," at least in the context of the accompanying concepts of conjunction

[1] Symbolized in logic by the wedge, "v." The statement $p \vee q$ is true if either or both of p and q is true.

[2] As opposed to using a barbarism like "and/or." Preliminary studies with junior high school students showed them to be uncomfortable with the and/or device.

[3] In propositional logic, "if p then q" (symbolized "$p \rightarrow q$") is true just in the case p is not true, or q is true, or both; that is, $p \rightarrow q$ is false only if p is true and q is false.

[4] Frase (1966) has also instructed subjects as to the intended meaning of key logical words in arguments to be evaluated. Not surprisingly, subjects' opinions as to the validity or invalidity of inferences was thereby brought into closer conformity with standard logics based on those same concepts. See also Ceraso and Provitera (1971) for a similar result.

and negation. On the other hand, the propositional-logic version of conditionals is minimally imaginative. So we have not imposed a standard interpretation of "if. . .then. . ." on our subjects. We hope instead to make use of something closer to their spontaneous concept.[5]

6.3   MEASURES OF ARGUMENT DIFFICULTY

The additivity requirement of Section 5.2 presupposes a measure of the difficulty subjects have in evaluating arguments. In Volume 2 the measure of difficulty was error rate. To make this measure theoretically coherent, it was necessary to assume that an argument was incorrectly evaluated (from the point of view of the model) only when it was too complex to give rise to a firm intuition of either validity or invalidity. There was some evidence supporting this idea (see Volume 2, Sections 6.5, 6.6, and 11.4), and much theorizing exploited it (Volume 2, Chapter 6). But in general this measure of difficulty has little to recommend it. First, Section 20.4 presents evidence contradicting the conclusion of Volume 2 that mislabeling an argument is due primarily to computational overload. Second, use of error rate invalidates the inventory analysis (see Section 7.3, Footnote 1, Volume 2). With respect to the inventory analysis, derivations with different operations can never be functionally identical. On the other hand, the processing complexity of derivations with different operations may be the same. Third, error rate or acceptance rate of arguments is a between-subjects measure. Since the theory concerns individuals, the difficulty measure should at least in principle apply to data based on one subject.

One experiment reported in Volume 2 employed latency of response. This measure of difficulty has two drawbacks. To diminish variability, it is necessary to ask for fast responding. Rushing the subject in this way can lead to an ill-considered response, or to decisions based on situation-specific strategies that are remote from processes used in relaxed circumstances. Furthermore, for the arguments used in Volume 2, there were large order effects. This necessitated averaging latencies across subjects.

In the present research, subjects construct a scale for perceived difficulty of arguments. The size of the number assigned is taken to be linearly related to the complexity of the derivation for the subject. There are two dangers in this procedure. First, adolescents may find rating to be difficult or confusing. Second, work by Banks and Hill (1974) raises the possibility that subjects' assignment of numbers to subjective continua is nonlinear.

Regarding the first danger, subjects in our experiments seem comfortable with the rating procedure. Moreover, Experiment 1 (Chapter 8) shows that use of rating as a measure of difficulty gives the same theoretical results

---

[5] But see the remarks on the properties of conditionals in our system, in Chapter 21, Footnote 9.

as did error rate and latency in Volume 2. Regarding the second danger, we have computed logarithmic and exponential transformations of the raw scores provided by our subjects, in case the ratings contained one of these kinds of nonlinearities. These transformations affected the results of the additivity analysis only marginally, generally in the wrong direction. We shall proceed on the assumption that there is a linear relationship between the numbers used by the subjects and the mental complexity of derivations.[6] The smallness of the numbers employed in the rating (usually less than 100) makes this assumption the more plausible.[7]

Our rating procedure allows within-subject analyses, because order effects are reduced by an initial ranking procedure (see Section 7.3).

6.4 ROLE OF INVALID ARGUMENTS

In our model, deciding that an inference is valid depends on much the same mechanism as deciding that an inference is invalid (see Section 4.2, Remark 5). The difficulty of each is a function of the number and kind of operations used in an argument's derivation. The conclusion of an argument labeled valid by the theory is the last line in its derivation. For an invalid argument, the executive exits before reaching the conclusion as soon as legal and helpful operations can no longer be found. The predicted difficulty of an invalid inference thus depends on the helping conditions. The fewer the requirements for the application of an operation, the longer a "blind alley" the derivation for an invalid argument becomes. This incomplete derivation represents the implicit and unsuccessful attempt by the subject to find a deductive connection between the argument's premise and conclusion. By appropriately reformulating helping conditions it is possible to increase or decrease to some extent the predicted difficulty of invalid arguments, without affecting the predicted difficulty of valid arguments.

The theory of Volume 2 was used to predict the difficulty of both valid and invalid arguments. The present research is restricted to valid arguments. This is theoretically simpler because it allows us, temporarily, to write helping conditions with only valid arguments in mind. Methodologically, it is simpler for subjects to make comparisons of perceived difficulty among arguments that are all valid, than among a logically heterogeneous set of arguments.

In every experiment, subjects received 5 or 6 invalid arguments drawn from a pool of 10 or 18 invalid arguments. These arguments are intuitively invalid for most people. They are also invalid from the point of view of both propositional logic and our theory. They are not considered in data

[6] The same post hoc considerations lead us to the "city block" over the Euclidean version of our additivity requirement. See Section 5.2.

[7] In general, we take the orderly experimental results to be reported as support for all the sets of assumptions, including linearity, that predict them.

analyses. Their purpose is to keep subjects alert to the possibility of invalid arguments as they evaluate the valid arguments. The great majority of subjects labeled the invalid arguments correctly.

Despite our exclusive concern in this book with valid arguments, it must be admitted that a complete theory will deal equally with the psychology of both valid and invalid inferences.

6.5   CONTENT OF THE ARGUMENTS

A schema like

$$(1) \quad \frac{p \rightarrow (q \,\&\, r)}{-q \rightarrow -p}$$

gives only an argument's logical structure.[8] The content of the argument, that is, the sentences for which p, q, and r stand, is obscured. Thus, Schema (1) represents the structure of both the arguments

> <u>If Harry left, then Martha stayed and Florence is happy.</u>
> If Martha did not stay, then Harry did not leave.

and

> <u>If the valence of carbon is less than that of magnesium, then the compound is unstable and the theory must be wrong.</u>
> If the compound is not unstable, then the valence of carbon is not less than that of magnesium.

Despite their translation into common propositional notation, these arguments are likely to have different psychological properties. Different content can affect the difficulty subjects have in evaluating arguments with the same logical structure. Wason and Johnson-Laird (1972) provide an excellent review of the complex literature documenting this phenomenon. One powerful variable is the extent to which propositions in an argument fit into a causal nexus familiar to the subject.[9]

---

[8] At least, as much of that structure as propositional logic reveals.

[9] Experiments are not required to see that the propositional form of an argument is not sufficient to explain its difficulty. This is made evident by the following logically isomorphic arguments:

> (2)   <u>Either the dog is asleep or Jane is washing the dishes.</u>
> If the dog is not asleep, then Jane is washing the dishes.

> (3)   <u>Either you sit down or I'll leave.</u>
> If you don't sit down, I'll leave.

The validity of (3) is easier to apprehend that the validity of (2). [For a chronometric study of "pseudoimperatives" like (3), see Springston & Clark, in press.]

In order to facilitate development of the model, we have attempted, initially, to neutralize the effects of content. All the arguments in Part 2 will deal with a sterile and artificial situation. As described in the next chapter, subjects are asked to imagine a blackboard in another room, upon which any consonant of the alphabet can be written. All statements in the arguments deal with this blackboard. Thus, the argument in Schema (1) becomes

If there is a Z, then there is both a Q and an H.

If there is not a Q, then there is not a Z.

In some experiments an alternative sentence structure was used, as follows:

If Z is there, then both Q and H are there.

If Q is not there, then Z is not there.

The difference in wording had no discernible effect on results. This kind of argument was developed and used by Taplin and Staudenmayer (1973).[10] In Part 3, we consider again arguments with familiar content.

For all its interest, the distinction between the logical form of a statement and its content is not absolute, but relative instead to the logical system at hand (see Katz, 1972, Preface). Questions concerning the effects of content on inferential reasoning blend into questions concerning the presence of a different logic. Returning to the issue of causal inference, if people systematically reason differently when using causal conditionals, as opposed to more arbitrary conditionals, it might be desirable to introduce a causal operator in the fashion of other modal operators (as does Burks, 1951), or to modify the system some other way. We might thereby hope to capture structurally this erstwhile content variable and be better able to investigate the possibility of a distinct set of logical operations underlying causal inferences.

---

[10] In pilot work, we used the same paradigm but employed nonsense syllables rather than letters. The initial model performs equally well in either paradigm.

7

Method

All the experiments reported here employed essentially the same method. For special purposes, there were minor departures from the standard procedure and these will be described as needed. The general procedure is given in this chapter for all experiments. It has five parts: introduction, sorting, ranking, scaling, and debriefing.

7.1   INTRODUCTION

Subjects came from high schools and junior high schools in the San Francisco Bay Area. Classes were selected from these schools so that (*a*) they included no seniors, (*b*) they were not mathematics classes, and (*c*) the students in the classes were considered by the principal and teacher to be cooperative. The great majority of subjects were middle-class. They participated in the experiment in groups as large as 50. The size of the groups as well as the grade and school of the students are noted with each experiment. Janet Davis and the present author performed the experiments together, except occasionally when only one could be present.

To begin the procedure, the experimenters introduced themselves to the students and thanked them for their willingness to participate in the experiment.[1] The following points were made:

(a) The experiment is designed to test a theory about how people reason, in particular, about how they draw conclusions from evidence.

[1] Technically, subjects were volunteers. But more accurately, they were volunteered by their principal and teacher. Virtually all the students were eager to participate, however, partly because, we believe, the experiments were performed during regular class hours.

(b) To test this theory, we need to have the opinion of (junior) high school students about the best answer to a set of reasoning problems, and their estimate of the difficulty of each problem.

(c) The correct answers to the problems are matters of opinion. The experiment does not, in any known way, measure students' "intelligence."

(d) No comparisons based on the experiment are made between students or between schools. Indeed, the experiment is performed anonymously. Names of students are not recorded.

(e) If the experiment is going to serve its purpose, it is important that each student think carefully about the problems. The experiment is moderately enjoyable, but it requires close attention. It is far preferable not to participate in the experiment than to perform carelessly or haphazardly.[2] If the experiment is upsetting in any way, the student should feel free to stop, no matter how far along into the experiment.[3]

(f) If at any time during the experiment, the student is unsure of what to do, or is confused by the instructions, he should raise his hand. One of the experimenters will confer individually with the student (or, if the question arose during the instructions, it was answered publically).[4]

These instructions were not a speech. One of the experimenters spoke informally from notes. In different experiments there was different phrasing. The wording and emphasis depended on the group of students being addressed, their demeanor, apparent interest, etc. This same semiformal procedure was employed for all the instructions. It was clear that any attempt to read instructions to the students would have invited apathy and loss of attention. Moreover, different ages and classes of students require different emphases and clarifications of the instructions. As Olson (1970) has maintained, the important thing to standardize in an experiment is the information each subject ultimately receives, not the exact words that reach his ears.

7.2 SORTING

Next, subjects were told about the nature of the experimental task by means of the following points:

(a) Each student was told they would receive an envelope containing about 30 slips of paper. On each slip would be typed a reasoning problem

[2] Very rarely, a student excercised the option at this point not to participate in the experiment. The vast majority remained.

[3] This point was added after an early experiment in which a junior high school student wept openly at the difficulty of the problems. This student insisted on finishing the experiment, however. Occasionally, a student would choose to discontinue the experiment in the middle. This was rare, however.

[4] Questions relating to the theory behind the experiment or to psychology in general were deferred.

involving inference. The experimenter said (roughly): "A person engages in inference when he takes the truth of one statement to guarantee the truth of another statement; that is, given that you believe a sentence, you infer a second sentence, if you believe that the second sentence has to be true, given that the first one is true." This point was elaborated as needed.

(b) The experimenter continued: "On each slip, there are two sentences, one above the other, separated by a solid black line. The top line is the *premise* of the problem. *The top line is always assumed to be true.* Your task is to decide whether the bottom sentence, called the *conclusion,* must be true, given the truth of the top line. So, always assume that the top line is true, and then ask yourself: 'Can I be sure that the bottom line is also true?' This is the same thing as asking yourself whether the conclusion of the problem follows logically from the problem's premise. Depending on your decision, we will be asking you to do different things with each slip."

(c) "The sentences in the problems all refer to a blackboard that you can imagine is in some other part of the school. Any letter of the alphabet can be written on that blackboard, and the sentences in the problems give you information about which letters appear there.[5] So, for example, the top line of a problem might be: There is both an *F* and a *B*.' That means that on the blackboard, there is written both an *F* and a *B*."

(d) "Your job is to read the top line of the problem and assume that it is true. Then read the bottom line of the problem and decide whether the bottom line must be true, given that the top line is true."

(e) In deciding each problem, the students were warned against using a previous problem to decide about a current one. Each problem was to be self-contained. ("Imagine that the blackboard has been erased between problems.")

(f) Subjects were asked to ignore a string of symbols placed at the top right of each problem. It was explained that these were assigned randomly to slips to allow the experimenters to code the data.

At this point, $8\frac{1}{2}$- by 11-inch sheets of paper were distributed to the subjects, which they placed on the desk (or table) in front of them. Spaced on the sheet were three expressions: CANNOT DECIDE, THE CONCLUSION DOES NOT FOLLOW, and THE CONCLUSION MUST BE TRUE. The instructions continued as follows:

(g) "Depending on your decision about each of the problems, you should place each slip in one of three piles on the sheet that we have given you. If you think that the bottom line of a problem must be true, given the truth of the top line, then place that slip underneath the line that says

---

[5] In fact, only consonants appeared in the problems.

THE CONCLUSION MUST BE TRUE. If you think that it is possible for the bottom line to be false, despite the truth of the top line, then place that slip under the line that says THE CONCLUSION DOES NOT FOLLOW. Finally, if a problem is too hard for you, if it seems too difficult to decide about, then place that slip under the line that says CANNOT DECIDE. If you cannot understand a problem, place it in the CANNOT DECIDE pile."

These instructions were amplified as necessary in order to respond to questions. In addition, it was remarked that few of the problems were very difficult, so that few, if any, of them would appear in the CANNOT DECIDE pile. It was also mentioned that a majority of the problems would likely appear to the students to belong in the CONCLUSION MUST BE TRUE pile. This was a perfectly acceptable outcome, but it was important to judge each problem separately.

At this point, instructions as to the intended meaning of the logical expressions "and," "or," and "if. . .then. . ." were given.

(h) The experimenter said (roughly): "Before giving out the envelopes, we would like to explain the meaning of three important phrases that occur in the problems. The first one is simple. It is just the word 'and.' If a line in a problem says that 'There is both an S and a C,' that means that both S and C are written on the board. Let's take an example. If one of the problems has the premise 'There is both a D and an R,' can you be sure that the conclusion 'There is a D' is true?" It was explained that the correct answer is "Yes." This slip, therefore, would be placed in the pile of slips for which the conclusion must be true. Other examples were given as needed, although there was hardly any difficulty with "and."

(i) The experimenter said (roughly): "The difficult word is 'or.' We are using this word in a slightly different way than it is ordinarily used. If a problem says: 'There is either a T or a Q,' that means that at least one of T and Q is on the board, maybe both; that is, the sentence 'There is either a T or a Q' is true if there is a T but not a Q, or if there is a Q but not a T, or if there is both a T and a Q. Remember that if there is both a T and a Q, then the sentence 'There is either a T or a Q' is true. To make certain that you understand, suppose that you receive the premise: 'There is an H.' Given that statement, can you be sure that the sentence: 'There is either an H or a V' is true?" The answer to this question is affirmative, and the reason for the answer was explained. At least one other example, with explanation, was given before proceeding.

(j) The experimenter said (roughly): "Finally, you should be careful about the 'if. . .then. . .' expression. If a line reads 'If there is a T, then there is an F,' that means that if you knew that there was a T written on the blackboard, then you can be sure that there is an F written there as well. To say that 'If there is a T, then there is an F' is not the same thing as saying that if there is not a T then there is not an F. There might be other reasons for F being written on the board than the presence of T. To say that 'If there is a T then there is an F' only means that if a T is there, then F will be there also. But F can be there without T. So, 'If there is a T, then there is an F' does not mean that if there is an F, then there is a T." These instructions were elaborated as necessary. The subjects seemed to have little difficulty grasping the point.

Following this clarification of the logical words, parts (d) and (g) of the instructions were recapitulated. Then the envelopes containing the slips were passed out and the subjects began work. The experimenters answered questions that arose by referring to the instructions. The sorting task took roughly 20 minutes. The half-way mark and other marks were announced. Subjects who finished early were asked to check their work.

Each slip was $8\frac{1}{2}$ by roughly 3 inches. They were typed with an IBM Selectrix typewriter with the "orator" element. This element produces characters $\frac{1}{4}$ inch high. The order of slips within each envelope was random.

The sorting task allows us to test the inventory requirement of Section 5.1. The additivity requirement of Section 5.2 is tested by means of the next two procedures.

7.3 RANKING

Upon completion of the sorting part of the experiment, subjects were instructed as follows:

(a) The slips piled under the line CANNOT DECIDE, if there were any, were to be folded in half (with a crease) and returned to the envelope. The slips piled under the line THE CONCLUSION DOES NOT FOLLOW were to be returned to the envelope without folding. The slips piled under the line THE CONCLUSION MUST BE TRUE were to remain on the subject's desk. The white sheet used for piling was returned. Subjects were informed that if they changed their minds during the remaining procedures about the status of one of the slips originally deemed valid, it was proper to return the slip to the envelope.

(b) The experimenter said (roughly): "Now we have an idea of which inferences you find legitimate or good, and which you find illegitimate. We would like now to find out how difficult each problem was for you to decide about. To do this, we would like you to make a column on your desk out of the slips that you think represent arguments whose conclusions must be true. At the bottom of the column, closest to you, put the slip for the easiest problem. Second closest to you, put the second easiest problem. Third closest to you put the third easiest problem. And so on, until at the top of the column, place the most difficult problem. To see whether you understand, what will you do if two slips are the exact same difficulty?" The correct answer, which was almost always given, was that slips of identical difficulty would be stacked on top of each other at the appropriate place in the column.[6] Amplification of these instructions was provided as necessary.

Before allowing subjects to construct the column, two injunctions were given:

(c) Subjects should not use the number of words in a problem as a measure of its difficulty. It is quite possible that a very long and wordy problem would be easy to decide about, whereas a short problem could be difficult. Instead of using the number of words in a problem as a basis for judging its difficulty, subjects were asked to think about the difficulty they experienced in deciding whether the conclusion had to be true, given the truth of the premise.

(d) In constructing the column, subjects should make an attempt to compare every slip with every other slip. In deciding about the relative difficulty of a given slip, the subject should go up the column comparing the given slip with every slip already in the column. The purpose of this admonition was to eliminate order effects. By comparing every slip to every other slip, the effect on relative difficulty of the order in which they are examined is, theoretically, nullified. Within-subject analyses are thus made feasible (see Section 6.3).

The ranking procedure lasted about 15 minutes.

7.4 SCALING

After ranking, subjects were instructed as follows:

(a) "We now have a rough idea of how difficult you found each inference that you judged to be legitimate. We would like to get an even more precise idea of your opinion about their difficulty by using numbers. In general, you will be assigning numbers to the slips so that the size of the number reflects the difficulty you experienced with that problem. The larger the number you give the slip, the more difficult that inference seemed to you. The smaller the number you give the slip, the easier that inference seemed to you."

At this juncture, a large diagram was displayed, comparable to Fig. 7.1. Figure 7.1 represents the column of slips on each student's desk. This figure

[6] Students occasionally suggested that identically difficult slips be placed side by side (short edges contiguous), thereby holding the same place in the column.

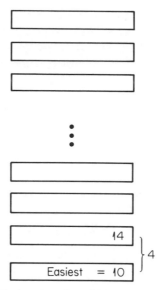

FIG. 7.1.   Diagram displayed to the subjects during the scaling procedure.

was referred to during the explanation of the scaling procedure. The instructions continued as follows:

(b) "When we ask you to begin, write the number 10 in the margin of the easiest slip. If you have more than one problem in the first pile, write the number 10 on each slip in that pile. The number 10 represents 10 units of difficulty. Unfortunately, we cannot tell you exactly what a unit of difficulty is, but whatever it means to you, the easiest problems gave you 10 units of difficulty."

(c) "For the second slip (or pile of slips) in your column, you may assign any number you please. If the difference in difficulty between the first and second slip is small, then assign a number to the second slip only a little larger than 10. If the difference between the first two slips is large, then assign a number to the second slip that is considerably more than 10. To have an example, we shall use the number 14, but you have your choice of any number."

(d) "Now the difference in number of units of difficulty between the first two slips (or pile of slips) is 4, in our example. Suppose that the difference between the second and third slips is exactly the same as the difference between the first and second slips; that is, suppose that the third slip is harder than the second slip by exactly the same amount as the second slip is harder than the first. What number would you write on the third slip?" The correct answer is 18, which the students usually offered spontaneously. "Suppose the difference between the second and third problems is less than the difference between the first and second problems. What can you say about the number that you would write on the third slip?" The correct answer is that the number would be less than 18. Explanation was given as needed. The complementary question, for the second difference being larger than the first, was also posed. "You decide what number to write on the third slip by asking yourself how much the third problem differs from the second. If it differs by a lot, compared to the difference between the first two problems, then you increase the number you gave to the second problem by a big amount and write it on the third slip. If the third slip differs from the second slip by only a little, compared to the difference between the first two problems, then you make the third slip's number only a little bigger than the second slip's number. You should feel free to use decimals, if you like. In the same way, you compare the fourth slip (or pile of slips) with the third slip (or pile of slips); and so on, up the column. In general, the idea is that a big jump in the difficulty of problems next to each other in the column is marked by a big jump in the numbers you write on the slips, and a little jump is marked by a little jump in the numbers you write on the slips. Always use the difference between the first and second slips to decide what counts as a big or a small increase." These instructions were amplified as necessary.

(e) Several admonitions were given before the subjects began scaling. First, slips in the same pile must get the same number (unless the subject wished to change his mind at that point about the ranking, which was permissible). Second, every slip must eventually have a number written on it, including every slip in a pile. Third, as the subject proceeded up the column, the numbers must get larger. If they do not, he is doing something wrong and should raise his hand.

We shall assume that the resulting scale has equal-interval properties, even though our instructions do not entirely conform to this kind of metric. We wished to avoid the additional complexity of explicit proportionality judgments between differences. The results of the experiments indicate that the scales that subjects produced were close enough to linearity for present purposes.

The actual scaling required about 10 minutes. The experimenters answered questions from the instructions as necessary.

7.5 DEBRIEFING

Following the scaling procedure, the slips were returned to their envelope. Subjects were then asked to write on the back of their envelopes whether they had taken a course in symbolic logic, or studied it in any of their mathematics classes. Some students stated that in geometry classes they had spent a few sessions on logic, but there was no mention of a symbolic approach. These latter subjects were asked, further, whether they thought they used the logic taught in their mathematics classes to help solve the problems. Throughout the experiments, only a few students indicated that they attempted to apply logic they had learned to some of the problems. Hence, this factor will be ignored hereafter.

Subjects were also asked to indicate on their envelopes whether they used mental imagery (which was explained to them), in solving the problems.[7] In particular, it was asked whether they imaged the blackboard upon which the letters were written. Roughly half the students reported the use of some mental imagery. We have performed within-subject analyses on imagery and nonimagery groups and found no appreciable differences in the results. Consequently, the use of imagery will be considered epiphenomenal and ignored hereafter.

At this point, the envelopes were turned in and the experimenters talked informally with the students about the experiment. There was little consensus concerning the techniques used to solve the problems. Usually, the most that students could report was careful study of the premise and conclusion, consisting mainly of its repetition. Some of the students' introspections, however, did resemble proof finding (see Section 2.2).

This concluded the experiment. It usually lasted about one hour, with sessions varying from 50 minutes to an hour and a half. Within two months after a given experiment, the present author returned to the school to lecture on the theory behind the experiment. No school was involved in two experiments.

With a few exceptions, the experiment engendered a spirit of cooperation among the students. Most found it enjoyable to be working with psychologists on a problem in human reasoning.

---

[7] Regrettably, this part of the debriefing procedure was omitted in the first two experiments.

Part II

PROPOSITIONAL ARGUMENTS

8

Experiment 1:
Validation of Methodology,
and the Question
of Alternative Operations

A model for adolescent logical judgment is developed in Part 2. The model is based on data from five experiments. The arguments figuring in these experiments are of the noncausal, "arbitrary" variety described in Section 6.5. Part 3 deals with arguments of more familiar content, as well as with arguments based on class inclusion.

8.1   AIMS OF THE EXPERIMENT

The experiments presented in this volume employ a different methodology than those described in Volume 2. We thought it worthwhile to attempt to replicate the chief theoretical finding of the previous study with the new procedures. The initial model of Section 4.2 is a close approximation to the model of Volume 2. It was tested in the present experiment. Given the executive described in Section 4.2, the model may be thought of as an ordered list of operations, along with their helping conditions. Table 8.1 summarizes the model underlying Experiment 1.[1]

The second aim of the experiment was to shed light on an issue raised in Section 11.2 of Volume 2. There it was pointed out that the model of Table 8.1 could not derive either of the arguments

(A) $\dfrac{(p \mathbin{\&} r) \to q}{(p \mathbin{\&} r) \to (q \mathbin{\&} r)}$

(B) $\dfrac{p \to (q \vee r)}{(p \vee r) \to (q \vee r)}$

[1] The helping conditions in Table 8.1 include the amendments discussed in Section 4.3.

TABLE 8.1
Theory for Experiments 1 and 2

1. $A \rightarrow (B \ \& \ C)/A \rightarrow B$

No subformula of C occurs conjoined to B in the conclusion.

2. $(A \lor B) \rightarrow C/A \rightarrow C$

No subformula of B occurs disjoined to A in the conclusion.

3. $A \rightarrow B/-B \rightarrow -A$

A subformula of A and a subformula of B occur in the conclusion, each with a changed sign.

4. $A \rightarrow B/(A \ \& \ C) \rightarrow (B \ \& \ C)$

$(A \ \& \ F)$ and $(B \ \& \ F)$ occur in the conclusion, for some formula F. Then C equals F in line l_{i+1}.

5. $A \rightarrow B/(A \lor C) \rightarrow (B \lor C)$

$(A \lor F)$ and $(B \lor F)$ occur in the conclusion, for some formula F. Then C equals F in line l_{i+1}.

6. $A \rightarrow B/(A \ \& \ C) \rightarrow B$

$(A \ \& \ F)$ occurs in the conclusion, for some formula F. Then C equals F in line l_{i+1}.

7. $A \rightarrow B/A \rightarrow (B \lor C)$

$(B \lor F)$ occurs in the conclusion, for some formula F. Then C equals F in line l_{i+1}.

This can be remedied by adding the following operations to the theory, with the given helping conditions:

(8) $(A \ \& \ B) \rightarrow C/(A \ \& \ B) \rightarrow (C \ \& \ B)$:   A subformula of B occurs conjoined to C in the conclusion.

(9) $A \rightarrow (B \lor C)/(A \lor C) \rightarrow (B \lor C)$:   A subformula of C occurs disjoined to A in the conclusion.

Adding these operations, however, makes Operations (4) and (5) of Table 8.1 logically redundant. The result of any application of Operation (4) can be achieved through the use of Operation (6) followed by Operation (8). This is shown by the following derivation:

(i) $p \rightarrow q$
$\quad (p \ \& \ r) \rightarrow q$ \qquad (Operation 6)
$\quad (p \ \& \ r) \rightarrow (q \ \& \ r)$ \qquad (Operation 8)

Similarly, Operation (5) is redundant with Operations (7) and (9), as the following derivation shows:

(ii) $p \rightarrow q$
$\quad p \rightarrow (q \vee r)$ \qquad (Operation 7)
$\quad (p \vee r) \rightarrow (q \vee r)$ \qquad (Operation 9)

These facts suggest a different theory than that shown in Table 8.1, namely, the alternative theory shown in Table 8.2.

TABLE 8.2
Alternative Version of the Theory for Experiments 1 and 2

1. $A \rightarrow (B \ \& \ C)/A \rightarrow B$

No subformula of C occurs conjoined to B in the conclusion.

2. $(A \vee B) \rightarrow C/A \rightarrow C$

No subformula of B occurs disjoined to A in the conclusion.

3. $A \rightarrow B/-B \rightarrow -A$

A subformula of A and a subformula of B occur in the conclusion, each with a changed sign.

6. $A \rightarrow B/(A \ \& \ C) \rightarrow B$

$(A \ \& \ F)$ occurs in the conclusion, for some formula F. Then C equals F in line l_{i+1}.

7. $A \rightarrow B/A \rightarrow (B \vee C)$

$(B \vee F)$ occurs in the conclusion, for some formula F. Then C equals F in line l_{i+1}.

8. $(A \ \& \ B) \rightarrow C/(A \ \& \ B) \rightarrow (C \ \& \ B)$

$(C \ \& \ B)$ occurs in the conclusion.

9. $A \rightarrow (B \vee C)/(A \vee C) \rightarrow (B \vee C)$

$(A \vee C)$ occurs in the conclusion.

Logical redundancy is not the same as psychological redundancy, however. Operations (4) and (5) may exist in the subjects' competence along with Operations (8) and (9), or Arguments (A) and (B) may be derived by other means than Operations (8) and (9). Only experimentation can decide the issue. To the extent that the additivity and inventory requirements of Chapter 5 are fulfilled by a theory that substitutes derivations like (i) and (ii) for those based on Operations (4) and (5) in Table 8.1, the new operations can be attributed to the subjects' competence in place of Operations (4) and (5). Experiment 1 was designed also to test the theory of Table 8.2.

To test the additivity and inventory requirements, 16 multiple-operation arguments were generated from the two theories. Table 8.3 gives the derivations for these arguments, according to the theory of Table 8.1. All the derivations in Table 8.3 are based on two operations. Table 8.4 provides derivations for the same arguments, according to the theory of Table 8.2. Derivations for the two erstwhile single-operation arguments are listed last. Derivations differing between the two theories are starred in Tables 8.3 and 8.4.

A subsidiary aim of Experiment 1 was to determine whether subjects were assessing the difficulty of arguments on the basis of the number of words they contained, contrary to instructions (see Section 7.3). Several arguments were prepared of the same logical structure as other arguments in the experiment, but more wordy. If subjects were judging difficulty on the basis of the logic of a problem, and not on the basis of the number of words, then the verbose and taciturn forms of the same argument should be judged equally difficult.

8.2   METHOD

Subjects were 35 volunteer students from a summer school program in Palo Alto, California. They ranged from the 8th to the 11th grades. Subjects were seen in groups of about four.[2] There was only one experimenter per group. Each subject received 34 arguments. The arguments had two premises: one major premise, along with a minor premise that could as easily be part of the conclusion. To illustrate with an argument based on Operation (1), instead of the argument

(1) $\dfrac{p \rightarrow (q \mathbin{\&} r)}{p \rightarrow q}$

[2] This is considerably less than the size of groups in later experiments. Group size increased across the experiments as the experimenters' confidence and experience with the procedures grew.

TABLE 8.3
Derivations of Multiple-Operations Argument According to the
Model of Table 8.1

Derivation	Operation	Derivation	Operation
(1) $p \rightarrow (q \ \& \ r)/-q \rightarrow -p$		(9) $p \rightarrow (q \ \& \ r)/p \rightarrow (q \lor s)$	
$p \rightarrow (q \ \& \ r)$	Premise	$p \rightarrow (q \ \& \ r)$	Premise
$p \rightarrow q$	(1)	$p \rightarrow q$	(1)
$-q \rightarrow -p$	(3)	$p \rightarrow (q \lor s)$	(7)
(2) $(p \lor q) \rightarrow r/-r \rightarrow -p$		*(10) $p \rightarrow (q \ \& \ r)/(p \ \& \ s) \rightarrow (q \ \& \ s)$	
$(p \lor q) \rightarrow r$	Premise	$p \rightarrow (q \ \& \ r)$	Premise
$p \rightarrow r$	(2)	$p \rightarrow q$	(1)
$-r \rightarrow -p$	(3)	$(p \ \& \ s) \rightarrow (q \ \& \ s)$	(4)
(3) $p \rightarrow q/(-q \ \& \ r) \rightarrow -p$		*(11) $p \rightarrow (q \ \& \ r)/(p \lor s) \rightarrow (q \lor s)$	
$p \rightarrow q$	Premise	$p \rightarrow (q \ \& \ r)$	Premise
$-q \rightarrow -p$	(3)	$p \rightarrow q$	(1)
$(-q \ \& \ r) \rightarrow -p$	(6)	$(p \lor s) \rightarrow (q \lor s)$	(5)
(4) $p \rightarrow q/-q \rightarrow (-p \lor r)$		(12) $(p \lor q) \rightarrow r/(p \ \& \ s) \rightarrow r$	
$p \rightarrow q$	Premise	$(p \lor q) \rightarrow r$	Premise
$-q \rightarrow -p$	(3)	$p \rightarrow r$	(2)
$-q \rightarrow (-p \lor r)$	(7)	$(p \ \& \ s) \rightarrow r$	(6)
(5) $p \rightarrow q/(-q \ \& \ r) \rightarrow (-p \ \& \ r)$		(13) $(p \lor q) \rightarrow r/p \rightarrow (r \lor s)$	
$p \rightarrow q$	Premise	$(p \lor q) \rightarrow r$	Premise
$-q \rightarrow -p$	(3)	$p \rightarrow r$	(2)
$(-q \ \& \ r) \rightarrow (-p \ \& \ r)$	(4)	$p \rightarrow (r \lor s)$	(7)
(6) $p \rightarrow q/(-q \lor r) \rightarrow (-p \lor r)$		*(14) $(p \lor q) \rightarrow r/(p \ \& \ s) \rightarrow (r \ \& \ s)$	
$p \rightarrow q$	Premise	$(p \lor q) \rightarrow r$	Premise
$-q \rightarrow -p$	(3)	$p \rightarrow r$	(2)
$(-q \lor r) \rightarrow (-p \lor r)$	(5)	$(p \ \& \ s) \rightarrow (r \ \& \ s)$	(4)
(7) $(p \lor q) \rightarrow (r \ \& \ s)/p \rightarrow r$		*(15) $(p \lor q) \rightarrow r/(p \lor s) \rightarrow (r \lor s)$	
$(p \lor q) \rightarrow (r \ \& \ s)$	Premise	$(p \lor q) \rightarrow r$	Premise
$(p \lor q) \rightarrow r$	(1)	$p \rightarrow r$	(2)
$p \rightarrow r$	(2)	$(p \lor s) \rightarrow (r \lor s)$	(5)
(8) $p \rightarrow (q \ \& \ r)/(p \ \& \ s) \rightarrow q$		(16) $p \rightarrow q/(p \ \& \ r) \rightarrow (q \lor s)$	
$p \rightarrow (q \ \& \ r)$	Premise	$p \rightarrow q$	Premise
$p \rightarrow q$	(1)	$(p \ \& \ r) \rightarrow q$	(6)
$(p \ \& \ s) \rightarrow q$	(6)	$(p \ \& \ r) \rightarrow (q \lor s)$	(7)

TABLE 8.4
Derivations of Multiple-Operation Arguments According to the Model of Table 8.2

Derivation	Operation	Derivation	Operation
(1) $p \rightarrow (q \& r)/-q \rightarrow -p$		*(10) $p \rightarrow (q \& r)/(p \& s) \rightarrow (q \& s)$	
$\quad p \rightarrow (q \& r)$	Premise	$\quad p \rightarrow (q \& r)$	Premise
$\quad p \rightarrow q$	(1)	$\quad p \rightarrow q$	(1)
$\quad -q \rightarrow -p$	(3)	$\quad (p \& s) \rightarrow q$	(6)
		$\quad (p \& s) \rightarrow (q \& s)$	(8)
(2) $(p \vee q) \rightarrow r/-r \rightarrow -p$			
$\quad (p \vee q) \rightarrow r$	Premise	*(11) $p \rightarrow (q \& r)/(p \vee s) \rightarrow (q \vee s)$	
$\quad p \rightarrow r$	(2)	$\quad p \rightarrow (q \& r)$	Premise
$\quad -r \rightarrow -p$	(3)	$\quad p \rightarrow q$	(1)
		$\quad p \rightarrow (q \vee s)$	(7)
(3) $p \rightarrow q/(-q \& r) \rightarrow -p$		$\quad (p \vee s) \rightarrow (q \vee s)$	(9)
$\quad p \rightarrow q$	Premise		
$\quad -q \rightarrow -p$	(3)	(12) $(p \vee q) \rightarrow r/(p \& s) \rightarrow r$	
$\quad (-q \& r) \rightarrow -p$	(6)	$\quad (p \vee q) \rightarrow r$	Premise
		$\quad p \rightarrow r$	(2)
(4) $p \rightarrow q/-q \rightarrow (-p \vee r)$		$\quad (p \& s) \rightarrow r$	(6)
$\quad p \rightarrow q$	Premise		
$\quad -q \rightarrow -p$	(3)	(13) $(p \vee q) \rightarrow r/p \rightarrow (r \vee s)$	
$\quad -q \rightarrow (-p \vee r)$	(7)	$\quad (p \vee q) \rightarrow r$	Premise
		$\quad p \rightarrow r$	(2)
*(5) $p \rightarrow q/(-q \& r) \rightarrow (-p \& r)$		$\quad p \rightarrow (r \vee s)$	(7)
$\quad p \rightarrow q$	Premise		
$\quad -q \rightarrow -p$	(3)	*(14) $(p \vee q) \rightarrow r/(p \& s) \rightarrow (r \& s)$	
$\quad (-q \& r) \rightarrow -p$	(6)	$\quad (p \vee q) \rightarrow r$	Premise
$\quad (-q \& r) \rightarrow (-p \& r)$	(8)	$\quad p \rightarrow r$	(2)
		$\quad (p \& s) \rightarrow r$	(6)
*(6) $p \rightarrow q/(-q \vee r) \rightarrow (-p \vee r)$		$\quad (p \& s) \rightarrow (r \& s)$	(8)
$\quad p \rightarrow q$	Premise		
$\quad -q \rightarrow -p$	(3)	*(15) $(p \vee q) \rightarrow r/(p \vee s) \rightarrow (r \vee s)$	
$\quad -q \rightarrow (-p \vee r)$	(7)	$\quad (p \vee q) \rightarrow r$	Premise
$\quad (-q \vee r) \rightarrow (-p \vee r)$	(9)	$\quad p \rightarrow r$	(2)
		$\quad p \rightarrow (r \vee s)$	(7)
(7) $(p \vee q) \rightarrow (r \& s)/p \rightarrow r$		$\quad (p \vee s) \rightarrow (r \vee s)$	(9)
$\quad (p \vee q) \rightarrow (r \& s)$	Premise		
$\quad (p \vee q) \rightarrow r$	(1)	*(16) $p \rightarrow q/(p \& r) \rightarrow (q \vee s)$	
$\quad p \rightarrow r$	(2)	$\quad p \rightarrow q$	Premise
		$\quad (p \& r) \rightarrow q$	(6)
(8) $p \rightarrow (q \& r)/(p \& s) \rightarrow q$		$\quad (p \& r) \rightarrow (q \vee s)$	(7)
$\quad p \rightarrow (q \& r)$	Premise		
$\quad p \rightarrow q$	(1)	*(17) $p \rightarrow q/(p \& r) \rightarrow (q \& r)$	
$\quad (p \& s) \rightarrow q$	(6)	$\quad p \rightarrow q$	Premise
		$\quad (p \& r) \rightarrow q$	(6)
(9) $p \rightarrow (q \& r)/p \rightarrow (q \vee s)$		$\quad (p \& r) \rightarrow (q \& r)$	(8)
$\quad p \rightarrow (q \& r)$	Premise		
$\quad p \rightarrow q$	(1)	*(18) $p \rightarrow q/(p \vee r) \rightarrow (q \vee r)$	
$\quad p \rightarrow (q \vee s)$	(7)	$\quad p \rightarrow q$	Premise
		$\quad p \rightarrow (q \vee r)$	(7)
		$\quad (p \vee r) \rightarrow (q \vee r)$	(9)

subjects were presented with the argument

$$p \rightarrow (q \& r)$$
$$\underline{p}$$
$$q$$

In general, any argument of the form

$$\frac{A \rightarrow B}{C \rightarrow D}$$

was replaced by one of the form

$$A \rightarrow B$$
$$\underline{C}$$
$$D$$

This variation in argument form is minor and requires only the use of the rule Modus Ponens at the end of a derivation:

$$A \rightarrow B$$
$$\underline{A}$$
$$B$$

For example, the derivation of Argument (1) is simply

$p \rightarrow (q \& r)$	(Premise)
$p \rightarrow q$	(Operation 1)
p	(Premise)
q	(Modus Ponens)

The same holds for all the other derivations; the last operation to be applied is Modus Ponens.[3]

Because of this modification of the arguments, the instructions were cast in terms of two-premise arguments, rather than one-premise arguments, as described in Chapter 7. Obviously, this change is minor. The only other deviation from the instructions of Chapter 7 was that in this first experiment, and only in this experiment, subjects were not given the CANNOT DECIDE option in the sorting procedure. All arguments had to be judged valid or invalid.

The arguments in the experiment were as follows: Subjects received one argument for each of the seven operations of Table 8.1, and one argument for each of Operations (8) and (9) in Table 8.2. These nine single-operation arguments are presented in Table 8.5. Subjects also received the 16 multiple-operation arguments given derivations in Tables 8.3 and 8.4.

---

[3] We thought this form of argument would be more intuitive for the subjects. Addition of the two-premise rule Modus Ponens to the theory is unlikely to be controversial.

TABLE 8.5
Single-Operation Arguments for Experiment 1

1. $p \rightarrow q, -q/-p$

If there is an M, there is a V.
There is not a V.
There is not an M.

2. $p \rightarrow (q \& r), p/q$

If there is a P, there is a V and an F.
There is a P.
There is a V.

3. $(p \lor q) \rightarrow r, p/r$

If there is either an R or an S, there is an M.
There is an R.
There is an M.

4. $p \rightarrow q, p \& r/q$

If there is a D, there is a P.
There is a D and a K.
There is a P.

5. $p \rightarrow q, p/q \lor r$

If there is an S, there is an M.
There is an S.
There is either an M or a Y.

6. $p \rightarrow q, p \& r/q \& r$

If there is a Y, there is an H.
There is a Y and a Z.
There is an H and a Z.

7. $p \rightarrow q, p \lor r/q \lor r$

If there is a D, there is an L.
There is either a D or a B.
There is either an L or a B.

8. $(p \& q) \rightarrow r, p \& q/r \& q$

If there is an X and a B, there is a J.
There is an X and a B.
There is a J and a B.

9. $p \rightarrow (r \lor q), p \lor q/r \lor q$

If there is an R, there is either a Z or a J.
There is either an R or a J.
There is either a Z or a J.

These arguments are presented in Table 8.6. Finally, there was one problem based on Modus Ponens, three *wordy* arguments that have the logic of other valid arguments but are untypically verbose, and five invalid arguments with no derivation within the theory. For each subject, the five invalid arguments were drawn randomly from a pool of ten invalid problems. The invalid, wordy, and Modus Ponens arguments are presented in Table 8.7.

8.3   PRELIMINARY ANALYSIS OF RESULTS

1. Dropped subjects.   Two subjects were dropped because they were uncooperative. The decision to drop them was made prior to examination of their data. Data analyses refer to the remaining 33 subjects.[4]

[4] We have not hesitated to drop subjects from the analysis for a variety of reasons. We did not attempt to formulate rules in advance for determining whether a subject should be dropped, since we suspected that there would be unforeseen but legitimate grounds for ignoring certain subjects' data. This proved to be correct. In all cases, the decision to drop a subject was made prior to any data analyses relevant to the theories to be discussed.

TABLE 8.6
Multiple-Operation Arguments for Experiment 1

1. $p \rightarrow (q \ \& \ r), -q/-p$

   If there is an F, there is a P and a J.
   There is not a P.
   _____
   There is not an F.

2. $(p \lor q) \rightarrow r, -r/-p$

   If there is either an N or a Z, there is a K.
   There is not a K.
   _____
   There is not an N.

3. $p \rightarrow q, -q \ \& \ r/-p$

   If there is an L, there is a T.
   There is not a T, and there is a Q.
   _____
   There is not an L.

4. $p \rightarrow q, -q/-p \lor r$

   If there is an F, there is a T.
   There is not a T.
   _____
   Either there is not an F or there is an X.

5. $p \rightarrow q, -q \ \& \ r/-p \ \& \ r$

   If there is an F, there is a B.
   There is not a B, and there is a D.
   _____
   There is not an F, and there is a D.

6. $p \rightarrow q, -q \lor r/-p \lor r$

   If there is a Y, there is a Q.
   Either there is not a Q or there is an S.
   _____
   Either there is not a Y or there is an S.

7. $(p \lor q) \rightarrow (r \ \& \ s), p/r$

   If there is either an R or a D, there is both a P and a K.
   There is an R.
   _____
   There is a P.

8. $p \rightarrow (q \ \& \ r), p \ \& \ s/q$

   If there is an M, there is a P and a T.
   There is an M and a Q.
   _____
   There is a P.

9. $p \rightarrow (q \ \& \ r), p/q \lor s$

   If there is a T, there is an N and a K.
   There is a T.
   _____
   There is either an N or a D.

(continued)

TABLE 8.6 *(continued)*

10. $p \rightarrow (q \ \& \ r)$, $p \ \& \ s/q \ \& \ s$

If there is a G, there is a C and a P.
There is a G and an S.

There is a C and an S.

11. $p \rightarrow (q \ \& \ r)$, $p \ \vee \ s/q \ \vee \ s$

If there is a C, there is an N and a G.
There is either a C or a Z.

There is either an N or a Z.

12. $(p \ \vee \ q) \rightarrow r$, $p \ \& \ s/r$

If there is either an N or a Y, there is an L.
There is an N and a C.

There is an L.

13. $(p \ \vee \ q) \rightarrow r$, $p/r \ \vee \ s$

If there is an H or an S, there is a C.
There is an H.

There is either a C or a Y.

14. $(p \ \vee \ q) \rightarrow r$, $p \ \& \ s/r \ \& \ s$

If there is either an R or a D, there is a G.
There is an R and a K.

There is a G and a K.

15. $(p \ \vee \ q) \rightarrow r$, $p \ \vee \ s/r \ \vee \ s$

If there is either a C or an M, there is a B.
There is either a C or a Q.

There is either a B or a Q.

16. $p \rightarrow q$, $p \ \& \ r/q \ \vee \ s$

If there is an N, there is a P.
There is an N and an S.

There is either a P or a T.

2.   Acceptance rate for arguments.   Table 8.8 shows the number of subjects accepting each valid argument. The invalid arguments (invalid from the point of view of the theory and of propositional logic) are not listed in Table 8.8, since very few subjects judged them to be valid.

3.   Difficulty of the arguments.   The best index of an argument's difficulty is the average value assigned to it by the subjects during the scaling procedure. However, since subjects were free to choose the size of the first difference, that is, the difference between the first and second slips (see Section 7.4), it is possible for some subjects to have higher numbers than others, and thereby unduly influence the average score. For this reason, the scores assigned by each subject were normalized to run from 0.0 to 100.0. This was achieved by the following linear transformation for the value assigned by subject S to problem p:

(1) Normalized value of p for $S = (100.0/(\max_S - \min_S)) \times (p_S' - \min_S)$

where $\max_S$ is the maximum number assigned by S to any valid argument; $\min_S$ is the minimum number assigned by S to any valid argument ($= 10.0$, by Section 7.4); p_S' is the number S assigned to problem p.

This normalization transformation was applied to each valid argument that the subject accepted, except for the three wordy arguments. The arguments given derivations by the theory but labeled invalid by the subject were not involved in the normalization, since the subject had assigned no number to them. None of the theoretically invalid arguments were included either. On the other hand, the problem Modus Ponens was involved in the normalization of a subject's data. Since Modus Ponens was almost always assigned the lowest number by the subjects, it almost always takes the normalized value of 0.0. This causes the normalized difficulty score for each argument to represent its difficulty for the subject over and above the difficulty experienced with Modus Ponens, the easiest problem. Since the argument Modus Ponens is based solely on an operation common to all of the problems, this normalizing procedure subtracts from each argument some additive constants that all the problems share.[5]

To summarize, each subject's numerical assignments were constrained to run from 0.0 to 100.0. The easiest problem (almost always Modus Ponens) received the score of 0.0. The most difficult problem for the subject received the score of 100.0. Between these extremes lay the other arguments accepted by the subject (but no wordy or invalid arguments). The normalization was accomplished by the linear transformation given in Eq. (1) above. Arguments with the same difficulty rating before normalization still have identical numbers after normalization.

Table 8.9 presents the mean and standard deviation for these normalized numerical assignments. The entries in Table 8.9 are based on unequal N's.

[5] Ignoring the subject who found Modus Ponens more difficult than another argument, the normalized numerical assignments represent the difficulty of an argument minus the difficulty due to factors common to all the arguments; see Section 5.2, Footnote 2. Starting with Experiment 3, we dropped subjects who found baseline arguments like Modus Ponens relatively difficult. Including such subjects in the present experiment, however, has little effect. The additivity correlations are unchanged if the residual mean normalized numerical assignment for Modus Ponens is subtracted from the mean normalized numerical assignments of the other arguments, before entering them into the additivity correlation. In general, normalizing subjects' ratings has only a small effect on the additivity analyses to be reported in this volume.

TABLE 8.7
Invalid, Wordy, and Baseline Arguments for Experiment 1

Invalid arguments

1. $p \rightarrow (q \vee r), -r / -p \ \& \ s$

    If there is an N, there is either an F or an X.
    There is not an X.

    There is not an N and there is a D.

2. $p \rightarrow (q \vee r), p \vee s / q \vee r$

    If there is a G, there is either a C or an M.
    There is either a G or a J.

    There is either a C or an M.

3. $p \rightarrow q, -p / -q \vee r$

    If there is a V, there is a P.
    There is not a V.

    Either there is not a P or there is a K.

4. $(p \vee q) \rightarrow r, p / q$

    If there is an H and an L, there is a Q.
    There is an H.

    There is an L.

5. $p \rightarrow q, p \vee r / q$

    If there is a Y, there is a T.
    There is either a Y or a Z.

    There is a T.

6. $p \rightarrow q, p / q \ \& \ r$

    If there is an S, there is an R.
    There is an S.

    There is an R and a B.

7. $p \rightarrow (q \vee r), p / q$

    If there is a P, there is either a K or an S.
    There is a P.

    There is a K.

(*continued*)

TABLE 8.7 (*continued*)

---

8. $p \rightarrow q, p \& r/q \& s$

If there is a C, there is an M.
There is a C and a J.
___
There is an M and a Y.

9. $(p \& q) \rightarrow r, p/r$

If there is a D and a G, there is an X.
There is a D.
___
There is an X.

10. $(p \& q) \rightarrow r, -r/-p$

If there is a Q and an F, there is an N.
There is not an N.
___
There is not a Q.

Wordy arguments
1. $(p \vee q) \rightarrow r, p/r$

If either a C or a Q has been written on the paper, then a T has been too.
A C has been written down on the paper.
___
A T has been written down on the paper.

2. $p \rightarrow q, -q \& r/-p$

If a T occurs on the paper, then so does a C.
In fact, a C does not occur, and an N does.
___
There is not a T on the paper.

3. $(p \vee q) \rightarrow r, p \& s/r$

If either one of R or D is there, then so is a G.
Now, there is an R and there is also an H.
___
There is a G.

Baseline argument (Modus Ponens)
      $p \rightarrow q, p/q$

If there is a T, there is an H.
There is a T.
___
There is an H.

TABLE 8.8

Acceptance Rates for Valid Arguments of Experiment 1 ($N = 33$)

	No. accepted	No. rejected
Single-operation arguments		
1. $p \rightarrow q, -q/-p$	22	11
2. $p \rightarrow (q \ \& \ r), p/q$	31	2
3. $(p \lor q) \rightarrow r, p/r$	33	0
4. $p \rightarrow q, p \ \& \ r/q$	32	1
5. $p \rightarrow q, p/q \lor r$	24	9
6. $p \rightarrow q, p \ \& \ r/q \ \& \ r$	32	1
7. $p \rightarrow q, p \lor r/q \lor r$	29	4
8. $(p \ \& \ q) \rightarrow r, p \ \& \ q/r \ \& \ q$	29	4
9. $p \rightarrow (r \lor q), p \lor q/r \lor q$	25	8
Total:	257	40
Mean:	28.6	
Multiple-operation arguments		
1. $p \rightarrow (q \ \& \ r), -q/-p$	21	12
2. $(p \lor q) \rightarrow r, -r/-p$	20	13
3. $p \rightarrow q, -q \ \& \ r/-p$	24	9
4. $p \rightarrow q, -q/-p \lor r$	17	16
5. $p \rightarrow q, -q \ \& \ r/-p \ \& \ r$	28	5
6. $p \rightarrow q, -q \lor r/-p \lor r$	27	6
7. $(p \lor q) \rightarrow (r \ \& \ s), p/s$	27	6
8. $p \rightarrow (q \ \& \ r), p \ \& \ s/q$	31	2
9. $p \rightarrow (q \ \& \ r), p/q \lor s$	23	10
10. $p \rightarrow (q \ \& \ r), p \ \& \ s/q \ \& \ s$	31	2
11. $p \rightarrow (q \ \& \ r), p \lor s/q \lor s$	27	6
12. $(p \lor q) \rightarrow r, p \ \& \ s/r$	33	0
13. $(p \lor q) \rightarrow r, p/r \lor s$	24	9
14. $(p \lor q) \rightarrow r, p \ \& \ s/r \ \& \ s$	32	1
15. $(p \lor q) \rightarrow r, p \lor s/r \lor s$	32	1
16. $p \rightarrow q, p \ \& \ r/q \lor s$	24	9
Total:	421	107
Mean:	26.3	
Baseline argument		
$p \rightarrow q, p/q$	33	0
Wordy arguments		
1. $(p \lor q) \rightarrow r, p/r$	32	1
2. $p \rightarrow q, -q \ \& \ r/-p$	27	6
3. $(p \lor q) \rightarrow r, p \ \& \ s/r$	32	1
Total:	91	8

Only problems judged to be valid during the sorting procedure were given numbers by subjects during the scaling procedure. The number of subjects figuring in each average may be determined from Table 8.8; in each case, it is simply the number of subjects accepting the argument.

4. *Wordy arguments.* Each wordy argument may be paired with a normal argument that has the same logical structure. Thirty-two subjects accepted both the first wordy item and its mate, Argument (3) in Table 8.5. A correlated t test on the untransformed numerical assignments for the wordy and normal argument reveals no significant difference between the arguments ($t = -1.1$). Indeed, the wordy argument was slightly easier. The same situation obtains for the two other wordy items: 20 subjects accepted both the second wordy item and its mate, 32 subjects accepted both the third wordy item and its mate. There are no significant differences between the wordy and normal arguments, with the wordy items tending to be slightly easier ($t = -.4$, $t = -.9$). These results discredit the idea that subjects use the number of words in an argument as the basis of their scaling (despite explicit instructions not to do so). More evidence for the same conclusion is presented in Section 20.2.

5. *Comparison with the data of Volume 2.* Thirteen valid arguments figured in both Volume 2 and the present experiment, provided that we ignore "extra negations" in formulas from Volume 2 (see Section 6.3 thereof). Seven of these formulas come from Experiment 1 of Volume 2, namely, Formulas (1), (2), (4), and (8)–(11) of Section 2.1. The remaining six formulas come from Experiment 2, namely, Formulas (38), (40), (45), (47), and (48) of Section 8.1. Experiments 1 and 2 of Volume 2 used acceptance rate as a measure of these formulas' difficulty. We shall combine results from the two experiments in order to give each formula an acceptance rate from Volume 2 (see Tables 1 and 12 in Volume 2 for these acceptance rates). The correlation of acceptance rates for these arguments from Experiments 1 and 2 of Volume 2 and the present experiment is .73 ($N = 13$). The correlation between Volume 2 acceptance and the mean normalized numerical assignments of the present experiment is −.74 ($N = 13$).

In Experiment 3 of Volume 2, all 13 formulas appeared. The difficulty of the formulas was assessed by means of latency (see Volume 2, Section 10.3). The correlation between Volume 2 latency and the mean normalized numerical assignments of the present experiment is .87 ($N = 13$).

At a superficial level, the results of Experiment 1 are thus similar to those of Volume 2, so far as can be determined with the partially overlapping set of arguments used in the two places. A more important issue is whether the results of this first experiment support the theory of Table 8.1, a theory similar to that of Volume 2.

TABLE 8.9
Mean Normalized Numerical Assignments for
Valid Arguments of Experiment 1 ($N = 33$)

	Mean normalized numerical assignments	Standard deviations of mean normalized numerical assignments
Single-operation arguments		
1. $p \rightarrow q, -q/-p$	23.84	23.90
2. $p \rightarrow (q \& r), p/q$	19.08	22.75
3. $(p \vee q) \rightarrow r, p/r$	19.56	20.95
4. $p \rightarrow q, p \& r/q$	21.82	20.44
5. $p \rightarrow q, p/q \vee r$	43.67	25.93
6. $p \rightarrow q, p \& r/q \& r$	30.07	21.30
7. $p \rightarrow q, p \vee r/q \vee r$	54.17	23.08
8. $(p \& q) \rightarrow r, p \& q/r \& q$	31.23	22.90
9. $p \rightarrow (r \vee q), p \vee q/r \vee q$	67.68	26.90
Multiple-operation arguments		
1. $p \rightarrow (q \& r), -q/-p$	33.68	21.99
2. $(p \vee q) \rightarrow r, -r/-p$	54.31	22.87
3. $p \rightarrow q, -q \& r/-p$	40.01	26.78
4. $p \rightarrow q, -q/-p \vee r$	58.04	23.97
5. $p \rightarrow q, -q \& r/-p \& r$	54.41	28.91
6. $p \rightarrow q, -q \vee r/-p \vee r$	85.87	22.39
7. $(p \vee q) \rightarrow (r \& s), p/s$	34.18	22.30
8. $p \rightarrow (q \& r), p \& s/q$	28.43	22.23
9. $p \rightarrow (q \& r), p/q \vee s$	49.93	21.22
10. $p \rightarrow (q \& r), p \& s/q \& s$	48.34	25.12
11. $p \rightarrow (q \& r), p \vee s/q \vee s$	62.22	19.30
12. $(p \vee q) \rightarrow r, p \& s/r$	39.65	23.96
13. $(p \vee q) \rightarrow r, p/r \vee s$	44.13	25.64
14. $(p \vee q) \rightarrow r, p \& s/r \& s$	39.59	23.05
15. $(p \vee q) \rightarrow r, p \vee s/r \vee s$	69.64	25.02
16. $p \rightarrow q, p \& r/q \vee s$	60.64	22.81
Baseline argument		
$p \rightarrow q, p/q$	0.54	2.51
Wordy arguments	(not normalized)	
1. $(p \vee q) \rightarrow r, p/r$	13.20	2.68
2. $p \rightarrow q, -q \& r/-p$	18.24	8.29
3. $(p \vee q) \rightarrow r, p \& s/r$	17.95	8.77

8.4 INVENTORY AND ADDITIVITY ANALYSES
FOR THE THEORY OF TABLE 8.1

1. The inventory analysis. The derivations of Table 8.3 provide the inventory predictions of the theory of Table 8.1. As described in Section 5.1, the inventory requirement is that for each multiple-operation argument, a subject will either (a) accept the multiple-operation argument and accept all the single-operation arguments based on operations that figure in the derivation of the multiple-operation argument, or (b) reject the multiple-operation argument (on principle, rather than because of overload) and reject at least one of the single-operation arguments based on operations that figure in the derivation of that multiple-operation argument. All together, there are 528 inventory predictions (33 subjects × 16 multiple-operation arguments). The theory predicts correctly 442 times, for an accuracy rate of 83.7%.

A question that we faced in Volume 1, Section 7.2 arises again. How impressed should we be with this degree of fulfillment of the inventory requirement? To help answer this question, we calculated the expected number of true inventory predictions based on the marginal totals of Table 8.8. We asked how many true inventory predictions would be expected knowing the total number of acceptances for each argument across the 33 subjects, and assuming that acceptances of arguments are stochastically independent. For each multiple-operation argument, m, Eq. (2) gives the number of expected true inventory predictions on this basis, where p_m is the probability (as measured by relative frequency) of accepting the multiple-operation argument, and each q_i is the probability of accepting the i-th single-operation argument relevant to it.

(2)   Expected number of true inventory predictions involving multiple-operation argument m

$$= [(p_m \times q_1 \times \cdots \times q_k) + [(1 - p_m) \times (1 - (q_1 \times \cdots \times q_k))]] \times (\text{number of subjects evaluating argument } m)$$

The expected value given by Eq. (2) was calculated for each multiple-operation argument and summed across the 16 multiple-operation arguments to give the total number of expected true inventory predictions. The result was an expected value of 365.2, or 69.2% true predictions.

This procedure amounts to a "rival theory" analysis like that performed in Volume 1 (Section 7.2). It determines how much of the within-subject predictive success of the theory might be due to between-subject totals. The results show that the theory of Table 8.1 is 14.5% better in its predictions than a theory that could predict the marginal totals of Table 8.8 with no within-subject patterning. If we bear in mind that such a "rival" theory is rather powerful, and does not yet exist, the inventory analysis provides support for the theory of Table 8.1.

On the other hand, null hypotheses more powerful than that of Eq. (2) are possible, and will, in general, increase the number of expected true predictions (cf. Volume 1, Section 7.2). In this regard, Ewart Thomas (personal communication) has given convincing arguments that the rival theory of Eq. (2) may be too weak. This will not affect our conclusions, however, because the inventory results, overall, are too poor (on any null hypothesis) to provide much support for our theory (see, e.g., Sections 10.4 and 11.4). In any event, the use of Eq. (2) will enable us to take into consideration the effects of overall acceptance rate when evaluating the number of true inventory predictions.

2. The additivity analysis. The derivations of Table 8.3 provide the basis for testing the additivity requirement of Section 5.2. We report within-subject correlations first. For each subject, those triples of arguments were isolated for which the subject accepted the multiple-operation argument and both single-operation arguments associated with it. Only for these triples of arguments could the relation between the scaled difficulty of the multiple-operation argument be compared to the sum of the difficulties of the relevant single-operation arguments. For these arguments, the normalized numerical assignment to the multiple-operation arguments was correlated with the sum of the normalized numerical assignments given to the relevant single-operation arguments. Thus, different subjects had different numbers of correlated observations. The number of degrees of freedom depended on the number of argument-triples that the subject accepted. One subject accepted only three such argument-triples and was excluded from the analysis.

Of the 32 remaining correlations, the average number of degrees of freedom was 11.4, with a standard deviation of 3.1. Twenty-one of these correlations were positive and significant beyond the 5% level by a one-tailed test.[6] Two additional positive correlations were significant at the 10% level. The mean value of all 32 correlations was .48, $s = .37$. There were two marginally significant negative correlations.

These results are disappointing. We expect a theory of individual subjects to perform powerfully at the individual level. On the other hand, the scaling procedure is a "noisy" affair, with distraction of the subjects possible at every moment. We hope that the mediocre performance of the theory

---

[6] We felt justified in using a one-tailed test because the theory already had support from the results of Volume 2. Moreover, the small number of correlated observations requires a substantial correlation for significance even with one-tailed tests. In any event, statistical significance is used in this volume primarily as a benchmark, since it is unclear to what extent the assumptions underlying sound statistical inference in these cases have been met.

at the individual level is due to such "noise." The best test of this hypothesis is the between-subject additivity analysis.[7]

For the between-subject analysis, the mean normalized numerical assignment (from Table 8.9) of each multiple-operation argument is correlated with the sum of the mean normalized numerical assignments for the single-operation arguments that should add up to it (according to the derivations in Table 8.3).[8] The resulting correlation is .88 ($N = 16$). Figure 8.1 provides a scatter plot for this correlation. The high correlation supports the model of Table 8.1. (When the nonnormalized mean numerical assignments are used, the correlation is .85.)

8.5 INVENTORY AND ADDITIVITY ANALYSES
FOR THE THEORY OF TABLE 8.2

As explained in Section 8.1, the theory of Table 8.1 may be considered a special case of the theory of Table 8.2. If the latter theory is correct, Operations (4) and (5) are not psychologically primitive but are composed of Operations (6) and (8), and (7) and (9), respectively. The best way to test this claim is to determine whether the theory of Table 8.2 fulfills the inventory and additivity requirements as well as does the theory of Table 8.1. If so, the theory of Table 8.2 would account for more arguments than does the theory of Table 8.1, namely, for arguments like (4) and (5) in Table 8.5. These are single-operation arguments for the former theory, but double-operation arguments for the revised theory, as Table 8.4 shows. For the present analysis, therefore, there are 18 multiple-operation arguments instead of 16. Under the theory of Table 8.1, all 16 multiple-operation arguments are composed of two operations. Under the revised theory, 6 of the multiple-operation arguments are based on 3 operations, and the remaining 12 on 2 operations. The derivations in Table 8.4 pair each multiple-operation argument with the set of single-operation arguments that are relevant to it under the revised theory.

1. The inventory analysis. To make comparison easier, we first performed the inventory analysis with only the 16 multiple-operation

[7] If the theory of Table 8.1 is correct, the mediocre performance of the theory for individual subjects provides some support for the idea that the mental derivations of these arguments are implicit, and not usually open to introspection (see Chapter 2). A more conscious approach would likely lead to a systematic rating of argument difficulty that would give correlations close to unity (assuming that the theory is correct about these mental derivations).

[8] An alternative method of combining data is to average a subject's argument into the total only if it figures in the within-subject correlation. We prefer the present procedure because it allows every valid argument accepted by a subject to be represented in the between-subject correlation.

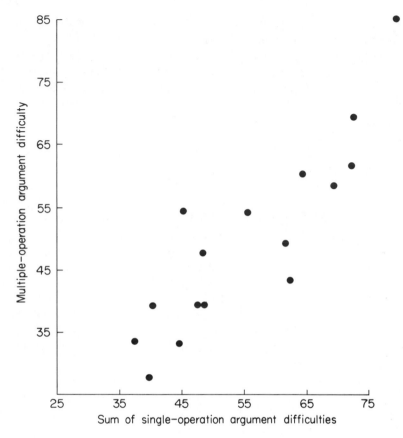

FIG. 8.1. Scatter plot for the additivity analysis of Experiment 1, based on the theory of Table 8.1.

arguments that arise from the theory of Table 8.1., that is, only those arguments appearing in Table 8.3 were considered. The logic of this analysis is the same as before except that some multiple-operation arguments are paired with three single-operation arguments rather than two.

The inventory requirement is better fulfilled under the revised model than under the former model. Of the 528 predictions, 469, or 88.8%, are true. The former theory produced 83.7% true predictions. We used Eq. (2) of Section 8.4 to determine the number of true predictions that could be expected on the basis of the acceptance rate of each argument, assuming independence. On the basis of this "rival" theory, we would expect 335.4 or 63.5% true predictions. The margin of superiority is thus 25.3% for the theory of Table 8.2, as opposed to 14.5% for the theory of Table 8.1. The revised theory is superior. When Arguments (4) and (5) of Table

8.5 are added as multiple-operation arguments to the inventory analysis, the results are almost exactly the same.

2. The additivity analysis. The within-subject additivity analysis for the 18 multiple-operation arguments of the revised theory gives results comparable to those for the theory of Table 8.1. Again, one subject had to be eliminated because there were too few observations to correlate. Of the remaining 32 subjects, 20 produced correlations significant beyond the 5% level. However, any comparison of the results of the within-subject analyses for the two theories is complicated by the fact that four subjects rejected the argument based on Operation (8), eight subjects rejected the argument based on Operation (9), one subject rejected the argument based on Operation (4), and nine rejected the argument based on Operation (5). The outcome is that for many subjects the additivity predictions of the two theories are almost identical.

The between-subject additivity analysis is more revealing. The correlation is .85 between the mean normalized numerical assignments for the 16 original multiple-operation arguments and the sums of the mean normalized numerical assignments for the single-operation arguments paired with them by the revised theory. When the full 18 arguments are employed (i.e., including the two erstwhile single-operation arguments of the former theory), the correlation is .83. Figure 8.2 provides a scatter plot of this

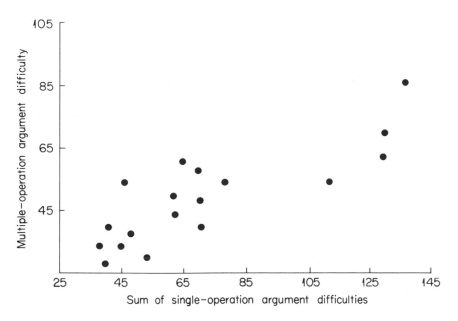

FIG. 8.2. Scatter plot for the additivity analysis of Experiment 1, based on the theory of Table 8.2.

latter correlation. Although this .83 correlation is five points below that of the former theory, the additivity analysis provides support for the revised theory as well.

8.6   CONCLUSIONS OF EXPERIMENT 1

Two major conclusions can be drawn from the results of Experiment 1. First, the methodological innovations discussed in Chapters 6 and 7 provide interpretable data. Not only do the measures of difficulty used in Volume 2 correlate with those of the present volume, the theoretical findings of Volume 2 have been replicated with our new methodology as well, in that comparable operations were used to predict argument difficulty.

The second finding of Experiment 1 is that the revision to the theory proposed in Volume 2, Section 11.2, seems to be correct. The theory of Table 8.2 fulfills the inventory and additivity requirements roughly as well as does the original theory of Table 8.1. Since the theory of Table 8.2 allows the derivation of more arguments, it is preferred. Moreover, the revised theory does not contain a greater number of operations than the former theory.

The operations of a deduction model should be psychologically primitive. An operation is primitive if no combination of other operations can be substituted for it without either reducing the number of intuitively valid arguments that can be derived or diminishing conformity to the inventory and additivity requirements. Although psychologically primitive operations may be reducible to more fundamental information-processing schemes in the nervous system, a set of primitive logical operations would provide the ultimate nonreductionist explanation of logical judgment. It is in this sense that the theory of Table 8.2 is superior to that of Table 8.1.

Despite the superiority of the revised theory, we shall continue to construct experiments around the operations of Table 8.1, that is, with Operations (4) and (5) treated as underlying single-operation arguments. The genuine Operations (8) and (9) will not underlie any single-operation arguments. The reason is that no multiple-operation arguments investigated in later experiments are built from Operation (8) without a prior application of Operation (4); similarly, all arguments derived with the help of Operation (9) employ a prior application of Operation (5). Hence, the net result is one application of either of the (nonprimitive) Operations (4) and (5), ordered before (6) and (7), as in Table 8.1. But our official theory for arguments based on conditionals is given in Table 8.2, with the new derivations of Table 8.4.

9

Experiment 2: Within-Subject Consistency and Complex, Single-Operation Arguments

9.1 AIMS OF THE EXPERIMENT

Before attempting to expand the theory, we thought it worthwhile to perform another experiment based on the model of Table 8.1. The same 16 multiple-operation arguments were employed. This allows one more check on methodology. In addition, two interesting issues can be explored without the distraction of theoretical innovation.

One issue concerns within-subject consistency. Would subjects respond the same way to two presentations of the same arguments on different days (where the arguments take slightly different forms in order to make recognition less likely)? There are three kinds of consistency at issue. First, and most important, we may determine whether the theory performs equally well for the two test situations. Second, we may examine the consistency with which subjects accept and reject arguments between the two sessions. Third, we may examine the consistency with which subjects scale the difficulty of arguments. The theory of this volume has no stake in the latter two kinds of consistency. The theory specifies only the pattern of acceptances and the pattern of argument difficulties. It does not predict whether any given argument, by itself, will be accepted or be judged difficult. A subject's configuration of acceptances and argument difficulties could change without a change occurring in this crucial pattern. Indeed, we expect some change in the profile of argument difficulties on the basis of the order effects found for latencies in Experiment 3 of Volume 2 (see Volume 2, Section 10.4). With practice, arguments become easier to evaluate. Different operations may have different time courses in this regard, and since the several operations do not occur the same number of times across the arguments, differential learning effects are likely. The outcome would be low consistency in argument difficulty.

The second issue addressed by the present study is the effect of different substitution instances in the use of an operation. Consider the following two uses of Operation (6):

(i) $(p \vee q) \rightarrow r$
     $p \rightarrow r$ (Operation 2)
     $(p \ \& \ s) \rightarrow r$ (Operation 6)

(ii) $p \rightarrow q$
      $-q \rightarrow -p$ (Operation 3)
      $(-q \ \& \ s) \rightarrow -p$ (Operation 6)

Operation (6) is written in formula variables, as follows: $A \rightarrow B/(A \ \& \ C) \rightarrow B$. The use of Operation (6) in Argument (i) to turn $p \rightarrow r$ into $(p \ \& \ s) \rightarrow r$ is a particular substitution instance of that operation (see Sections 4.2 and 4.3). The use of Operation (6) in Argument (ii) to turn $-q \rightarrow -p$ into $(-q \ \& \ s) \rightarrow -p$ is a different substitution instance.

In Experiment 1 we used the simplest substitution instances to estimate the difficulty of an operation, regardless of the substitution instance actually employed in a derivation. The simple argument used for estimation involved replacing each formula variable A, B, C in an operation with a single proposition letter, p, q, r. In the present experiment, we attempted to estimate the difficulty of each particular operation application by constructing an argument based directly on that intervening step in the derivation. For example, referring again to Operation (6), to estimate the difficulty of its application in Argument (i), we used the simple argument $p \rightarrow q/(p \ \& \ s) \rightarrow q$. But to estimate the difficulty of applying Operation (6) in Argument (ii), we used the argument $-q \rightarrow -p/(-q \ \& \ s) \rightarrow -p$. The same holds for the other operations and arguments.

9.2   METHOD

Subjects were 43 volunteer students from the 10th grade of Leland High School in San Jose, California. They were seen in groups of about seven. Subjects participated in two sessions, at least one week apart. In each session they received 37 arguments.. All the arguments were in two-premise form, as described in Section 8.2.

The method was the same as that described in Chapter 7, except that the instructions were modified to speak of two premises rather than one. Unlike Experiment 1 (which was an exception), subjects were given the CANNOT DECIDE option during sorting.

The arguments in the two sessions were identical except that the letters (on the blackboard) were changed randomly for each argument so as to inhibit recognition of specific arguments. We shall enumerate only the first session arguments. Each subject received 37 arguments. There was one

TABLE 9.1
Complex Single-Operation Arguments for Experiment 2

1. $(p \lor q) \to (r \& s), p \lor q/s$

   If there is either a V or an F,
      there is both an X and an M.
   There is either a V or an F.
   ___
   There is an M.

2. $(p \lor q) \to (r \& s), p/r \& s$

   If there is either a B or an L,
      there is both a T and a J.
   There is a B.
   ___
   There is a T and a J.

3. $-q \to -p, -q \& r/-p$

   If there is not a W, there is not a V.
   There is not a W and there is an L.
   ___
   There is not a V.

4. $p \to (q \lor s), p \& r/q \lor s$

   If there is a Z, there is either a D or an R.
   There is a Z and a C.
   ___
   There is either a D or an R.

5. $-q \to -p, -q/-p \lor r$

   If there is not an R, there is not a Q.
   There is not an R.
   ___
   There is either not a Q or there is a J.

6. $(p \& r) \to q, p \& r/q \lor s$

   If there is an S and a P, there is an X.
   There is an S and a P.
   ___
   There is either an X or a K.

7. $-q \to -p, -q \& r/-p \& r$

   If there is not an N, there is not an H.
   There is not an N and there is a Z.
   ___
   There is not an H and there is a Z.

8. $-q \to -p, -q \lor r/-p \lor r$

   If there is not a Y, there is not a P.
   There is either not a Y or there is a T.
   ___
   There is either not a P or there is a T.

simple, single-operation argument for each of the seven operations of Table 8.1. These simple arguments had one proposition letter instancing each formula letter of the operation. These arguments appear as the first seven arguments of Table 8.5.[1] Each subject received the 16 multiple-operation arguments whose derivations are given in Table 8.3. These arguments are presented in Table 8.6. There was one argument based on Modus Ponens and five invalid arguments drawn randomly from a pool of ten; Table 8.7 presents these arguments. Finally, each subject received eight arguments based on complex substitution instances of operations. Table 9.1 presents these arguments.

The arguments in Table 9.1 will be called *complex, single-operation arguments*. Each is based on one operation, representing a complex substitution

___

[1] Operations (8) and (9) of Table 8.2 are not represented in the experiment as separate arguments, in accord with the remarks of Section 8.6.

instance of it. All the substitution instances of operations that occur in the derivations for the 16 multiple-operation arguments are present among the simple and complex single-operation arguments. (See the derivations in Table 8.3.) One of the arguments in Table 9.1 does not appear in a derivation of Table 8.3, namely, the argument $(p \lor q) \to (r \& s)/p \to (r \& s)$. This complex single-operation argument was used to test whether the derivation of the argument $(p \lor q) \to (r \& s)/p \to r$ was either

(A) $(p \lor q) \to (r \& s)$
      $(p \lor q) \to r$
      $p \to r$

or

(B) $(p \lor q) \to (r \& s)$
      $p \to (r \& s)$
      $p \to r$

Derivation (A) conforms to the ordering of operations given in Table 8.1. Derivation (B) reverses the order of Operations (1) and (2). Since the two orders have consequences as to which operation is applied through a simple substitution instance and which through a complex substitution instance, the question of rule ordering in this case can in principle be answered. But in practice, the difference made no difference in the results, and we shall not dwell on the issue. (For the question of rule ordering, see Section 4.3.)

9.3 PRELIMINARY ANALYSIS OF RESULTS

1. Dropped subjects.   Forty-three students participated in both sessions of the study. None of these subjects was dropped. An additional 16 students participated in the first session but were reluctant to participate in the second session, mostly from boredom, we believe. The data from these students were discarded. Hence there is selection for cooperativeness (as in all our experiments). Subjects in Experiment 2 did not seem to enjoy the procedure as much as subjects in other experiments.

2. Acceptance rates for arguments.   Table 9.2 shows the number of subjects in Session 1 who judged each of the 32 arguments derivable from the theory to be either valid, invalid, or undecidable. Table 9.3 gives the same information for Session 2. The invalid arguments were seldom accepted.

3. Difficulty of the arguments.   For the two sessions separately, each subject's numerical assignments were normalized to run between 0.0 and 100.0, as explained in Section 8.3. All but the invalid arguments figured in the normalization. Table 9.4 gives the mean normalized numerical assignment for each valid problem in Session 1. The value in Table 9.4 for

TABLE 9.2
Acceptance Rates for Valid Arguments of Experiment 2,
Session 1 ($N = 43$)

	No. accepted	No. rejected	No. cannot decide
Single-operation arguments			
1. $p \to q, -q/-p$	33	9	1
2. $p \to (q \& r), p/q$	41	2	0
3. $(p \vee q) \to r, p/r$	43	0	0
4. $p \to q, p \& r/q$	42	1	0
5. $p \to q, p/q \vee r$	27	15	1
6. $p \to q, p \& r/q \& r$	40	3	0
7. $p \to q, p \vee r/q \vee r$	36	6	1
Total: 262		36	3
Mean: 37.4			
Multiple-operation arguments			
1. $p \to (q \& r), -q/-p$	31	12	0
2. $(p \vee q) \to r, -r/-p$	28	13	2
3. $p \to q, -q \& r/-p$	26	15	2
4. $p \to q, -q/-p \vee r$	16	24	3
5. $p \to q, -q \& r/-p \& r$	31	12	0
6. $p \to q, -q \vee r/-p \vee r$	32	7	4
7. $(p \vee q) \to (r \& s), p/s$	39	3	1
8. $p \to (q \& r), p \& s/q$	37	6	0
9. $p \to (q \& r), p/q \vee s$	25	16	2
10. $p \to (q \& r), p \& s/q \& s$	36	6	1
11. $p \to (q \& r), p \vee s/q \vee s$	30	8	5
12. $(p \vee q) \to r, p \& s/r$	40	3	0
13. $(p \vee q) \to r, p/r \vee s$	29	12	2
14. $(p \vee q) \to r, p \& s/r \& s$	40	2	1
15. $(p \vee q) \to r, p \vee s/r \vee s$	32	9	2
16. $p \to q, p \& r/q \vee s$	25	13	5
Total: 497		161	30
Mean: 31.1			
Complex single-operation arguments			
1. $(p \vee q) \to (r \& s), p \vee q/s$	39	4	0
2. $(p \vee q) \to (r \& s), p/r \& s$	42	1	0
3. $-q \to -p, -q \& r/-p$	40	2	1
4. $p \to (q \vee s), p \& r/q \vee s$	40	3	0
5. $-q \to -p, -q/-p \vee r$	24	15	4
6. $(p \& r) \to q, p \& r/q \vee s$	28	14	1
7. $-q \to -p, -q \& r/-p \& r$	42	1	0
8. $-q \to -p, -q \vee r/-p \vee r$	36	3	4
Total: 291		43	10
Mean: 36.4			
Baseline argument			
$p \to q, p/q$	43	0	0

TABLE 9.3
Acceptance Rates for Valid Arguments of Experiment 2,
Session 2 ($N = 43$)

	No. accepted	No. rejected	No. cannot decide
Single-operation arguments			
1. $p \to q, -q/-p$	33	10	0
2. $p \to (q \& r), p/q$	42	1	0
3. $(p \lor q) \to r, p/r$	43	0	0
4. $p \to q, p \& r/q$	43	0	0
5. $p \to q, p/q \lor r$	33	9	1
6. $p \to q, p \& r/q \& r$	42	1	0
7. $p \to q, p \lor r/q \lor r$	40	3	0
Total: 276		24	1
Mean: 39.4			
Multiple-operation arguments			
1. $p \to (q \& r), -q/-p$	28	15	0
2. $(p \lor q) \to r, -r/-p$	24	18	1
3. $p \to q, -q \& r/-p$	27	16	0
4. $p \to q, -q/-p \lor r$	24	18	1
5. $p \to q, -q \& r/-p \& r$	28	14	1
6. $p \to q, -q \lor r/-p \lor r$	34	5	4
7. $(p \lor q) \to (r \& s), p/s$	39	4	0
8. $p \to (q \& r), p \& s/q$	40	3	0
9. $p \to (q \& r), p/q \lor s$	29	13	1
10. $p \to (q \& r), p \& s/q \& s$	39	4	0
11. $p \to (q \& r), p \lor s/q \lor s$	35	5	3
12. $(p \lor q) \to r, p \& s/r$	41	2	0
13. $(p \lor q) \to r, p/r \lor s$	35	8	0
14. $(p \lor q) \to r, p \& s/r \& s$	42	1	0
15. $(p \lor q) \to r, p \lor s/r \lor s$	38	3	2
16. $p \to q, p \& r/q \lor s$	31	9	3
Total: 534		138	16
Mean: 33.4			
Complex single-operation arguments			
1. $(p \lor q) \to (r \& s), p \lor q/s$	35	7	1
2. $(p \lor q) \to (r \& s), p/r \& s$	42	1	0
3. $-q \to -p, -q \& r/-p$	42	1	0
4. $p \to (q \lor s), p \& r/q \lor s$	41	2	0
5. $-q \to -p, -q/-p \lor r$	32	9	2
6. $(p \& r) \to q, p \& r/q \lor s$	33	9	1
7. $-q \to -p, -q \& r/-p \& r$	41	2	0
8. $-q \to -p, -q \lor r/-p \lor r$	34	3	6
Total: 300		34	10
Mean: 37.5			
Baseline argument			
$p \to q, p/q$	43	0	0

TABLE 9.4
Mean Normalized Numerical Assignments for Valid Arguments
of Experiment 2, Session 1

	Mean normalized numerical assignments	Standard deviations of mean normalized numerical assignments
Single-operation arguments		
1. $p \rightarrow q,\ -q/-p$	16.66	20.55
2. $p \rightarrow (q\ \&\ r),\ p/q$	20.59	23.27
3. $(p\ v\ q) \rightarrow r,\ p/r$	16.53	20.99
4. $p \rightarrow q,\ p\ \&\ r/q$	22.52	23.66
5. $p \rightarrow q,\ p/q\ v\ r$	38.25	25.76
6. $p \rightarrow q,\ p\ \&\ r/q\ \&\ r$	30.22	22.92
7. $p \rightarrow q,\ p\ v\ r/q\ v\ r$	54.90	25.14
Multiple-operation arguments		
1. $p \rightarrow (q\ \&\ r),\ -q/-p$	38.44	20.74
2. $(p\ v\ q) \rightarrow r,\ -r/-p$	39.08	24.96
3. $p \rightarrow q,\ -q\ \&\ r/-p$	40.47	27.78
4. $p \rightarrow q,\ -q/-p\ v\ r$	58.67	25.77
5. $p \rightarrow q,\ -q\ \&\ r/-p\ \&\ r$	55.18	28.62
6. $p \rightarrow q,\ -q\ v\ r/-p\ v\ r$	73.70	29.59
7. $(p\ v\ q) \rightarrow (r\ \&\ s),\ p/s$	35.96	27.09
8. $p \rightarrow (q\ \&\ r),\ p\ \&\ s/q$	35.72	21.96
9. $p \rightarrow (q\ \&\ r),\ p/q\ v\ s$	53.71	29.43
10. $p \rightarrow (q\ \&\ r),\ p\ \&\ s/q\ \&\ s$	42.68	25.81
11. $p \rightarrow (q\ \&\ r),\ p\ v\ s/q\ v\ s$	66.36	25.37
12. $(p\ v\ q) \rightarrow r,\ p\ \&\ s/r$	36.17	25.40
13. $(p\ v\ q) \rightarrow r,\ p/r\ v\ s$	46.18	29.65
14. $(p\ v\ q) \rightarrow r,\ p\ \&\ s/r\ \&\ s$	40.48	25.38
15. $(p\ v\ q) \rightarrow r,\ p\ v\ s/r\ v\ s$	59.54	31.86
16. $p \rightarrow q,\ p\ \&\ r/q\ v\ s$	57.92	24.04
Complex single-operation arguments		
1. $(p\ v\ q) \rightarrow (r\ \&\ s),\ p\ v\ q/s$	43.95	26.92
2. $(p\ v\ q) \rightarrow (r\ \&\ s),\ p/r\ \&\ s$	27.42	26.62
3. $-q \rightarrow -p,\ -q\ \&\ r/-p$	32.46	24.44
4. $p \rightarrow (q\ v\ s),\ p\ \&\ r/q\ v\ s$	43.98	22.55
5. $-q \rightarrow -p,\ -q/-p\ v\ r$	45.43	26.12
6. $(p\ \&\ r) \rightarrow q,\ p\ \&\ r/q\ v\ s$	50.58	29.88
7. $-q \rightarrow -p,\ -q\ \&\ r/-p\ \&\ r$	50.11	28.13
8. $-q \rightarrow -p,\ -q\ v\ r/-p\ v\ r$	73.48	26.13
Baseline argument		
$p \rightarrow q,\ p/q$	4.76	12.51

the argument Modus Ponens is not exactly zero. The reason is that a few subjects, inexplicably, found that argument more difficult than some of the easier single-operation arguments. Table 9.5 gives the mean normalized numerical assignment for each valid argument in Session 2. Again, Modus Ponens is not exactly zero.

TABLE 9.5
Mean Normalized Numerical Assignments for Valid Arguments
of Experiment 2, Session 2

	Mean normalized numerical assignments	Standard deviations of mean normalized numerical assignments
Single-operation arguments		
1. $p \to q, -q/-p$	22.12	28.30
2. $p \to (q \& r), p/q$	16.14	17.99
3. $(p \lor q) \to r, p/r$	16.48	21.83
4. $p \to q, p \& r/q$	21.62	19.81
5. $p \to q, p/q \lor r$	48.28	29.45
6. $p \to q, p \& r/q \& r$	32.63	21.16
7. $p \to q, p \lor r/q \lor r$	50.87	26.46
Multiple-operation arguments		
1. $p \to (q \& r), -q/-p$	40.25	27.98
2. $(p \lor q) \to r, -r/-p$	41.05	30.21
3. $p \to q, -q \& r/-p$	49.85	22.08
4. $p \to q, -q/-p \lor r$	57.27	24.64
5. $p \to q, -q \& r/-p \& r$	53.40	30.99
6. $p \to q, -q \lor r/-p \lor r$	73.68	27.58
7. $(p \lor q) \to (r \& s), p/s$	35.40	27.70
8. $p \to (q \& r), p \& s/q$	37.95	26.75
9. $p \to (q \& r), p/q \lor s$	58.26	24.68
10. $p \to (q \& r), p \& s/q \& s$	42.36	24.80
11. $p \to (q \& r), p \lor s/q \lor s$	57.40	21.39
12. $(p \lor q) \to r, p \& s/r$	27.35	18.79
13. $(p \lor q) \to r, p/r \lor s$	50.39	25.91
14. $(p \lor q) \to r, p \& s/r \& s$	45.66	27.25
15. $(p \lor q) \to r, p \lor s/r \lor s$	58.27	30.59
16. $p \to q, p \& r/q \lor s$	45.85	28.84
Complex single-operation arguments		
1. $(p \lor q) \to (r \& s), p \lor q/s$	38.90	31.55
2. $(p \lor q) \to (r \& s), p/r \& s$	31.64	27.90
3. $-q \to -p, -q \& r/-p$	37.86	24.69
4. $p \to (q \lor s), p \& r/q \lor s$	46.72	28.75
5. $-q \to -p, -q/-p \lor r$	56.97	25.91
6. $(p \& r) \to q, p \& r/q \lor s$	51.16	25.18
7. $-q \to -p, -q \& r/-p \& r$	48.46	30.36
8. $-q \to -p, -q \lor r/-p \lor r$	61.11	33.19
Baseline argument		
$p \to q, p/q$	2.25	8.28

9.4   WITHIN-SUBJECT CONSISTENCY

Conversations with students after the experiment revealed that few, if any, realized that the arguments of the two sessions had identical logical structures. Many thought that the second session's problems were easier than those in Session 1. To assess consistency in sorting (i.e., consistency in accepting and rejecting arguments), phi correlations were computed for each subject between the acceptance–rejection patterns of each session for the 32 valid arguments. In this analysis, the arguments that could not be decided about were lumped with the rejected arguments. For nine subjects the phi coefficient was meaningless because of two or more empty cells. Of the remaining 34 subjects, the mean correlation was .39 ($N = 32$), which would be significant at the 5% level. Of the 34 correlations, 17 were individually significant at this level.

To assess consistency in scaling for each subject, the valid arguments that were accepted in both sessions were isolated and their numerical assignments correlated. The number of correlated observations thus varies over subjects, depending on how many valid arguments were accepted by the subject in both sessions (and thus scaled in both sessions). Across subjects, the mean number of valid arguments accepted in both sessions was 23.4, with $s = 5.2$. Of the 43 product-moment correlations calculated in this way, 21 were significant at the 5% level, one-tailed test. In addition, there were six correlations significant at the 10% level. The mean correlation for all correlations is .36, $s = .25$.

These analyses reveal only moderate within-subject consistency. Taken as a group, however, the subjects were quite consistent from Session 1 to Session 2. The correlation for the acceptance rates of valid arguments between the sessions is .88 ($N = 32$). The correlation for the mean normalized numerical assignments of valid arguments between the sessions is .94 ($N = 32$).

9.5   INVENTORY AND ADDITIVITY ANALYSES USING SIMPLE, SINGLE-OPERATION ARGUMENTS

The inventory and additivity analyses were first performed with simple single-operation arguments only. The logic of these analyses is the same as that of Section 8.4.

1.   Inventory analysis.   The derivations of Table 8.3 specify the inventory predictions. As observed in Section 5.1, if a multiple-operation argument is too complex to be judged by à subject, then the theory makes no prediction about that subject's acceptance or rejection of that argument's relevant single-operation arguments. Thus, the total number of inventory predictions in the present experiment is equal to the number of subjects multiplied by the 16 multiple-operation arguments, from which is subtracted the total number of multiple-operation arguments that the subjects judged to be too complex for a decision.[2] Thus, in Session 1, the total number of predictions is 658 [(43 subjects) $\times$ (16 multiple operation arguments) — 30 multiple-operation arguments too complex for judgment]. In Session 2, it is 672 [(43 subjects) $\times$ (16 multiple-operation arguments) — 16 multiple-operation arguments too complex for judgment].

In Session 1, 574 (87.2%) of the 658 predictions are true. Equation (2) of Section 8.4 was used to calculate the number of true inventory predictions that would be expected on the basis of the overall acceptance rate for arguments. For the logic of this "rival" theory analysis, see Section 8.4. The probability of accepting an argument was estimated from the ratio of the number of times it was accepted to the number of times it was either accepted or rejected. This excludes the number of CANNOT DECIDE responses. Similarly, the "number of subjects evaluating argument m" referred to in Eq. (2) is equal to the number of subjects either accepting or rejecting the multiple-operation argument, m. The number of expected true inventory predictions for Session 1 is 445.6, or 67.7%. The model of Table 8.1 performs 19.5% better than expected from the marginal totals, assuming independence.

In Session 2, 604 (89.9%) of the 672 inventory predictions are true. The expected number of true predictions is 490.1, or 72.9%. The model of Table 8.1 performs 17.0% better than expected from the marginal totals, assuming independence.

   2. Additivity analysis.   The additivity analysis proceeds as in Section 8.4. We consider the within-subject correlations first.

In Session 1, one subject provided only three observations to correlate because he rejected many arguments. Of the remaining 42 subjects, the mean number of observations to be correlated was 10.8 per subject, with $s = 3.3$. Twenty-three of these subjects gave correlations significant beyond the 10% level, of which 14 were significant beyond the 5% level. The average correlations over all 42 subjects was .30, $s = .38$. In Session 2,

---

[2] In determining the number of possible predictions, we do not take into consideration the number of single-operation agruments that were too complex for judgment, but only the number of multiple-operation arguments. The reason is that, theoretically, a single-operation argument should not be too complex for judgment unless every multiple-operation argument based on that operation is also too complex for judgment.

the average number of correlatable observations was 11.9, $s = 3.2$. Of the 43 subjects, 20 had correlations significant beyond the 10% level, of which 12 were significant beyond the 5% level. The mean correlation over all 43 subjects was .29, $s = .42$.

These results are not impressive. Hopefully, the low correlations result from random perturbations during scaling (see Section 8.4). Subjects with high additivity correlations in Session 1 were no more likely to have high additivity correlations in Session 2 than were subjects with low additivity correlations in Session 1. This fact is consistent with the "noise" explanation for the poor within-subject results. There is also no relationship between the consistency of subjects' numerical assignments between sessions and how high their additivity correlations are in either session.

For the between-subjects test of the additivity requirement, the mean normalized numerical assignment for multiple-operation arguments was correlated with the sums of the mean normalized numerical assignments for relevant single-operation arguments. For Session 1, the additivity correlation is .90 ($N = 16$). Figure 9.1 provides the scatter plot. For Session 2,

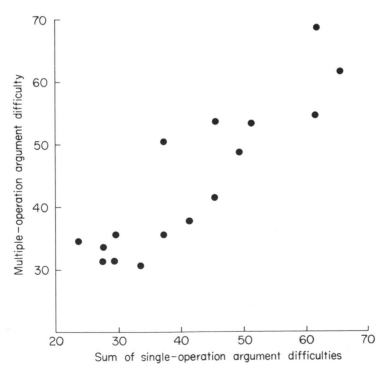

FIG. 9.1. Scatter plot for the additivity analysis of Experiment 2 (Session 1), based on the theory of Table 8.1.

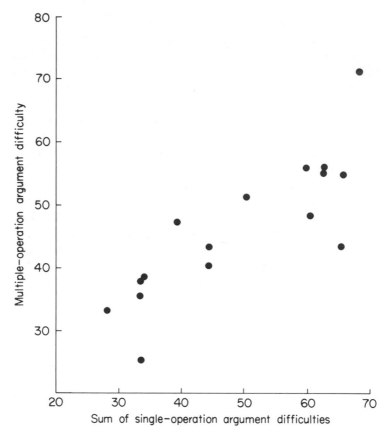

FIG. 9.2.   Scatter plot for the additivity analysis of Experiment 2 (Session 2), based on the theory of Table 8.1.

the additivity correlation is .83 ($N = 16$). Figure 9.2 provides the scatter plot.

Both sessions result in high additivity correlations for averaged data. In this important sense, the results of Sessions 1 and 2 are consistent with each other.

9.6   INVENTORY AND ADDITIVITY ANALYSES USING COMPLEX, SINGLE-OPERATION ARGUMENTS

Table 9.6 shows the difference between the mean normalized numerical assignment of the simple and complex versions of single-operation arguments based on the same operation. From Table 8.3 it can be

TABLE 9.6

Comparison of Simple and Complex Single-Operation Arguments,
Experiment 2

Relevant simple, single-operation argument	Complex, single-operation argument	Difference in mean normalized numerical assignment	
		Session 1	Session 2
(2) $p \rightarrow (q \,\&\, r), p/q$	(1) $(p \vee q) \rightarrow (r \,\&\, s), p \vee q/s$	23.36	22.76
(3) $(p \vee q) \rightarrow r, p/r$	(2) $(p \vee q) \rightarrow (r \,\&\, s), p/r \,\&\, s$	10.09	15.16
(4) $p \rightarrow q, p \,\&\, r/q$	(3) $-q \rightarrow -p, -q \,\&\, r/-p$	9.94	16.24
	(4) $p \rightarrow (q \vee s), p \,\&\, r/q \vee s$	21.46	25.10
(5) $p \rightarrow q, p/q \vee r$	(5) $-q \rightarrow -p, -q/-p \vee r$	7.18	8.69
	(6) $(p \,\&\, r) \rightarrow q, p \,\&\, r/q \vee s$	12.33	2.88
(6) $p \rightarrow q, p \,\&\, r/q \,\&\, r$	(7) $-q \rightarrow -p, -q \,\&\, r/-p \,\&\, r$	19.89	15.83
(7) $p \rightarrow q, p \vee r/q \vee r$	(8) $-q \rightarrow -p, -q \vee r/-p \vee r$	18.58	10.24

determined which derivations employ complex substitution instances of arguments.[3]

If complex substitution instances are taken into account, the inventory and additivity analyses proceed exactly as before. Of the 658 inventory predictions, 567 (86.2%) are fulfilled in Session 1. This is compared with 445.1 or 67.7% expected true predictions on the basis of argument acceptance rates. The margin of superiority is thus 18.5%, compared to 19.5% when only simple, single-operation arguments are considered. In Session 2, 576 (85.7%) of the 672 inventory predictions are fulfilled. The rival model based on acceptance rates would predict correctly 484.0, or 72.0%

[3] In accordance with the theory of Table 8.1 we have given the argument $(p \vee q) \rightarrow (r \,\&\, s)/p \rightarrow r$ the derivation

$$(p \vee q) \rightarrow (r \,\&\, s)$$
$$(p \vee q) \rightarrow r$$
$$p \rightarrow r$$

rather than the derivation

$$(p \vee q) \rightarrow (r \,\&\, s)$$
$$p \rightarrow (r \,\&\, s)$$
$$p \rightarrow r$$

The same holds true for the argument $p \rightarrow q/(p \,\&\, r) \rightarrow (q \vee s)$. Thus, the derivations reflect the operation order in Table 8.1. There is little in the data to support the chosen order, however. If we use the alternative derivations the results to be reported are only slightly weaker.

of the time. Thus, the margin of superiority is 13.7% compared to 17.8% for the analysis performed with only simple, single-operation arguments. There is, therefore, little effect on the results of the inventory analysis when complex substitution instances of operations are taken into account. If anything, the results are slightly worse.

The within-subject additivity correlations are the same as before. The between-subject additivity analysis yields a correlation of .90 for Session 1 (compared to .90 when simple, single-operation arguments are used) and .83 for Session 2 (compared to the same .83 when only simple, single-operation arguments are used).

9.7 CONCLUSIONS OF EXPERIMENT 2

Experiment 2 yields three major findings. First, within-subject consistency with respect to the sorting and scaling of arguments is only moderate. However, taking subjects as a group, the inventory and additivity requirements are fulfilled equally well by the data of the two sessions.

Second, as in Experiment 1, the theory does not perform impressively on the level of the individual subject. Averaging of data across subjects is required before high correlations in the additivity analysis result. We shall continue to assume that the need to average data arises from "noise" in the subject's scaling.

Third, substitution of complex, single-operation arguments for simple ones does not improve the results of the inventory and additivity analyses. Indeed, in other experiments, use of complex, single-operation arguments disrupts the performance of the model. This suggests that, at least for the arguments figuring in the current experiments, the difficulty of applying an operation resides in its transformation of one formula into another. The antecedent step of parsing a line to make it match the upper formula of the operation seems not to count toward the difficulty of applying that operation. Doubtless, this principle breaks down in more complicated cases, although these more complicated arguments may escape logical judgment altogether in favor of proof finding. But for the simple arguments employed here, the complexity of the substitution instance seems not to matter within a derivation. Only the nature of the particular operation being instanced contributes to the difficulty of a multiple-operation argument.[4]

[4] This conclusion comports well with the finding in Volume 2 (see Sections 6.3–6.5, 9.3, and 10.6, and Tables 9, 10, 15, and 21) that "extranegations" in formulas have little effect on problem difficulty. The presence of such extranegations did not affect which operations of the model of Volume 2 applied in the formula's derivation.

But we are left with the fact that complex, single-operation arguments are somewhat more difficult than corresponding simple, single-operation arguments. Table 9.6 shows this. If only the transformation and not the parsing processes of an operation account for its difficulty, how can this be? As one possible explanation, note that the application of an operation in multiple-operation derivations is at least partially "buried," that is, the substitution instance of at least one of the upper or lower formulas of an operation is neither the premise nor conclusion of the argument.[5] For single-operation arguments, on the other hand, the upper formula of the operation applies to the argument's premise, and the lower formula applies to the argument's conclusion. Hence, for single-operation arguments, the complexity of the parse is fully visible as well as being available to conscious reflection. However, the parse is not visible in the substitution instance of an operation's application during a multiple-operation derivation, regardless of the complexity of that substitution instance. If subjects are sensitive to the difficulty of a complex parse when both sides of the operation are visible, then the results of Table 9.6 would be explained. If subjects are not sensitive to the difficulty of a parse when one side of the operation is buried, then using complex, single-operation arguments in the additivity analysis would not help the additivity correlation and it might in fact reduce it (cf. Footnote 2, Chapter 6).

We favor this explanation of the results. Intuitively it says that during the scaling procedure, subjects are impressed by the complexity of the premise or of the conclusion or of both in the complex, single-operation arguments because this complexity is out in the open (showing extraneous negations, added conjuncts, and so forth). Beyond the difficulty of applying the operation then, these arguments' scaled difficulty represents a factor of parsing complexity that is present in neither the simple, single-operation arguments nor in the implicit application of operations in the middle of multiple-operation derivations.[6]

The same considerations apply to the use of operations on proper subformulas within lines of a derivation. Operations to be introduced in the next chapter apply either to a whole line or to just a proper part of it (see Section 4.3). We shall assume that an operation applies equally easily to a part of a line as to a whole line, provided that the "excess baggage" is hidden

---

[5] To say it another way, in a multiple-operation derivation in which line l_i is transformed by an operation into line l_{i+1}, it is not possible for l_i to be the premise of the argument and l_{i+1} to be the conclusion; for, in that case, the argument would not involve multiple operations.

[6] The upper formula of an operation may count more than the lower formula in parsing complexity. Also, operations that either end or begin a derivation might involve more parsing complexity than totally embedded operations, since the lower and upper formulas, respectively, of these operations are visible. But such subtle properties of operation application are unlikely to have testable consequences.

within interior lines of the derivation. In contrast, single-operation arguments like p & $--q/p$ & q, which show additional complexity in both the premise and conclusion, will likely be rated more difficult than $--p/p$.

For the remainder of this volume, we shall have little to say about the problem of substitution instances or subformula application. A few complex, single-operation arguments are included in Experiments 4 and 5. With them, we again attempted to improve the results of the additivity and inventory analyses. The attempt failed, and these arguments will be largely ignored. In addition, we have performed an experiment with 70 subjects that was devoted exclusively to the difference in difficulty of simple and complex arguments, and part- and whole-line applications of operations. The arguments were based on operations discussed in the next chapter. We had hoped to use the results of this study to improve the additivity correlation in Experiment 3. Again the attempt failed. Since this experiment has little independent interest, we shall not describe it (except occasionally in notes).

10

Experiment 3: New Operations

10.1 AIMS OF THE EXPERIMENT

The arguments of Experiments 1 and 2 as well as the arguments of Volume 2 have the form $A \rightarrow B/C \rightarrow D$, where A, B, C, and D stand for conjunctions or disjunctions with either prime propositions or negated prime propositions as constituents. Accordingly, the operations discussed so far are such that both the upper and lower formulas are conditionals. The present experiment was designed to extend the theory to operations pertinent to a broader class of arguments. A new set of operations was used to derive new experimental arguments. In Chapter 11 these new operations are intercalated with the old operations of Table 8.1 to produce a still more powerful theory.

On intuitive, introspective grounds, a set of operations and two executives were devised. Table 10.1 gives one theory. Some of the operations apply to proper subformulas of lines in a derivation.[1] A variation of the theory, which appeared equally plausible, is given in Table 10.2. The two theories differ (a) in that the operations are in a different order, and (b) in regard to the helping condition for operation $A \& (B \vee C)/(A \& B) \vee (A \& C)$.

Operation (1) in Table 10.1 [Operation (2) in Table 10.2] has two versions, namely, $A \& B/A$ and $A \& B/B$. Since a pilot study indicated that their level of difficulty was almost identical, only one single-operation argument will be used to represent them (see Table 10.5).

The derivations for 17 multiple-operation arguments according to the theory of Table 10.1 are provided by Table 10.3. Table 10.4 provides derivations according to the theory of Table 10.2. Those derivations that differ from one theory to another are starred in Tables 10.3 and 10.4.

[1] In general, an operation is applicable to proper subformulas of a line just in case the upper and lower formulas of the operation are logically equivalent, instead of simply being such that the upper formula implies the lower formula.

TABLE 10.1
Theory for Experiment 3

---

1. $A \& B/A$

A subformula of A occurs in the conclusion, with no subformula of B conjoined to it.

1′ (variant of 1). $A \& B/B$

A subformula of B occurs in the conclusion, with no subformula of A conjoined to it.

2. $A \& B/B \& A$

A and B occur in reverse order in the conclusion (not necessarily conjoined or disjoined to each other), or, if only one appears, B [A] occurs to the immediate right [left] of a connective that A [B] occurred to the immediate right [left] of in l_i. (Bracketed material provides an alternative helping condition.) Applies to subformulas.

3. $A \vee B/B \vee A$

A and B occur in reverse order in the conclusion (not necessarily conjoined or disjoined to each other), or, if only one appears, B [A] occurs to the immediate right [left] of a connective that A [B] occurred to the immediate right [left] of in l_i. (Bracketed material provides an alternative helping condition.) Applies to subformulas.

4. $A \& (B \vee C)/(A \& B) \vee (A \& C)$

Either $(A \& B)$ or $(A \& C)$ occurs in the conclusion. Applies to subformulas.

5. $A \vee (B \& C)/A \vee B$

No subformula of C occurs conjoined to B in the conclusion.

6. $--A/A$

A occurs in the conclusion, under the scopes of two fewer negations than in line l_i. Applies to subformulas.

7. $-A \vee -B/-(A \& B)$

$-(A \& B)$ occurs in the conclusion. Applies to subformulas.

8. $-(A \vee B)/-A \& -B$

A subformula of A [B] occurs in the conclusion, not disjoined to B [A]. (Bracketed material provides an alternative helping condition.) Applies to subformulas.

(continued)

TABLE 10.1 (*continued*)

---

9. $-(A \& B)/-A \lor -B$

A subformula of A [B] occurs in the conclusion, not conjoined to B [A]. (Bracketed material provides an alternative helping condition.) Applies to subformulas.

10. $A/A \lor B$

Any of the following holds:
   (a) The conclusion has the form $A \lor F$, for some formula F. Then B equals F in line l_{i+1} .
   (b) The conclusion has the form $-A \rightarrow F$, for some formula F. Then B equals F in line l_{i+1} .
   (c) The conclusion has the form $-F \rightarrow A$, for some formula F. Then B equals F in line l_{i+1} .
   (d) The conclusion has the form $-(A' \& F)$, for some formula F, where A' equals A with changed sign. Then B equals $-F$ in line l_{i+1} .

11. $A \lor B/-A \rightarrow B$

A subformula of A occurs in the conclusion under the scope of a changed sign, this occurence being within the antecedent of a conditional whose consequent contains a subformula of B. Applies to subformulas.

   In both theories there is only partial distribution of disjuncts through conjuncts, that is, we have the operation $A \lor (B \& C)/A \lor B$, but not $A \lor (B \& C)/(A \lor B) \& (A \lor C)$. The latter operation is logically valid, but it does not seem psychologically primitive. The reader may verify this by constructing the appropriate natural-language arguments. The other distribution principle in both theories, namely, $A \& (B \lor C)/(A \& B) \lor (A \& C)$, is unrestricted. Hence, on the present theory, Arguments (1) and (2) below, although formally analogous, have different length derivations psychologically:

   (1) $\dfrac{p \& (q \lor r)}{(p \& q) \lor (p \& r)}$

   (2) $\dfrac{p \lor (q \& r)}{(p \lor q) \& (p \lor r)}$

   This apparent asymmetry in distributivity operations is connected to the difference in ease of processing conjunctive versus disjunctive information

TABLE 10.2

Alternative Version of the Theory for Experiment 3

---

1. $--A/A$

A occurs in the conclusion, under the scopes of two fewer negations than in line l_i .
Applies to subformulas.

2. $A \& B/A$

A subformula of A occurs in the conclusion, with no subformula of B conjoined to it.

2′ (variant of 2). $A \& B/B$

A subformula of B occurs in the conclusion, with no subformula of A conjoined to it.

3. $A \& (B \lor C)/(A \& B) \lor (A \& C)$

$A[-A]$ occurs conjoined [disjoined] to $B[-B]$ or $C[-C]$ in the conclusion. (Bracketed
material provides an alternative helping condition.) Applies to subformulas.

4. $A \lor (B \& C)/A \lor B$

No subformula of C occurs conjoined to B in the conclusion.

5. $-A \lor -C/-(A \& C)$

$-(A \& C)$ occurs in the conclusion. Applies to subformulas.

6. $-(A \lor B)/-A \& -B$

A subformula of A $[B]$ occurs in the conclusion, not disjoined to $B[A]$. (Bracketed material provides an alternative helping condition.) Applies to subformulas.

7. $-(A \& B)/-A \lor -B$

A subformula of A $[B]$ occurs in the conclusion, not conjoined to $B[A]$. (Bracketed
material provides an alternative helping condition.) Applies to subformulas.

8. $A \& B/B \& A$

A and B occur in reverse order in the conclusion (not necessarily conjoined or disjoined to
each other), or, if only one appears, $B[A]$ occurs to the immediate right [left] of a connective that A $[B]$ occurred to the immediate right [left] of in l_i. (Bracketed material
provides an alternative helping condition.) Applies to subformulas.

(*continued*)

TABLE 10.2 (*continued*)

---

9. $A \vee B/B \vee A$

A and B occur in reverse order in the conclusion (not necessarily conjoined or disjoined to each other), or, if only one appears, $B[A]$ occurs to the immediate right [left] of a connective that $A[B]$ occurred to the immediate right [left] of in l_i. (Bracketed material provides an alternative helping condition.) Applies to subformulas.

10. $A/A \vee B$

Any of the following holds:
     (a) The conclusion has the form $A \vee F$, for some formula F. Then B equals F in line l_{i+1}.
     (b) The conclusion has the form $-A \rightarrow F$, for some formula F. Then B equals F in line l_{i+1}.
     (c) The conclusion has the form $-F \rightarrow A$, for some formula F. Then B equals F in line l_{i+1}.
     (d) The conclusion has the form $-(A' \& F)$, for some formula F, where A' equals A with changed sign. Then B equals $-F$ in line l_{i+1}.

11. $A \vee B/-A \rightarrow B$

A subformula of A occurs in the conclusion under the scope of a changed sign, this occurrence being within the antecedent of a conditional whose consequent contains a subformula of B. Applies to subformulas.

(cf. Bourne, 1966). Beyond that truism, we cannot explain or justify our choice of operations.[2]

10.2   METHOD

Subjects were 35 7th- and 8th-grade students from a junior high school in Menlo Park, California. They formed a random sample from 105

[2] In the experiment mentioned at the end of Section 9.6, the argument

(1) $\dfrac{p \vee (q \& r)}{p \vee q}$

was found to be somewhat easier than the argument

(2) $\dfrac{p \vee (q \& r)}{(p \vee q) \& (p \vee r)}$

This is consistent with the hypothesis that Argument (1) is not derived from Argument (2), but, if anything, Argument (2) is based on Argument (1).

TABLE 10.3
Derivations for Multiple-Operation Arguments According to the Theory of Table 10.1

Derivation	Operation	Derivation	Operation
(1) $p \& -(q \vee r)/-r$		(7) $-(p \vee q)/-(p \& r)$	
$p \& -(q \vee r)$	Premise	$-(p \vee q)$	Premise
$-(q \vee r)$	(1)′	$-p \& -q$	(8)
$-q \& -r$	(8)	$-p$	(1)
$-r$	(1)′	$-p \vee -r$	(10)
(2) $p \vee (q \& r)/-p \to q$		$-(p \& r)$	(7)
$p \vee (q \& r)$	Premise	(8) $p \& q/p \vee r$	
$p \vee q$	(5)	$p \& q$	Premise
$-p \to q$	(11)	p	(1)
(3) $-(p \vee -q)/-p \& q$		$p \vee r$	(10)
$-(p \vee -q)$	Premise	*(9) $-(p \vee q)/-q \& -p$	
$-p \& --q$	(8)	$-(p \vee q)$	Premise
$-p \& q$	(6)	$-(q \vee p)$	(3)
(4) $-(p \& -q)/-p \vee q$		$-q \& -p$	(8)
$-(p \& -q)$	Premise	*(10) $-(p \& q)/-q \vee -p$	
$-p \vee --q$	(9)	$-(p \& q)$	Premise
$-p \vee q$	(6)	$-(q \& p)$	(2)
*(5) $-(p \vee -q)/q$		$-q \vee -p$	(9)
$-(p \vee -q)$	Premise	(11) $-(p \& q)/p \to -q$	
$-p \& --q$	(8)	$-(p \& q)$	Premise
$--q$	(1)′	$-p \vee -q$	(9)
q	(6)	$--p \to -q$	(11)
(6) $-(p \vee q)/-p \vee r$		$p \to -q$	(6)
$-(p \vee q)$	Premise	(12) $-p \vee q/p \to q$	
$-p \& -q$	(8)		
$-p$	(1)	$-p \vee q$	Premise
$-p \vee r$	(10)	$--p \to q$	(11)
		$p \to q$	(6)

(*continued*)

TABLE 10.3 (*continued*)

Derivation	Operation	Derivation	Operation
*(13) $p \& (q \vee r)/(p \& r) \vee (p \& q)$		(16) $p \vee (q \& r)/p \vee r$	
$p \& (q \vee r)$	Premise	$p \vee (q \& r)$	Premise
$p \& (r \vee q)$	(3)	$p \vee (r \& q)$	(2)
$(p \& r) \vee (p \& q)$	(4)	$p \vee r$	(5)
(14) $-[p \vee (q \& r)]/-q \vee -r$		(17) $-(p \vee q)/-q$	
$-[p \vee (q \& r)]$	Premise	$-(p \vee q)$	Premise
$-p \& -(q \& r)$	(8)	$-p \& -q$	(8)
$-(q \& r)$	$(1)'$	$-q$	$(1)'$
$-q \vee -r$	(9)		
*(15) $-[p \& (q \vee r)]/-p \vee -q$			
$-[p \& (q \vee r)]$	Premise		
$-p \vee -(q \vee r)$	(9)		
$-p \vee (-q \& -r)$	(8)		
$-p \vee -q$	(5)		

students seen in groups of about 25. The remaining students were participating simultaneously in a different experiment.[3] The subjects received 34 arguments as follows: Ten of the arguments were single-operation arguments based directly on Operations (1)–(8) and (10)–(11) in Table 10.1. A single-operation argument for Operation (9) of Table 10.1 was omitted due to an oversight. Table 10.5 gives the ten single-operation arguments. Subjects also received 17 multiple-operation arguments derivable from the theories of Tables 10.1 and 10.2. These arguments are given in Table 10.6. Finally, subjects received one argument of the form p/p to serve as a baseline in the scaling procedure, analogous to Modus Ponens in Experiments 1 and 2, and six invalid arguments drawn randomly from the 18 invalid arguments shown in Table 10.7.

[3] Namely, the experiment mentioned at the end of Section 9.6. Since the instructions were identical for the two experiments, they could be run simultaneously. Envelopes containing the arguments for the different experiments were handed out randomly.

(*Text continued on page 126*)

TABLE 10.4
Derivations for Multiple-Operation Arguments According to the
Theory of Table 10.2

Derivation	Operation	Derivation	Operation
(1) $p \& -(q \lor r)/-r$		*(10) $-(p \& q)/-q \lor -p$	
$p \& -(q \lor r)$	Premise	$-(p \& q)$	Premise
$-(q \lor r)$	(2)′	$-p \lor -q$	(7)
$-q \& -r$	(6)	$-q \lor -p$	(9)
$-r$	(2)′		
		(11) $-(p \& q)/p \to -q$	
(2) $p \lor (q \& r)/-p \to q$		$-(p \& q)$	Premise
$p \lor (q \& r)$	Premise	$-p \lor -q$	(7)
$p \lor q$	(4)	$--p \to -q$	(11)
$-p \to q$	(11)	$p \to -q$	(1)
(3) $-(p \lor -q)/-p \& q$		(12) $-p \lor q/p \to q$	
$-(p \lor -q)$	Premise	$-p \lor q$	Premise
$-p \& --q$	(6)	$--p \to q$	(11)
$-p \& q$	(1)	$p \to q$	(1)
(4) $-(p \& -q)/-p \lor q$		(13) $p \& (q \lor r)/(p \& r) \lor (p \& q)$	
$-(p \& -q)$	Premise	$p \& (q \lor r)$	Premise
$-p \lor --q$	(7)	$(p \& q) \lor (p \& r)$	(3)
$-p \lor q$	(1)	$(p \& r) \lor (p \& q)$	(9)
*(5) $-(p \lor -q)/q$		(14) $-[p \lor (q \& r)]/-q \lor -r$	
$-(p \lor -q)$	Premise	$-[p \lor (q \& r)]$	Premise
$-p \& --q$	(6)	$-p \& -(q \& r)$	(6)
$-p \& q$	(1)	$-(q \& r)$	(2)′
q	(2)′	$-q \lor -r$	(7)
(6) $-(p \lor q)/-p \lor r$		(15) $-[p \& (q \lor r)]/-p \lor -q$	
$-(p \lor q)$	Premise	$-[p \& (q \lor r)]$	Premise
$-p \& -q$	(6)	$-[(p \& q) \lor (p \& r)]$	(3)
$-p$	(2)	$-(p \& q) \& -(p \& r)$	(6)
$-p \lor r$	(10)	$-(p \& q)$	(2)
		$-p \lor -q$	(7)
(7) $-(p \lor q)/-(p \& r)$			
$-(p \lor q)$	Premise	(16) $p \lor (q \& r)/p \lor r$	
$-p \& -q$	(6)	$p \lor (q \& r)$	Premise
$-p$	(2)	$p \lor (r \& q)$	(8)
$-p \lor -r$	(10)	$p \lor r$	(4)
$-(p \& r)$	(5)		
		(17) $-(p \lor q)/-q$	
(8) $p \& q/p \lor r$		$-(p \lor q)$	Premise
$p \& q$	Premise	$-p \& -q$	(6)
p	(2)	$-q$	(2)′
$p \lor r$	(10)		
*(9) $-(p \lor q)/-q \& -p$			
$-(p \lor q)$	Premise		
$-p \& -q$	(6)		
$-q \& -p$	(8)		

TABLE 10.5
Single-Operation Arguments for Experiment 3

1. $p \& (q \vee r)/(p \& q) \vee (p \& r)$

   P is there and either M is there or Y is there.
   Either both P is there and M is there, or both P is there and Y is there.

2. $p \vee (q \& r)/p \vee q$

   Either J is there or both N is there and R is there.
   Either J is there or N is there.

3. $-(p \vee q)/-p \& -q$

   It is not true that either V is there or R is there.
   V is not there and R is not there.

4. $-p \vee -q/-(p \& q)$

   Either J is not there or D is not there.
   It is not true that both J is there and D is there.

5. $p \& q/q \& p$

   N is there and L is there.
   L is there and N is there.

6. $p \vee q/q \vee p$

   Either Z is there or H is there.
   Either H is there or Z is there.

7. $p \& q/p$

   H is there and M is there.
   H is there.

8. $p/p \vee q$

   C is there.
   Either C is there or H is there.

9. $--p/p$

   It is not true that M is not there.
   M is there.

10. $p \vee q/-p \rightarrow q$

    Either S is there or Y is there.
    If S is not there, then Y is there.

TABLE 10.6
Multiple-Operation Arguments for Experiment 3

---

1. $p \,\&\, -(q \lor r)/-r$

G is there, and it is not true that either R is there or Y is there.
Y is not there.

2. $p \lor (q \,\&\, r)/-p \rightarrow q$

Either N is there or both J is there and R is there.
If N is not there, then J is there.

3. $-(p \lor -q)/-p \,\&\, q$

It is not true that either L is there or P is not there.
L is not there and P is there.

4. $-(p \,\&\, -q)/ -p \lor q$

It is not true that both S is there and V is not there.
Either S is not there or V is there.

5. $-(p \lor -q)/q$

It is not true that either T is there or L is not there.
L is there.

6. $-(p \lor q)/-p \lor r$

It is not true that either V is there or F is there.
Either V is not there or H is there.

7. $-(p \lor q)/-(p \,\&\, r)$

It is not true that either P is there or S is there.
It is not true that both P is there and G is there.

8. $p \,\&\, q/p \lor r$

Y is there and Z is there.
Either Y is there or B is there.

9. $-(p \lor q)/-q \,\&\, -p$

It is not true that either M is there or Z is there.
Z is not there and M is not there.

(*continued*)

TABLE 10.6 (*continued*)

10. $-(p \& q)/-q \lor -p$

It is not true that both G is there and Y is there.

Either Y is not there or G is not there.

11. $-(p \& q)/p \rightarrow -q$

It is not true that both B is there and J is there.

If B is there, then J is not there.

12. $-p \lor q/p \rightarrow q$

Either T is not there or S is there.

If T is there, then S is there.

13. $p \& (q \lor r)/(p \& r) \lor (p \& q)$

H is there and either Q is there or X is there.

Either both H is there and X is there, or both H is there and Q is there.

14. $-[p \lor (q \& r)]/-q \lor -r$

It is not true that either C is there or both L is there and N is there.

Either L is not there or N is not there.

15. $-[p \& (q \lor r)]/-p \lor -q$

It is not true that both V is there and either P is there or F is there.

Either V is not there or P is not there.

16. $p \lor (q \& r)/p \lor r$

Either R is there or both D is there and H is there.

Either R is there or H is there.

17. $-(p \lor q)/-q$

It is not true that either V is there or K is there.

K is not there.

TABLE 10.7
Invalid and Baseline Arguments for Experiment 3

Invalid arguments

1. $-(p \lor q)/p \& -q$

    It is not true that either F is there or H is there.
    ___
    F is there and H is not there.

2. $p \lor -q/-(p \lor q)$

    Either Y is there or S is not there.
    ___
    It is not true that either Y is there or S is there.

3. $-(p \& q)/p \& -q$

    It is not true that both L is there and K is there.
    ___
    L is there and K is not there.

4. $p \& -q/-(p \& q)$

    G is there and Y is not there.
    ___
    It is not true that both G is there and Y is there.

5. $-p \& q/-(-p \lor -q)$

    L is not there and Q is there.
    ___
    It is not true that either L is not there or Q is not there.

6. $-(-p \lor -q)/-p \& q$

    It is not true that either H is not there or Z is not there.
    ___
    H is not there and Z is there.

7. $p \lor -q/-(-p \& -q)$

    Either V is there or Y is not there.
    ___
    It is not true that both V is not there and Y is not there.

8. $-(-p \& -q)/p \lor -q$

    It is not true that both D is not there and B is not there.
    ___
    Either D is there or B is not there.

9. $--p/-p \& -q$

    It is not true that N is not there.
    ___
    N is not there and V is not there.

10. $-p \& -q/--p$

    X is not there and T is not there.
    ___
    It is not true that X is not there.

(*continued*)

TABLE 10.7 (*continued*)

11. $--p/-q \lor -p$

It is not true that K is not there.
Either M is not there or K is not there.

12. $-q \lor -p/--p$

Either F is not there or C is not there.
It is not true that C is not there.

13   $p \lor (q \& r)/q \lor r$

Either B is there or both D is there and R is there.
Either D is there or R is there.

14. $q \lor r/p \lor (q \& r)$

Either Z is there or Y is there.
Either P is there or both Z is there and Y is there.

15. $p \& (q \lor r)/q \& r$

R is there and either G is there or N is there.
G is there and N is there.

16. $q \& r/p \& (q \lor r)$

L is there and C is there.
D is there and either L is there or C is there.

17. $-p \& q/-q \& p$

H is not there and Y is there.
Y is not there and H is there.

18. $p \lor -q/q \lor -p$

Either P is there or X is not there.
Either X is there or P is not there.

Baseline argument
p/p

K is there.
K is there.

10.3   PRELIMINARY ANALYSES OF RESULTS

No subjects were dropped. Table 10.8 shows the number of subjects accepting each valid argument.[4] Each subject's scaled numerical assignments were normalized from 0.0 to 100.0, as described in Section 8.3. The baseline argument p/p had the same role as Modus Ponens in the previous experiments. It was invariably assigned the lowest number and therefore was normalized to 0.0. Table 10.9 gives the mean normalized numerical assignments for valid arguments.

10.4   INVENTORY AND ADDITIVITY ANALYSES

A within-subject test of the additivity requirement is impractical because the rejection rate for arguments in this experiment was relatively high. The result is that many subjects did not provide enough observations to make a correlation meaningful. We turn instead to the between-subject additivity correlation.

As mentioned above, due to an oversight no argument based on Operation (9) of Table 10.1 [Operation (7) of Table 10.2] was administered. Yet a value for that operation is needed in order to perform the additivity analysis. We shall use the mean normalized numerical assignment for the argument based on Operation (7) of Table 10.1 to represent the difficulty of the missing argument, that is, we use the difficulty of the argument $-p \vee -q/ -(p \& q)$ to represent also the difficulty of the converse argument $-(p \& q)/ -p \vee -q$. It is plausible that the two arguments are mediated by the same understanding.[5] Table 10.9 shows that the first argument has a mean normalized numerical assignment of 47.6. Therefore, the missing argument $-(p \& q)/-p \vee -q$ shall be assigned the same number.

The derivations in Table 10.3 pair each multiple-operation argument with the set of single-operation arguments relevant to it according to the

---

[4] The acceptance rates for Arguments (7) and (8) of Table 10.5 are probably inflated by the fact that the instructions to subjects make direct reference to them (see Section 7.2). This inflation is of relatively minor importance, as we have indicated earlier. The theory of this volume makes neither direct claims about the frequency with which arguments are accepted nor claims about their difficulty. The theory, through its derivations, specifies only patterns of argument acceptability and difficulty. Thus, increasing the likelihood, through instruction, of accepting Arguments (7) and (8) of Table 10.5 should have consequences for the acceptability of all arguments built upon their underlying operations. The inventory analysis will test whether these consequences appear in the data. Similarly, the additivity analysis will test whether the theoretically appropriate consequences on rated difficulty occur.

[5] Results of the experiment mentioned at the end of Section 9.6 support the idea that the arguments $-p \vee -q/-(p \& q)$ and $-(p \& q)/-p \vee -q$ are of nearly equal difficulty.

	No. accepted	No. rejected	No. cannot decide
Single-operation arguments			
1. $p \& (q \lor r)/(p \& q) \lor (p \& r)$	30	4	1
2. $p \lor (q \& r)/p \lor q$	21	14	0
3. $-(p \lor q)/-p \& -q$	23	11	1
4. $-p \lor -q/-(p \& q)$	30	5	0
5. $p \& q/q \& p$	34	1	0
6. $p \lor q/q \lor p$	33	1	1
7. $p \& q/p$	32	3	0
8. $p/p \lor q$	17	18	0
9. $--p/p$	24	11	0
10. $p \lor q/-p \rightarrow q$	29	6	0
Total:	273	74	3
Mean:	27.3		
Multiple-operation arguments			
1. $p \& -(q \lor r)/-r$	26	7	2
2. $p \lor (q \& r)/-p \rightarrow q$	22	12	1
3. $-(p \lor -q)/-p \& q$	19	16	0
4. $-(p \& -q)/-p \lor q$	22	13	0
5. $-(p \lor -q)/q$	20	15	0
6. $-(p \lor q)/-p \lor r$	9	23	3
7. $-(p \lor q)/-(p \& r)$	18	16	1
8. $p \& q/p \lor r$	14	21	0
9. $-(p \lor q)/-q \& -p$	24	10	1
10. $-(p \& q)/ -q \lor -p$	16	17	2
11. $-(p \& q)/p \rightarrow -q$	17	17	1
12. $-p \lor q/p \rightarrow q$	8	26	1
13. $p \& (q \lor r)/(p \& r) \lor (p \& q)$	30	4	1
14. $-[p \lor (q \& r)]/-q \lor -r$	10	22	3
15. $-[p \& (q \lor r)]/-p \lor -q$	13	18	4
16. $p \lor (q \& r)/p \lor r$	26	9	0
17. $-(p \lor q)/-q$	21	14	0
Total:	315	260	20
Mean:	18.5		
Baseline argument			
p/p	35	0	0

TABLE 10.9
Mean Normalized Numerical Assignments for
Valid Arguments of Experiment 3 ($N = 35$)

	Mean normalized numerical assignments	Standard deviations of mean normalized numerical assignments
Single-operation arguments		
1. $p \& (q \vee r)/(p \& q) \vee (p \& r)$	61.48	32.86
2. $p \vee (q \& r)/p \vee q$	50.78	26.63
3. $-(p \vee q)/-p \& -q$	40.34	22.08
4. $-p \vee -q/-(p \& q)$	47.59	23.17
5. $p \& q/q \& p$	8.37	8.37
6. $p \vee q/q \vee p$	17.66	20.82
7. $p \& q/p$	12.73	15.56
8. $p/p \vee q$	26.78	24.15
9. $--p/p$	20.82	17.62
10. $p \vee q/-p \rightarrow q$	30.81	19.81
Multiple-operation arguments		
1. $p \& -(q \vee r)/-r$	58.28	28.80
2. $p \vee (q \& r)/-p \rightarrow q$	67.14	23.09
3. $-(p \vee -q)/-p \& q$	59.43	28.15
4. $-(p \& -q)/-p \vee q$	63.62	29.51
5. $-(p \vee -q)/q$	51.53	29.23
6. $-(p \vee q)/-p \vee r$	70.71	19.46
7. $-(p \vee q)/-(p \& r)$	74.73	29.28
8. $p \& q/p \vee r$	46.42	26.07
9. $-(p \vee q)/-q \& -p$	58.19	25.70
10. $-(p \& q)/-q \vee -p$	49.25	27.49
11. $-(p \& q)/p \rightarrow -q$	49.58	27.08
12. $-p \vee q/p \rightarrow q$	50.83	28.98
13. $p \& (q \vee r)/(p \& r) \vee (p \& q)$	57.57	30.13
14. $-[p \vee (q \& r)]/-q \vee -r$	65.99	31.09
15. $-[p \& (q \vee r)]/-p \vee -q$	76.02	24.19
16. $p \vee (q \& r)/p \vee r$	54.17	28.29
17. $-(p \vee q)/-q$	45.11	26.81
Baseline argument		
p/p	0.00	0.00

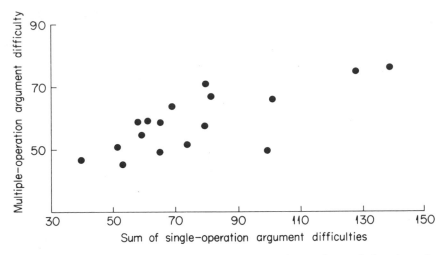

FIG. 10.1. Scatter plot for the additivity analysis of Experiment 3, based on the theory of Table 10.1.

theory of Table 10.1. The resulting additivity correlation is .76 ($N = 17$). Its scatter-diagram is shown in Fig. 10.1. This correlation is less than those in Experiments 1 and 2 but still respectable.

The derivations proper to the alternative theory of Table 10.2 are presented in Table 10.4. The derivations of Table 10.4 look very different from those of Table 10.5. However, most of the difference results from different substitution instances of the same operations. This is due to the different ordering of operations in the two theories. Only in three derivations is there a difference in the particular operations applied [namely, for Arguments (9), (10), and (15) of Table 10.6]. The resulting additivity correlation is .73 ($N = 17$).

For the inventory analysis, we made a decision similar to the one regarding the missing single-operation argument $-(p \ \& \ q)/-p \ \vee \ -q$: the judgment of a subject with respect to argument $-p \ \vee \ -q/-(p \ \& \ q)$ will represent his decision for the missing argument. If he accepts $-p \ \vee \ -q/-(p \ \& \ q)$, then he is counted as accepting $-(p \ \& \ q)/-p \ \vee \ -q$; the same holds for rejections and CANNOT DECIDE.

There are 575 inventory predictions [(35 subjects) $\times$ (17 multiple-operation arguments) — 20 multiple-operation arguments about which subjects could not decide]. Tables 10.3 and 10.4 provide the inventory predictions for the theories of Tables 10.1 and 10.2, respectively. The theory of Table 10.1 makes 352 (61.2%) true predictions. The number of true predictions expected on the basis of the overall acceptance rate of arguments is 304.0 or 52.9%. For the theory of Table 10.2, the number of true inventory predictions is 351, or 61.0%. The expected number of true predictions is 302.4, or 52.6%.

The results of the inventory analysis are less impressive than before. They do not, furthermore, distinguish between the theories of Tables 10.1 and 10.2.

10.5   CONCLUSIONS OF EXPERIMENT 3

In all, the results of Experiment 3 provide support for the new operations introduced into the theory. The between-subjects additivity analysis is most important in this regard. There is little basis for a decision, however, between the theories of Tables 10.1 and 10.2. Only three derivations of 17 differ between the two theories in terms of the operations applied. Still, substituting these three derivations from the theory of Table 10.2 for those of the theory of Table 10.1 weakens the correlation slightly. On this slender basis, we prefer the model of Table 10.1.[6]

[6] It should be clear that a vast number of possible sets of operations and executives exist, most of which are likely to be totally inaccurate in their attributions of argument difficulty and acceptance. We have not bothered to devise a palpably incorrect model for demonstration's sake because the resources necessary to test it are as great as for testing an accurate model. As for our luck in picking accurate models to a first approximation, it is presumably based on the fact that the author's logical intuitions are close to those of the subjects'.

11

Experiment 4:
Amalgamation of the Two Sets
of Operations

11.1 AIMS OF THE EXPERIMENT

In Chapters 8 and 9 a model close to that of Volume 2 was supported in two experiments. In Chapter 10, ten new operations and an executive were introduced. The two sets of operations were tested separately. It is necessary to determine whether the two models can be combined into one set of operations in the correct order. Some additional operations have also been included. To test proposals about the intercalation of operations, we shall use arguments that rely on at least one operation from each of the sets figuring in Experiments 1 and 3.

Before the experiment, two orderings of the operations seemed plausible. The two theories are presented in Tables 11.1 and 11.2. The same operations (with helping conditions) appear in each theory; only their orders differ. Note that the helping conditions for Operations (5) and (6) in Table 11.1 [Operations (7) and (8) in Table 11.2] are formulated differently than in Table 8.1. The new helping conditions allow the derivation of additional arguments [cf. Derivations (3) and (4) in Table 12.1]. A formula F occurring in line l_i of a derivation has a changed sign in the conclusion if either (a) $-F$ occurs in the conclusion, or (b) F has the form $-A$ in line l_i, and A occurs in the conclusion.[1] Finally, notice also that Operations (1)–(3), (6), and (7) from the theory of Table 10.1 are not included in Tables 11.1 and 11.2. They were left out in order to make the experiment more manageable in terms of the time required to complete it.[2]

[1] For example, p occurs with changed sign in the conclusion if $-p$ occurs in the conclusion: $-q$ occurs with changed sign in the conclusion if either $- -q$ or q occurs in the conclusion.

[2] At this point, it seemed to us that subjects had been somewhat rushed in previous experiments.

(*Text continued on page 141*)

TABLE 11.1
Theory for Experiments 4 and 5

---

1. $A \,\&\, (B \vee C)/(A \,\&\, B) \vee (A \,\&\, C)$

Either $(A \,\&\, B)$ or $(A \,\&\, C)$ occurs in the conclusion. Applies to subformulas.

2. $A \vee (B \,\&\, C)/A \vee B$

No subformula of C occurs conjoined to B in the conclusion.

$2'$ (variant of 2). $(A \,\&\, B) \vee C/A \vee C$

No subformula of B occurs conjoined to A in the conclusion.

3. $-(A \vee B)/-A \,\&\, -B$

A subformula of $A\,[B]$ occurs in the conclusion, not disjoined to $B\,[A]$. (Bracketed materia
provides an alternative helping condition.) Applies to subformulas.

4. $-(A \,\&\, B)/-A \vee -B$

A subformula of $A\,[B]$ occurs in the conclusion, not conjoined to $B\,[A]$. (Bracketed material provides an alternative helping condition.) Applies to subformulas.

5. $A \to (B \,\&\, C)/A \to B$

No subformula of C occurs conjoined to B in the conclusion, and no subformula of C'
occurs disjoined to B' in the conclusion, where B' equals B with changed sign, and C'
equals C with changed sign.

6. $(A \vee B) \to C/A \to C$

No subformula of B occurs disjoined to A in the conclusion, and no subformula of B'
occurs conjoined to A' in the conclusion, where A' equals A with changed sign, and B'
equals B with changed sign.

7. $A \to B/-B \to -A$

A subformula of A and a subformula of B occur in the conclusion, each with a changed
sign.

8. $A \to B/(A \,\&\, C) \to (B \,\&\, C)$

$(A \,\&\, F)$ and $(B \,\&\, F)$ occur in the conclusion, for some formula F. Then C equals F in
line l_{i+1} .

(*continued*)

TABLE 11.1 (*continued*)

---

9. $A \rightarrow B/(A \vee C) \rightarrow (B \vee C)$

$(A \vee F)$ and $(B \vee F)$ occur in the conclusion, for some formula F. Then C equals F in line l_{i+1} .

10. $A \rightarrow B/(A \And C) \rightarrow B$

$(A \And F)$ occurs in the conclusion, for some formula F. Then C equals F in line l_{i+1} .

11. $A \rightarrow B/A \rightarrow (B \vee C)$

$(B \vee F)$ occurs in the conclusion, for some formula F. Then C equals F in line l_{i+1} .

12. $A \vee B/-A \rightarrow B$

A subformula of A occurs in the conclusion under the scope of a changed sign, this occurrence   being within the antecedent of a conditional whose consequent contains a subformula of B. Applies to subformulas.

13. $-A \rightarrow B/A \vee B$

A subformula of A and a subformula of B occur disjoined to each other in the conclusion. Applies to subformulas.

14. $A \rightarrow B/-(A \And -B)$

A and $-B$ occur in the conclusion conjoined to each other, the conjunction occurring under the scope of negation. Applies to subformulas.

TABLE 11.2
Alternative Version of the Theory for Experiments 4 and 5

1. $A \lor B / -A \to B$

A subformula of A occurs in the conclusion under the scope of a changed sign, this occurrence being within the antecedent of a conditional whose consequent contains a subformula of B. Applies to subformulas.

2. $-A \to B / A \lor B$

A subformula of A and a subformula of B occur disjoined to each other in the conclusion. Applies to subformulas.

3. $A \& (B \lor C) / (A \& B) \lor (A \& C)$

Either $(A \& B)$ or $(A \& C)$ occurs in the conclusion. Applies to subformulas.

4. $A \lor (B \& C) / A \lor B$

No subformula of C occurs conjoined to B in the conclusion.

4' (variant of 4). $(A \& B) \lor C / A \lor C$

No subformula of B occurs conjoined to A in the conclusion.

5. $-(A \lor B) / -A \& -B$

A subformula of A [B] occurs in the conclusion, not disjoined to B[A]. (Bracketed material provides an alternative helping condition.) Applies to subformulas.

6. $-(A \& B) / -A \lor -B$

A subformula of A [B] occurs in the conclusion, not conjoined to B[A]. (Bracketed material provides an alternative helping condition.) Applies to subformulas.

7. $A \to (B \& C) / A \to B$

No subformula of C occurs conjoined to B in the conclusion, and no subformula of C' occurs disjoined to B' in the conclusion, where B' equals B with changed sign, and C' equals C with changed sign.

8. $(A \lor B) \to C / A \to C$

No subformula of B occurs disjoined to A in the conclusion, and no subformula of B' occurs conjoined to A' in the conclusion, where A' equals A with changed sign, and B' equals B with changed sign.

(continued)

TABLE 11.2 (*continued*)

---

9. $A \rightarrow B/-B \rightarrow -A$

A subformula of A and a subformula of B occur in the conclusion, each with a changed sign.

10. $A \rightarrow B/(A \,\&\, C) \rightarrow (B \,\&\, C)$

$(A \,\&\, F)$ and $(B \,\&\, F)$ occur in the conclusion, for some formula F. Then C equals F in line l_{i+1} .

11. $A \rightarrow B/(A \vee C) \rightarrow (B \vee C)$

$(A \vee F)$ and $(B \vee F)$ occur in the conclusion, for some formula F. Then C equals F in line l_{i+1} .

12. $A \rightarrow B/(A \,\&\, C) \rightarrow B$

$(A \,\&\, F)$ occurs in the conclusion, for some formula F. Then C equals F in line l_{i+1} .

13. $A \rightarrow B/A \rightarrow (B \vee C)$

$(B \vee F)$ occurs in the conclusion, for some formula F. Then C equals F in line l_{i+1} .

14. $A \rightarrow B/-(A \,\&\, -B)$

A and $-B$ occur in the conclusion conjoined to each other, the conjunction occurring under the scope of a negation. Applies to subformulas.

TABLE 11.3
Derivations for Multiple-Operation Arguments According
to the Theory of Table 11.1

Derivation	Operation	Derivation	Operation
(1) $-(p \& q) \to r/-p \to r$		(7) $p \vee q/(-p \& r) \to (q \& r)$	
$-(p \& q) \to r$	Premise	$p \vee q$	Premise
$(-p \vee -q) \to r$	(4)	$-p \to q$	(12)
$-p \to r$	(6)	$(-p \& r) \to (q \& r)$	(8)
(2) $p \to (q \vee r)/(-q \& -r) \to -p$		*(8) $(p \& q) \vee r/-p \to r$	
$p \to (q \vee r)$	Premise	$(p \& q) \vee r$	(Premise)
$-(q \vee r) \to -p$	(7)	$p \vee r$	Variant of (
$(-q \& -r) \to -p$	(3)	$-p \to r$	(12)
(3) $(p \& q) \to r/-r \to (-p \vee -q)$		*(9) $p \vee (q \& r)/-p \to (q \vee s)$	
$(p \& q) \to r$	Premise	$p \vee (q \& r)$	Premise
$-r \to -(p \& q)$	(7)	$p \vee q$	(2)
$-r \to (-p \vee -q)$	(4)	$-p \to q$	(12)
		$-p \to (q \vee s)$	(11)
(4) $(p \vee q) \to r/-(p \& -r)$		*(10) $p \vee (q \& r)/(-p \vee s) \to (q \vee s)$	
$(p \vee q) \to r$	Premise	$p \vee (q \& r)$	Premise
$p \to r$	(6)	$p \vee q$	(2)
$-(p \& -r)$	(14)	$-p \to q$	(12)
		$(-p \vee s) \to (q \vee s)$	(9)
(5) $(p \vee q) \to (r \& s)/-(p \& -r)$			
$(p \vee q) \to (r \& s)$	Premise	(11) $(-p \vee -q) \to r/p \vee r$	
$(p \vee q) \to r$	(5)	$(-p \vee -q) \to r$	Premise
$p \to r$	(6)	$-p \to r$	(6)
$-(p \& -r)$	(14)	$p \vee r$	(13)
(6) $p \vee q/(-p \& r) \to q$			
$p \vee q$	Premise	(12) $[p \& (q \vee r)] \to s/(p \& q) \to s$	
$-p \to q$	(12)	$[p \& (q \vee r)] \to s$	Premise
$(-p \& r) \to q$	(10)	$[(p \& q) \vee (p \& r)] \to s$	(1)
		$(p \& q) \to s$	(6)

TABLE 11.4
Derivations for Multiple-Operation Arguments According to the Theory of Table 11.2

Derivation	Operation	Derivation	Operation
(1) $-(p \& q) \rightarrow r/-p \rightarrow r$		(7) $p \vee q/(-p \& r) \rightarrow (q \& r)$	
$-(p \& q) \rightarrow r$	Premise	$p \vee q$	Premise
$(-p \vee -q) \rightarrow r$	(6)	$-p \rightarrow q$	(1)
$-p \rightarrow r$	(8)	$(-p \& r) \rightarrow (q \& r)$	(10)
(2) $p \rightarrow (q \vee r)/(-q \& -r) \rightarrow -p$		*(8) $(p \& q) \vee r/-p \rightarrow r$	
$p \rightarrow (q \vee r)$	Premise	$(p \& q) \vee r$	Premise
$-(q \vee r) \rightarrow -p$	(9)	$-(p \& q) \rightarrow r$	(1)
$(-q \& -r) \rightarrow -p$	(5)	$(-p \vee -q) \rightarrow r$	(6)
		$-p \rightarrow r$	(8)
(3) $(p \& q) \rightarrow r/-r \rightarrow (-p \vee -q)$		*(9) $p \vee (q \& r)/-p \rightarrow (q \vee s)$	
$(p \& q) \rightarrow r$	Premise	$p \vee (q \& r)$	Premise
$-r \rightarrow -(p \& q)$	(9)	$-p \rightarrow (q \& r)$	(1)
$-r \rightarrow (-p \vee -q)$	(6)	$-p \rightarrow q$	(7)
(4) $(p \vee q) \rightarrow r/-(p \& -r)$		$-p \rightarrow (q \vee s)$	(13)
$(p \vee q) \rightarrow r$	Premise	*(10) $p \vee (q \& r)/(-p \vee s) \rightarrow (q \vee s)$	
$p \rightarrow r$	(8)	$p \vee (q \& r)$	Premise
$-(p \& -r)$	(14)	$-p \rightarrow (q \& r)$	(1)
(5) $(p \vee q) \rightarrow (r \& s)/-(p \& -r)$		$-p \rightarrow q$	(7)
$(p \vee q) \rightarrow (r \& s)$	Premise	$(-p \vee s) \rightarrow (q \vee s)$	(11)
$(p \vee q) \rightarrow r$	(7)	(11) $(-p \vee -q) \rightarrow r/p \vee r$	
$p \rightarrow r$	(8)	$(-p \vee -q) \rightarrow r$	Premise
$-(p \& -r)$	(14)	$-p \rightarrow r$	(8)
(6) $p \vee q/(-p \& r) \rightarrow q$		$p \vee r$	(2)
$p \vee q$	Premise	(12) $[p \& (q \vee r)] \rightarrow s/(p \& q) \rightarrow s$	
$-p \rightarrow q$	(1)	$[p \& (q \vee r)] \rightarrow s$	Premise
$(-p \& r) \rightarrow q$	(12)	$[(p \& q) \vee (p \& r)] \rightarrow s$	(3)
		$(p \& q) \rightarrow s$	(8)

TABLE 11.5
Single-Operation Arguments for Experiments 4 and 5

1. $p \rightarrow (q \& r)/p \rightarrow q$

    If there is an L, then there is both a G and a D.

    If there is an L, then there is a G.

2. $(p \vee q) \rightarrow r/p \rightarrow r$

    If there is either an S or a Y, then there is a V.

    If there is an S, then there is a V.

3. $p \rightarrow q/-q \rightarrow -p$

    If there is a C, then there is a J.

    If there is not a J, then there is not a C.

4. $p \rightarrow q/(p \& r) \rightarrow (q \& r)$

    If there is an F, then there is an R.

    If there is both an F and a K, then there is both an R and a K.

5. $p \rightarrow q/(p \vee r) \rightarrow (q \vee r)$

    If there is a P, then there is a T.

    If there is either a P or a B, then there is either a T or a B.

6. $p \rightarrow q/(p \& r) \rightarrow q$

    If there is an X, then there is a G.

    If there is both an X and an H, then there is a G.

7. $p \rightarrow q/p \rightarrow (q \vee r)$

    If there is an N, then there is a C.

    If there is an N, then there is either a C or a Z.

8. $-(p \vee q)/-p \& -q$

    It is not true that: There is either a Q or a Z.

    There is not a Q and not a Z.

9. $-(p \& q)/-p \vee -q$

    It is not true that: There is both a C and an X.

    There is either not a C or not an X.

(*continued*)

TABLE 11.5 (*continued*)

10. $p \mathbin{\&} (q \vee r)/(p \mathbin{\&} q) \vee (p \mathbin{\&} r)$

There is a V and there is either a K or a D.

Either there is both a V and a K, or there is both a V and a D.

11. $p \vee (q \mathbin{\&} r)/p \vee q$

Either there is a J or there is both an M and an F.

There is either a J or an M.

12. $p \vee q/{-}p \rightarrow q$

There is either an S or a P.

If there is not an S, then there is a P.

13. $-p \rightarrow q/p \vee q$

If there is not an L, then there is an N.

There is either an L or an N.

14. $p \rightarrow q/{-}(p \mathbin{\&} {-}q)$

If there is a B, then there is a Y.

It is not true that: There is both a B and not a Y.

TABLE 11.6
Multiple-Operation Arguments for Experiment 4

1. $-(p \ \& \ q) \rightarrow r / -p \rightarrow r$

   If it is not true that there is both a T and a D, then there is an S.

   If there is not a T, then there is an S.

2. $p \rightarrow (q \vee r) / (-q \ \& \ -r) \rightarrow -p$

   If there is an N, then there is either an F or a J.

   If there is both not an F and not a J, then there is not an N.

3. $(p \ \& \ q) \rightarrow r / -r \rightarrow (-p \vee -q)$

   If there is both a B and a K, then there is an L.

   If there is not an L, then there is either not a B or not a K.

4. $(p \vee q) \rightarrow r / -(p \ \& \ -r)$

   If there is either a Y or an M, then there is an R.

   It is not true that: There is both a Y and not an R.

5. $(p \vee q) \rightarrow (r \ \& \ s) / -(p \ \& \ -r)$

   If there is either a P or a V, then there is both a Q and an H.

   It is not true that: There is both a P and not a Q.

6. $p \vee q / (-p \ \& \ r) \rightarrow q$

   There is either an X or a G.

   If there is not an X and there is a Z, then there is a G.

7. $p \vee q / (-p \ \& \ r) \rightarrow (q \ \& \ r)$

   There is either a D or a T.

   If there is not a D and there is an M, then there is both a T and an M.

8. $(p \ \& \ q) \vee r / -p \rightarrow r$

   Either there is both a C and a V, or there is a G.

   If there is not a C, then there is a G.

9. $p \vee (q \ \& \ r) / -p \rightarrow (q \vee s)$

   Either there is a J or there is both a P and an S.

   If there is not a J, then there is either a P or a Y.

(continued)

TABLE 11.6 (*continued*)

---

10. $p \vee (q \ \& \ r)/(-p \vee s) \rightarrow (q \vee s)$

Either there is an L or there is both an X and an H.

If there is either not an L or there is an R, then there is either an X or an R.

11. $(-p \vee -q) \rightarrow r/p \vee r$

If there is either not a Q or not an N, then there is a B.

There is either a Q or a B.

12. $[p \ \& \ (q \vee r)] \rightarrow s/(p \ \& \ q) \rightarrow s$

If there is a K and either a Z or an F, then there is a T.

If there is both a K and a Z, then there is a T.

The two theories produce different derivations for the same arguments with respect to the operations appearing in them. Table 11.3 provides derivations for 12 multiple-operation arguments, as determined by the theory of Table 11.1.[3] Table 11.4 provides derivations for the same arguments, as determined by the theory of Table 11.2. Derivations that differ from one theory to the other are starred. The aim of the present experiment was to determine which, if either, set of derivations is correct.

[3] In the derivation of multiple-operation Argument (8), there is an appeal to a commutative variant of Operation (2) of Table 11.1, rather than to Operation (2) directly. The reason is that this step in Derivation (8) is not technically a substitution instance of Operation (2). The required new operation for the step is $(A \ \& \ B) \vee C/A \vee C$, with the helping condition: No subformula of B occurs conjoined to A in the conclusion. The new operation is closely related to Operation (2) in Table 11.1. We have used the single-operation argument for Operation (2), viz., $p \vee (q \ \& \ r)/p \vee q$, to stand both for Operation (2) and for the new operation. The reason is to keep the analysis of the present experiment symmetrical to that of Experiment 5 (which has no need for the new operation). We are justified in collapsing these two operations onto the one single-operation argument because of the following fact: listed among the complex, single-operation arguments for this experiment is one based directly on the new operation, viz., $(p \ \& \ q) \vee r/p \vee r$. This argument has almost precisely the same mean normalized numerical assignment as the argument $p \vee (q \ \& \ r)/p \vee q$ (see Table 11.10). If the argument $(p \ \& \ q) \vee r/p \vee r$ is used to represent the one application of the new operation [instead of using the argument $p \vee (q \ \& \ r)/p \vee q$], the additivity and inventory results based on the theory of Table 11.1 are unchanged. These remarks do not apply to the derivations of Table 11.4, since the new operation is not required in any of the derivations based on the theory of Table 11.2.

11.2   METHOD

Subjects were 52 10th- and 11th-grade students from Woodside High School, in Woodside, California. The subjects were seen in one large group. Each subject received 34 arguments as follows: There were 14 single-operation arguments based on the operations of Table 11.1 (or, equivalently, Table 11.2). These are given in Table 11.5. The 12 multiple-operation arguments of the present experiment are given in Table 11.6. The baseline problem (like Modus Ponens in Experiments 1 and 2, and the Argument p/p in Experiment 3) was $p \to q/p \to q$. This argument, along with six complex, single-operation arguments, is given in Table 11.7. Finally, each subject received five invalid arguments chosen randomly from the ten arguments listed in Table 11.8.

11.3   PRELIMINARY ANALYSES OF RESULTS

1. Dropped subjects.   One subject was dropped because he rejected the baseline argument $p \to q/p \to q$. All subsequent data analyses refer to the 51 remaining subjects.

2. Acceptance rates and difficulty of arguments.   Table 11.9 shows the number of subjects accepting each valid argument in Experiment 4. Subjects' numerical assignments were normalized in the usual fashion (complex, single-operation arguments were included in the normalization). Table 11.10 shows the mean normalized numerical assignment for each valid argument.

11.4   INVENTORY AND ADDITIVITY ANALYSES

1. Inventory analysis.   Table 11.3 pairs each multiple-operation argument with the single-operation arguments relevant to it, according to the theory of Table 11.1. The derivations of Table 11.4 provide the same information for the theory of Table 11.2. The theory of Table 11.1 makes 382 (63.7%) true predictions out of a total of 600 inventory predictions [(51 subjects) $\times$ (12 multiple-operation arguments) $-$ 12 multiple-operation arguments about which subjects could not decide]. From Eq. (2) of Section 8.4, the expected number of true predictions calculated from the totals in Table 11.9 is 344.4 or 57.4%. The theory of Table 11.2 performs comparably. It makes 373 (62.2%) true predictions compared to 339.2 (56.5%) expected true predictions.[4]

[4] When the six complex, single-operation arguments are employed, the inventory results are virtually identical for each theory.

TABLE 11.7
Complex Single-Operation Arguments for Experiment 4

1. $p \rightarrow (q \vee r)/-(q \vee r) \rightarrow -p$

If there is a D, then there is either an N or a V.

If it is not true that there is either an N or a V, then there is not a D.

2. $(p \& q) \rightarrow r/-r \rightarrow -(p \& q)$

If there is both an X and a G, then there is a P.

If there is not a P, then it is not true that there is both an X and a G.

3. $(p \& q) \vee r/-(p \& q) \rightarrow r$

Either there is both a Y and an R or there is an L.

If it is not true that there is both a Y and an R, then there is an L.

4. $p \vee (q \& r)/-p \rightarrow (q \& r)$

Either there is a Q or there is both a J and an M.

If there is not a Q, then there is both a J and an M.

5. $(-p \vee -q) \rightarrow r/-p \rightarrow r$

If there is either not an S or not a Z, then there is a C.

If there is not an S, then there is a C.

6. $(p \& q) \vee r/p \vee r$

Either there is both a T and an L or there is a Q.

There is either a T or a Q.

The inventory results do not distinguish between the theories, being unimpressive for each. In neither case does the observed number of true predictions exceed the expected number by as much as 7%. Fortunately, the additivity analysis strongly supports one theory and disconfirms the other.

2.   *Additivity analysis.*   Because of the small number of multiple-operation arguments in the present experiment, within-subject tests of the additivity requirement are difficult. Few subjects provided enough observations to make the additivity correlation meaningful. We consider instead the between-subject correlations.

(*Text continued on page 148*)

TABLE 11.8

Invalid and Baseline Arguments for Experiments 4 and 5

Invalid Arguments

1. $p \rightarrow q / -p \rightarrow (-q \vee r)$

    If there is a C, then there is an R.

    If there is not a C, then there is either not an R or there is a Q.

2. $p \rightarrow q / p \rightarrow (q \& r)$

    If there is a V, then there is an M.

    If there is a V, then there is both an M and a D.

3. $-(p \& q) / -p \& -q$

    It is not true that: There is both an H and a J.

    There is not an H and not a J.

4. $(p \& q) \rightarrow r / p \rightarrow r$

    If there is both an N and an X, then there is a Z.

    If there is an N, then there is a Z.

5. $p \rightarrow (q \vee r) - p \rightarrow q$

    If there is a Y, then there is either an S or a B.

    If there is not a Y, then there is an S.

6. $-(p \vee q) / p \& -q$

    It is not true that: There is either a P or an F.

    There is a P and there is not an F.

7. $-p \& q / -q \& p$

    There is not an L and there is a G.

    There is not a G and there is an L.

8. $p \vee -q / -q \vee -p$

    Either there is a K or there is not a T.

    There is either not a T or not a K.

(*continued*)

TABLE 11.8 (*continued*)

9. $p \vee (q \& r)/p \& q$

Either there is an H or there is both a T and a Z.

There is both an H and a T.

10. $p \vee q/(-q \& r) \rightarrow -p$

There is either an X or a G.

If there is not a G and there is a C, then there is not an X.

Baseline Argument

$p \rightarrow q/p \rightarrow q$

If there is a K, then there is a T.

If there is a K, then there is a T.

TABLE 11.9
Acceptance Rates for Valid Arguments of
Experiment 4 ($N = 51$)

	No. accepted	No. rejected	No. cannot decide
Single-operation arguments			
1. $p \rightarrow (q \ \& \ r)/p \rightarrow q$	41	10	0
2. $(p \lor q) \rightarrow r/p \rightarrow r$	50	1	0
3. $p \rightarrow q/-q \rightarrow -p$	40	11	0
4. $p \rightarrow q/(p \ \& \ r) \rightarrow (q \ \& \ r)$	46	2	3
5. $p \rightarrow q/(p \lor r) \rightarrow (q \lor r)$	40	10	1
6. $p \rightarrow q/(p \ \& \ r) \rightarrow q$	48	3	0
7. $p \rightarrow q/p \rightarrow (q \lor r)$	18	33	0
8. $-(p \lor q)/-p \ \& \ -q$	27	24	0
9. $-(p \ \& \ q)/-p \lor -q$	30	20	1
10. $p \ \& \ (q \lor r)/(p \ \& \ q) \lor (p \ \& \ r)$	46	4	1
11. $p \lor (q \ \& \ r)/p \lor q$	33	18	0
12. $p \lor q/-p \rightarrow q$	45	5	1
13. $-p \rightarrow q/p \lor q$	40	11	0
14. $p \rightarrow q/-(p \ \& \ -q)$	31	20	0
Total:	535	172	7
Mean:	38.2		
Multiple-operation arguments			
1. $-(p \ \& \ q) \rightarrow r/-p \rightarrow r$	31	20	0
2. $p \rightarrow (q \lor r)/(-q \ \& \ -r) \rightarrow -p$	42	9	0
3. $(p \ \& \ q) \rightarrow r/-r \rightarrow (-p \lor -q)$	32	19	0
4. $(p \lor q) \rightarrow r/-(p \ \& \ -r)$	29	21	1
5. $(p \lor q) \rightarrow (r \ \& \ s)/-(p \ \& \ -r)$	31	18	2
6. $p \lor q/(-p \ \& \ r) \rightarrow q$	39	12	0
7. $p \lor q/(-p \ \& \ r) \rightarrow (q \ \& \ r)$	43	8	0
8. $(p \ \& \ q) \lor r/-p \rightarrow r$	36	14	1
9. $p \lor (q \ \& \ r)/-p \rightarrow (q \lor s)$	10	41	0
10. $p \lor (q \ \& \ r)/(-p \lor s) \rightarrow (q \lor s)$	12	33	6
11. $(-p \lor -q) \rightarrow r/p \lor r$	16	33	2
12. $[p \ \& \ (q \lor r)] \rightarrow s/(p \ \& \ q) \rightarrow s$	47	4	0
Total:	368	232	12
Mean:	30.7		
Complex single-operation arguments			
1. $p \rightarrow (q \lor r)/-(q \lor r) \rightarrow -p$	39	12	0
2. $(p \ \& \ q) \rightarrow r/-r \rightarrow -(p \ \& \ q)$	39	12	0
3. $(p \ \& \ q) \lor r/-(p \ \& \ q) \rightarrow r$	38	12	1
4. $p \lor (q \ \& \ r)/-p \rightarrow (q \ \& \ r)$	45	6	0
5. $(-p \lor -q) \rightarrow r/-p \rightarrow r$	38	13	0
6. $(p \ \& \ q) \lor r/p \lor r$	26	25	0
Total:	225	80	1
Mean:	37.5		
Baseline argument			
$p \rightarrow q/p \rightarrow q$	51	0	0

TABLE 11.10
Mean Normalized Numerical Assignments for
Valid Arguments of Experiment 4 ($N = 51$)

	Mean normalized numerical assignments	Standard deviations of mean normalized numerical assignments
Single-operation arguments		
1. $p \rightarrow (q \, \& \, r)/p \rightarrow q$	25.83	22.62
2. $(p \vee q) \rightarrow r/p \rightarrow r$	25.27	20.56
3. $p \rightarrow q/-q \rightarrow -p$	14.12	16.34
4. $p \rightarrow q/(p \, \& \, r) \rightarrow (q \, \& \, r)$	37.78	26.17
5. $p \rightarrow q/(p \vee r) \rightarrow (q \vee r)$	44.60	26.58
6. $p \rightarrow q/(p \, \& \, r) \rightarrow q$	28.40	20.04
7. $p \rightarrow q/p \rightarrow (q \vee r)$	22.86	17.78
8. $-(p \vee q)/-p \, \& \, -q$	45.82	34.14
9. $-(p \, \& \, q)/-p \vee -q$	51.32	27.71
10. $p \, \& \, (q \vee r)/(p \, \& \, q) \vee (p \, \& \, r)$	41.96	25.23
11. $p \vee (q \, \& \, r)/p \vee q$	41.39	24.34
12. $p \vee q/-p \rightarrow q$	12.29	13.16
13. $-p \rightarrow q/p \vee q$	22.32	17.60
14. $p \rightarrow q/-(p \, \& \, -q)$	53.09	28.08
Multiple-operation arguments		
1. $-(p \, \& \, q) \rightarrow r/-p \rightarrow r$	64.06	29.11
2. $p \rightarrow (q \vee r)/(-q \, \& \, -r) \rightarrow -p$	53.75	26.41
3. $(p \, \& \, q) \rightarrow r/-r \rightarrow (-p \vee -q)$	52.75	28.02
4. $(p \vee q) \rightarrow r/-(p \, \& \, -r)$	65.79	27.82
5. $(p \vee q) \rightarrow (r \, \& \, s)/-(p \, \& \, -r)$	80.76	21.95
6. $p \vee q/(-p \, \& \, r) \rightarrow q$	44.97	25.83
7. $p \vee q/(-p \, \& \, r) \rightarrow (q \, \& \, r)$	48.32	22.81
8. $(p \, \& \, q) \vee r/-p \rightarrow r$	31.93	22.95
9. $p \vee (q \, \& \, r)/-p \rightarrow (q \vee s)$	66.49	25.90
10. $p \vee (q \, \& \, r)/(-p \vee s) \rightarrow (q \vee s)$	90.36	16.24
11. $(-p \vee -q) \rightarrow r/p \vee r$	62.50	26.80
12. $[p \, \& \, (q \vee r)] \rightarrow s/(p \, \& \, q) \rightarrow s$	47.88	29.56
Complex single-operation arguments		
1. $p \rightarrow (q \vee r)/-(q \vee r) \rightarrow -p$	64.88	28.70
2. $(p \, \& \, q) \rightarrow r/-r \rightarrow -(p \, \& \, q)$	57.40	29.32
3. $(p \, \& \, q) \vee r/-(p \, \& \, q) \rightarrow r$	56.86	29.65
4. $p \vee (q \, \& \, r)/-p \rightarrow (q \, \& \, r)$	37.14	27.89
5. $(-p \vee -q) \rightarrow r/-p \rightarrow r$	42.46	26.69
6. $(p \, \& \, q) \vee r/p \vee r$	39.87	19.45
Baseline argument		
$p \rightarrow q/p \rightarrow q$	0.00	0.00

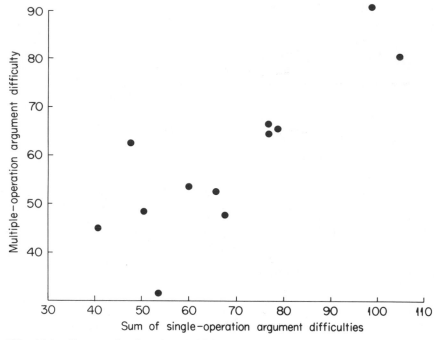

FIG. 11.1.   Scatter plot for the additivity analysis of Experiment 4, based on the theory of Table 11.1.

The derivations provide the bases for the additivity correlations for the two theories. The additivity correlation for the theory of Table 11.1 is .83 ($N = 12$). Figure 11.1 shows the scatter plot for this correlation. For the theory of Table 11.2, the correlation is only .40 ($N = 12$).[5]

11.5   CONCLUSIONS OF EXPERIMENT 4

On the basis of the additivity results, we prefer the theory of Table 11.1 to that of Table 11.2. The chosen theory has an interesting psychological property that we shall point out in the next chapter.

[5] When the six complex, single-operation arguments are employed, the additivity results are markedly poorer, dropping about 30 points for each theory.

12

Experiment 5:
Further Test of the Theory

12.1 AIMS OF THE EXPERIMENT

In Experiment 4 we found support for the theory of Table 11.1 by comparing it in a post hoc fashion to the theory of Table 11.2. In order to confirm the predictive power of the theory, 12 new multiple-operation arguments were generated. These were used in the present experiment.[1] As in Experiment 4, the new arguments all employed at least one operation from each of Chapters 8 and 10. Table 12.1 gives derivations for the 12 new arguments, in accordance with the theory of Table 11.1.

12.2 METHOD

Subjects were 49 10th- and 11th-grade students from Crestmoor High School in Burlingame, California. Subjects were seen in one large group. Each subject received 35 arguments as follows. There were 14 single-operation arguments based on the operations of Table 11.1. These are the same arguments employed in Experiment 4 and they are given in Table 11.5. The 12 multiple-operation arguments of the present experiment are given in Table 12.2. The baseline argument $p \rightarrow q/p \rightarrow q$, along with 7 complex, multiple-operation arguments are given in Table 12.3. Finally, each subject received five invalid arguments chosen randomly from the ten invalid arguments listed in Table 11.8.

---

[1] One of these multiple-operation arguments, namely, $p \vee (q \& r)/-p \rightarrow q$, is not entirely new, having figured in Experiment 3.

Derivation	Operation	Derivation	Operation
(1) $p \rightarrow -(q \vee r)/p \rightarrow -q$		*(8) $p \vee (q \& r)/-p \rightarrow q$	
$p \rightarrow -(q \vee r)$	Premise	$p \vee (q \& r)$	Premise
$p \rightarrow (-q \& -r)$	(3)	$p \vee q$	(2)
$p \rightarrow -q$	(5)	$-p \rightarrow q$	(12)
(2) $-(p \& q) \rightarrow r/p \vee r$		*(9) $p \vee (q \& r)/(-p \& s) \rightarrow (q \& s)$	
$-(p \& q) \rightarrow r$	Premise	$p \vee (q \& r)$	Premise
$(-p \vee -q) \rightarrow r$	(4)	$p \vee q$	(2)
$-p \rightarrow r$	(6)	$-p \rightarrow q$	(12)
$p \vee r$	(13)	$(-p \& s) \rightarrow (q \& s)$	(8)
(3) $(p \vee q) \rightarrow r/-r \rightarrow (-p \& -q)$		*(10) $p \vee (q \& r)/(-p \& s) \rightarrow q$	
$(p \vee q) \rightarrow r$	Premise	$p \vee (q \& r)$	Premise
$-r \rightarrow -(p \vee q)$	(7)	$p \vee q$	(2)
$-r \rightarrow (-p \& -q)$	(3)	$-p \rightarrow q$	(12)
(4) $p \rightarrow (q \& r)/(-q \vee -r) \rightarrow -p$		$(-p \& s) \rightarrow q$	(10)
$p \rightarrow (q \& r)$	Premise	*(11) $-p \rightarrow (q \& r)/p \vee q$	
$-(q \& r) \rightarrow -p$	(7)	$-p \rightarrow (q \& r)$	Premise
$(-q \vee -r) \rightarrow -p$	(4)	$-p \rightarrow q$	(5)
(5) $p \rightarrow (q \& r)/-(p \& -q)$		$p \vee q$	(13)
$p \rightarrow (q \& r)$	Premise	*(12) $p \& (q \vee r)/-(p \& q) \rightarrow (p \& r)$	
$p \rightarrow q$	(5)	$p \& (q \vee r)$	Premise
$-(p \& -q)$	(14)	$(p \& q) \vee (p \& r)$	(1)
(6) $p \vee q/(-p \vee r) \rightarrow (q \vee r)$		$-(p \& q) \rightarrow (p \& r)$	(12)
$p \vee q$	Premise		
$-p \rightarrow q$	(12)		
$(-p \vee r) \rightarrow (q \vee r)$	(9)		
(7) $p \vee q/-p \rightarrow (q \vee r)$			
$p \vee q$	Premise		
$-p \rightarrow q$	(12)		
$-p \rightarrow (q \vee r)$	(11)		

12.3 PRELIMINARY ANALYSIS OF RESULTS

1. Dropped subjects. Five subjects were dropped. Three were uncooperative. Two found the baseline argument rather difficult. Subsequent data analyses refer to the 44 remaining subjects.

2. Acceptance rates and difficulty of arguments. Table 12.4 shows the number of subjects accepting each valid argument in Experiment 5. The 14 simple, single-operation arguments figured in both Experiments 4 and 5. The correlation in acceptance rate for these arguments between the two experiments is .91 $(N = 14)$. Subjects' numerical assignments were normalized in the usual fashion. (The complex, single-operation arguments were included in the normalization.) Table 12.5 shows the mean normalized numerical assignment for each valid argument. The correlation in mean normalized numerical assignment between the 14 simple, single-operation arguments in Experiments 4 and 5 is .83 $(N = 14)$. These last two correlations indicate that subjects are relatively immune from context effects during sorting and scaling. The difference in multiple-operations arguments between Experiments 4 and 5 had little effect on subjects' judgments about single-operation arguments.

12.4 INVENTORY AND ADDITIVITY ANALYSES

1. Inventory analysis. The derivations of Table 12.1, which conform to the theory of Table 11.1, provide the inventory and additivity predictions. The theory is correct in 324 (62.4% of the time) out of 521 inventory predictions [(44 subjects) $\times$ (12 multiple-operation arguments) $-$ 7 multiple-operation arguments about which subjects could not decide]. The number of expected true predictions on the basis of the marginal totals of Table 12.4 is 268.6 or 51.6%.[2] The theory is thus 11% more accurate than expected on the basis of marginal totals.

2. Additivity analysis. Because of the small number of multiple-operation arguments in the present experiment, within-subject tests of the additivity requirement are impractical. The between-subject additivity correlation is .71 $(N = 12)$. Figure 12.1 shows the scatter plot for this correlation.[3] Although this result is not as strong as in previous experiments, it

---

[2] If the complex, single-operation arguments are employed in the inventory analysis instead of the corresponding simple, single-operation arguments, the results are almost identical.

[3] If the complex, single-operation arguments are employed in the addivity analysis, the results are considerably poorer.

TABLE 12.2
Multiple-Operation Arguments for Experiment 5

---

1. $p \rightarrow -(q \vee r)/p \rightarrow -q$

   If there is a T, then it is not true that there is either a Z or a B.
   _____
   If there is a T, then there is not a Z.

2. $-(p \;\&\; q) \rightarrow r/p \vee r$

   If it is not true that there is both an X and a G, then there is an L.
   _____
   There is either an X or an L.

3. $(p \vee q) \rightarrow r/-r \rightarrow (-p \;\&\; -q)$

   If there is either an N or an H, then there is a V.
   _____
   If there is not a V, then there is not an N and not an H.

4. $p \rightarrow (q \;\&\; r)/(-q \vee -r) \rightarrow -p$

   If there is an R, then there is both a J and a Y.
   _____
   If there is either not a J or not a Y, then there is not an R.

5. $p \rightarrow (q \;\&\; r)/-(p \;\&\; -q)$

   If there is an F, then there is both an S and a P.
   _____
   It is not true that: There is both an F and not an S.

6. $p \vee q/(-p \vee r) \rightarrow (q \vee r)$

   There is either a C or an M.
   _____
   If there is either not a C or there is a D, then there is either an M or a D.

7. $p \vee q/-p \rightarrow (q \vee r)$

   There is either a Q or a K.
   _____
   If there is not a Q, then there is either a K or a T.

8. $p \vee (q \;\&\; r)/-p \rightarrow q$

   Either there is an N or there is both an S and a Q.
   _____
   If there is not an N, then there is an S.

9. $p \vee (q \;\&\; r)/(-p \;\&\; s) \rightarrow (q \;\&\; s)$

   Either there is an H or there is both an R and an M.
   _____
   If there is not an H and there is a P, then there is both an R and a P.

(continued)

TABLE 12.2 (*continued*)

---

10. $p \vee (q \& r)/(-p \& s) \rightarrow q$

Either there is an X or there is both a D and a G.

If there is not an X and there is a B, then there is a D.

11. $-p \rightarrow (q \& r)/p \vee q$

If there is not a K, then there is both a C and a Y.

There is either a K or a C.

12. $p \& (q \vee r)/-(p \& q) \rightarrow (p \& r)$

There is an S and either an H or a Q.

If it is not true that there is both an S and an H, then there is both an S and a Q.

---

is still respectable and provides additional support for the theory of Table 11.1.[4]

12.5 CONCLUSIONS OF EXPERIMENT 5

The inventory and additivity analyses support our proposed theory of the operations underlying logical judgment. The full theory as elaborated to this point is presented in the Appendix, along with derivations of all arguments used in Experiments 1–5.

It is of interest to pool the results for all the arguments used and compute one grand correlation for the additivity analysis. Since the same arguments were used in both Experiment 2 and Experiment 1, we shall employ only the results of the latter. All together, 59 different arguments were employed. Pooling the results across experiments in this way is dangerous, of course, since the mean normalized numerical assignments for arguments depend to an unknown extent on the sample of subjects employed and particularly on the total set of arguments evaluated. Within any experiment these factors are held constant, but across experiments they vary. Our normalization procedure makes such a compilation of results doubly

---

[4] If the theory of Table 11.2 is used to provide derivations for the multiple-operation arguments of Experiment 5, the additivity correlation is about the same. However, the theory of Table 11.2 has already been discredited by the results of Experiment 4.

TABLE 12.3
Complex Single-Operation Arguments for Experiment 5

1. $(p \lor q) \rightarrow r/-r \rightarrow -(p \lor q)$

If there is either a Z or a B, then there is an M.

If there is not an M, then it is not true that there is either a Z or a B.

2. $p \rightarrow (q \And r)/-(q \And r) \rightarrow -p$

If there is a Y, then there is both a J and an X.

If it is not true that there is both a J and an X, then there is not a Y.

3. $p \lor (q \And r)/-p \rightarrow (q \And r)$

Either there is an F or there is both a D and a P.

If there is not an F, then there is both a D and a P.

4. $-p \rightarrow (q \And r)/p \lor (q \And r)$

If there is not an S, then there is both an H and a Q.

Either there is an S or there is both an H and a Q.

5. $(p \And q) \lor r/p \lor r$

Either there is both a T and an L or there is a Q.

There is either a T or a Q.

6. $-(p \And q) \rightarrow r/(p \And q) \lor r$

If it is not true that there is both an L and a T, then there is an N.

Either there is both an L and a T or there is an N.

7. $-p \rightarrow (q \And r)/-p \rightarrow q$

If there is not a G, then there is both a C and an R.

If there is not a G, then there is a C.

questionable. With this caveat, we may report that the overall correlation is .74 $(N = 59)$. The scatter plot for this correlation is given in Fig. 12.2.

As pointed out in Section 4.3, we cannot provide empirical justification for the total ordering of the operations in our theory. Indeed, some changes in ordering have no effect on the particular operations appearing in derivations for the multiple-operation arguments used in the present series of

	No. accepted	No. rejected	No. cannot decide
Single-operation arguments			
1. $p \rightarrow (q \& r)/p \rightarrow q$	38	6	0
2. $(p \vee q) \rightarrow r/p \rightarrow r$	42	2	0
3. $p \rightarrow q/-q \rightarrow -p$	32	11	1
4. $p \rightarrow q/(p \& r) \rightarrow (q \& r)$	37	6	1
5. $p \rightarrow q/(p \vee r) \rightarrow (q \vee r)$	27	16	1
6. $p \rightarrow q/(p \& r) \rightarrow q$	42	2	0
7. $p \rightarrow q/p \rightarrow (q \vee r)$	19	25	0
8. $-(p \vee q)/-p \& -q$	24	19	1
9. $-(p \& q)/-p \vee -q$	29	15	0
10. $p \& (q \vee r)/(p \& q) \vee (p \& r)$	35	9	0
11. $p \vee (q \& r)/p \vee q$	31	13	0
12. $p \vee q/-p \rightarrow q$	38	6	0
13. $-p \rightarrow q/p \vee q$	35	9	0
14. $p \rightarrow q/-(p \& -q)$	22	22	0
Total:	451	161	4
Mean:	32.2		
Multiple-operation arguments			
1. $p \rightarrow -(q \vee r)/p \rightarrow -q$	29	15	0
2. $-(p \& q) \rightarrow r/p \vee r$	24	20	0
3. $(p \vee q) \rightarrow r/-r \rightarrow (-p \& -q)$	30	14	0
4. $p \rightarrow (q \& r)/(-q \vee -r) \rightarrow -p$	30	13	1
5. $p \rightarrow (q \& r)/-(p \& -q)$	25	17	2
6. $p \vee q/(-p \vee r) \rightarrow (q \vee r)$	27	14	3
7. $p \vee q/-p \rightarrow (q \vee r)$	16	28	0
8. $p \vee (q \& r)/-p \rightarrow q$	26	18	0
9. $p \vee (q \& r)/(-p \& s) \rightarrow (q \& s)$	22	22	0
10. $p \vee (q \& r)/(-p \& s) \rightarrow q$	24	19	1
11. $-p \rightarrow (q \& r)/p \vee q$	29	15	0
12. $p \& (q \vee r)/-(p \& q) \rightarrow (p \& r)$	34	10	0
Total:	316	205	7
Mean:	26.3		
Complex single-operation arguments			
1. $(p \vee q) \rightarrow r/-r \rightarrow -(p \vee q)$	33	11	0
2. $p \rightarrow (q \& r)/-(q \& r) \rightarrow -p$	27	17	0
3. $p \vee (q \& r)/-p \rightarrow (q \& r)$	38	6	0
4. $-p \rightarrow (q \& r)/p \vee (q \& r)$	30	14	0
5. $(p \& q) \vee r/p \vee r$	33	11	0
6. $-(p \& q) \rightarrow r/(p \& q) \vee r$	22	21	1
7. $-p \rightarrow (q \& r)/-p \rightarrow q$	34	9	1
Total:	217	89	2
Mean:	31.0		
Baseline argument			
$p \rightarrow q/p \rightarrow q$	44	0	0

TABLE 12.5
Mean Normalized Numerical Assignments for
Experiment 5 ($N = 44$)

	Mean normalized numerical assignments	Standard deviations of mean normalized numerical assignments
Single-operation arguments		
1. $p \to (q \,\&\, r)/p \to q$	30.57	20.47
2. $(p \lor q) \to r/p \to r$	30.33	21.34
3. $p \to q/-q \to -p$	18.63	22.07
4. $p \to q/(p \,\&\, r) \to (q \,\&\, r)$	53.47	25.01
5. $p \to q/(p \lor r) \to (q \lor r)$	53.34	26.76
6. $p \to q/(p \,\&\, r) \to q$	32.81	29.10
7. $p \to q/p \to (q \lor r)$	39.41	24.83
8. $-(p \lor q)/-p \,\&\, -q$	32.68	26.93
9. $-(p \,\&\, q)/-p \lor -q$	49.97	32.04
10. $p \,\&\, (q \lor r)/(p \,\&\, q) \lor (p \,\&\, r)$	44.16	26.12
11. $p \lor (q \,\&\, r)/p \lor q$	35.35	22.90
12. $p \lor q/-p \to q$	17.39	19.04
13. $-p \to q/p \lor q$	24.19	25.39
14. $p \to q/-(p \,\&\, -q)$	55.36	29.36
Multiple-operation arguments		
1. $p \to -(q \lor r)/p \to -q$	52.01	32.91
2. $-(p \,\&\, q) \to r/p \lor r$	64.11	23.50
3. $(p \lor q) \to r/-r \to (-p \,\&\, -q)$	49.15	28.96
4. $p \to (q \,\&\, r)/(-q \lor -r) \to -p$	49.10	29.70
5. $p \to (q \,\&\, r)/-(p \,\&\, -q)$	67.43	24.38
6. $p \lor q/(-p \lor r) \to (q \lor r)$	73.12	25.92
7. $p \lor q/-p \to (q \lor r)$	44.27	30.32
8. $p \lor (q \,\&\, r)/-p \to q$	34.36	20.95
9. $p \lor (q \,\&\, r)/(-p \,\&\, s) \to (q \,\&\, s)$	71.65	23.88
10. $p \lor (q \,\&\, r)/(-p \,\&\, s) \to q$	61.35	25.88
11. $-p \to (q \,\&\, r)/p \lor q$	42.00	20.86
12. $p \,\&\, (q \lor r)/-(p \,\&\, q) \to (p \,\&\, r)$	67.44	27.60
Complex single-operation arguments		
1. $(p \lor q) \to r/-r \to -(p \lor q)$	63.14	25.96
2. $p \to (q \,\&\, r)/-(q \,\&\, r) \to -p$	52.79	26.95
3. $p \lor (q \,\&\, r)/-p \to (q \,\&\, r)$	37.94	26.88
4. $-p \to (q \,\&\, r)/p \lor (q \,\&\, r)$	40.83	26.56
5. $(p \,\&\, q) \lor r/p \lor r$	38.15	21.11
6. $-(p \,\&\, q) \to r/(p \,\&\, q) \lor r$	59.55	29.41
7. $-p \to (q \,\&\, r)/-p \to q$	33.50	20.78
Baseline argument		
$p \to q/p \to q$	0.19	1.24

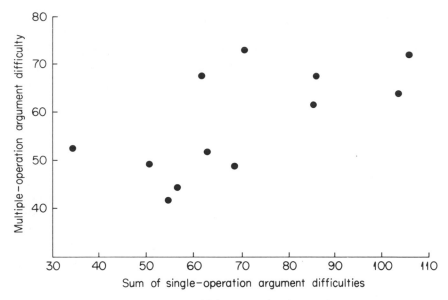

FIG. 12.1.   Scatter plot for the additivity analysis of Experiment 5, based on the theory of Table 11.1.

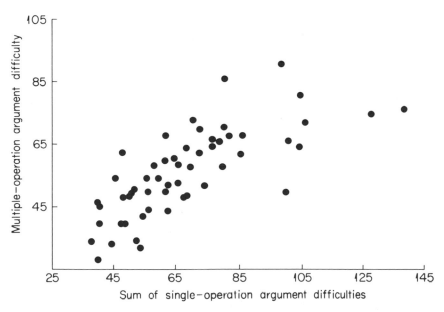

FIG. 12.2.   Scatter plot for the additivity analysis of Experiments 1, 3–5.

experiments; only the nature of the substitution instances of the operations are affected (see Sections 9.1 and 10.5).

On the other hand, some of the ordering is consequential. Consider, for example, the difference in ordering of operations distinguishing the theories of Tables 11.1 and 11.2. In the former theory, the operations $A \vee B/-A \rightarrow B$ and $-A \rightarrow B/A \vee B$ occur at the end of the ordering, whereas in the latter theory they occur toward the beginning. For the 24 multiple-operation arguments of Experiments 4 and 5, the difference in ordering results in different derivations for eight of these arguments. These alternative derivations are brought together in Table 12.6.[5]

The difference in the derivations between the two theories can be summarized this way. Other things equal, the theory of Table 11.1 is concerned first with eliminating propositions from the premise of an argument when they do not appear in the argument's conclusion, and subsequently with replacing the main connective of the formula with the connective that appears in the conclusion (if the premise and conclusion differ in these respects). The theory of Table 11.2 tends to perform these transformations in reverse order. This difference in derivational strategy between the two theories does not manifest itself in every derivation, but only in those in which more than one operation becomes legal and helpful for the same derivational line.

The results of Experiment 4 indicate that the derivational strategy of Table 11.1 is the correct one.[6] This is fortunate because it is related to a fact about the derivations of arguments in Experiments 1 and 2. Consider Arguments (i) and (ii), which appeared in these experiments:

(i) $(p \vee q) \rightarrow r/-r \rightarrow -p$
(ii) $p \rightarrow (q \& r)/-q \rightarrow -p$

The theory of Table 8.1 (as well as that of Table 11.1) gives them the Derivations (1) and (2), respectively:

(1) $(p \vee q) \rightarrow r$
      $p \rightarrow r$
      $-r \rightarrow -p$

(2) $p \rightarrow (q \& r)$
      $p \rightarrow q$
      $-q \rightarrow -p$

[5] Note that the derivations according to Table 11.1 are usually shorter than those provided by Table 11.2.

[6] Although this effect did not appear in Experiment 5 (see Footnote 3 of this chapter), it will emerge again in the causality experiments of Part 3.

TABLE 12.6
Derivations for the Two Theories Contrasted

Derivations according to the theory of Table 11.1		Derivations according to the theory of Table 11.2	
$(p \& q) \vee r / -p \rightarrow r$		$(p \& q) \vee r / -p \rightarrow r$	
$(p \& q) \vee r$	Premise	$(p \& q) \vee r$	Premise
$p \vee r$	Variant of (2)	$-(p \& q) \rightarrow r$	(1)
$-p \rightarrow r$	(12)	$(-p \vee -q) \rightarrow r$	(6)
		$-p \rightarrow r$	(8)
$p \vee (q \& r) / -p \rightarrow (q \vee s)$		$p \vee (q \& r) / -p \rightarrow (q \vee s)$	
$p \vee (q \& r)$	Premise	$p \vee (q \& r)$	Premise
$p \vee q$	(2)	$-p \rightarrow (q \& r)$	(1)
$-p \rightarrow q$	(12)	$-p \rightarrow q$	(7)
$-p \rightarrow (q \vee s)$	(11)	$-p \rightarrow (q \vee s)$	(13)
$p \vee (q \& r) / (-p \vee s) \rightarrow (q \vee s)$		$p \vee (q \& r) / (-p \vee s) \rightarrow (q \vee s)$	
$p \vee (q \& r)$	Premise	$p \vee (q \& r)$	Premise
$p \vee q$	(2)	$-p \rightarrow (q \& r)$	(1)
$-p \rightarrow q$	(12)	$-p \rightarrow q$	(7)
$(-p \vee s) \rightarrow (q \vee s)$	(9)	$(-p \vee s) \rightarrow (q \vee s)$	(11)
$-(p \& q) \rightarrow r / p \vee r$		$-(p \& q) \rightarrow r / p \vee r$	
$-(p \& q) \rightarrow r$	Premise	$-(p \& q) \rightarrow r$	Premise
$(-p \vee -q) \rightarrow r$	(4)	$(p \& q) \vee r$	(2)
$-p \rightarrow r$	(6)	$p \vee r$	Variant of (4)
$p \vee r$	(13)		
$p \vee (q \& r) / -p \rightarrow q$		$p \vee (q \& r) / -p \rightarrow q$	
$p \vee (q \& r)$	Premise	$p \vee (q \& r)$	Premise
$p \vee q$	(2)	$-p \rightarrow (q \& r)$	(1)
$-p \rightarrow q$	(12)	$-p \rightarrow q$	(7)
$p \vee (q \& r) / (-p \& s) \rightarrow (q \& s)$		$p \vee (q \& r) / (-p \& s) \rightarrow (q \& s)$	
$p \vee (q \& r)$	Premise	$p \vee (q \& r)$	Premise
$p \vee q$	(2)	$-p \rightarrow (q \& r)$	(1)
$-p \rightarrow q$	(12)	$-p \rightarrow q$	(7)
$(-p \& s) \rightarrow (q \& s)$	(8)	$(-p \& s) \rightarrow (q \& s)$	(10)
$p \vee (q \& r) / (-p \& s) \rightarrow q$		$p \vee (q \& r) / (-p \& s) \rightarrow q$	
$p \vee (q \& r)$	Premise	$p \vee (q \& r)$	Premise
$p \vee q$	(2)	$-p \rightarrow (q \& r)$	(1)
$-p \rightarrow q$	(12)	$-p \rightarrow q$	(7)
$(-p \& s) \rightarrow q$	(10)	$(-p \& s) \rightarrow q$	(12)
$-p \rightarrow (q \& r) / p \vee q$		$-p \rightarrow (q \& r) / p \vee q$	
$-p \rightarrow (q \& r)$	Premise	$-p \rightarrow (q \& r)$	Premise
$-p \rightarrow q$	(5)	$p \vee (q \& r)$	(2)
$p \vee q$	(13)	$p \vee q$	(4)

Arguments (i) and (ii) do not receive the Derivations (3) and (4), respectively, which would result from a different order of operations in Table 11.1:

(3) $(p \vee q) \rightarrow r$
$-r \rightarrow -(p \vee q)$
$-r \rightarrow (-p \And -q)$
$-r \rightarrow -p$

(4) $p \rightarrow (q \And r)$
$-(q \And r) \rightarrow -p$
$(-q \vee -r) \rightarrow -p$
$-q \rightarrow -p$

The strong results of Experiments 1 and 2 make it likely that Derivations (1) and (2) are correct and that (3) and (4) are incorrect.[7] The derivational strategy behind the correct derivations is similar to the one just discussed. It dictates first eliminating from the premise propositions that do not occur in the conclusion before straightening out which propositions appear under the scope of negations. Again, deleting irrelevant propositions has primacy.

The cognitive policy motivating these derivational strategies might be described this way. In attempting to transform one set of elements, S_1, with relations on them, into another set of elements, S_2, with relations on them, eliminate as soon as possible the elements from S_1 that do not occur in S_2. At any given step in the transformation of S_1 into S_2, the possibility of effecting a given change on S_1 is determined by the stock of admissible operations available to the subject.

What principle governs the addition to S_1 of new elements already present in S_2? It seems that propositions are added late in derivations, rather than early. Consider the argument $p \vee q / -p \rightarrow (q \vee r)$. The present theory gives it the derivation

$p \vee q$
$-p \rightarrow q$
$-p \rightarrow (q \vee r)$

in which the r is added last. However, if we assume an associativity operation, a different ordering of the operations produces the following derivation in which the needed proposition is added immediately:

$p \vee q$
$(p \vee q) \vee r$
$p \vee (q \vee r)$
$-p \rightarrow (q \vee r)$

[7] In addition, a pilot study performed with a small number of subjects indicates that (1) and (2) are the correct derivations rather than (3) and (4).

The latter derivation is counterintuitive; it seems to reflect clever proof finding more than logical judgment. If this is so, (and experimentation is obviously called for), an overall strategy emerges for manipulating propositions within a derivation: When you need to change the logical connectives of a formula, have as few propositions in the formula to be changed as possible; this is to be effected by deleting unwanted propositions before changing the connectives and adding wanted propositions after changing the connectives (compare Prawitz, 1965, p. 41). On this view, propositions are "excess baggage" whose presence adds to the difficulty of changing connectives. One physical analogy to this strategy involves the tasks of (a) interchanging the positions of two sets of shelves, (b) disposing of some items from one of these sets of shelves, and (c) adding some items to the other set of shelves. The sensible order in which to perform these tasks is (b), (a), (c). Were it only as plain what psychological principles relate the terms of the analogy to the derivational strategy!

These considerations are based on the results of Experiments 4 and 5, as well as on other experiments to be reported. It is worth emphasizing the tentative nature of our proposals. The theory of the Appendix needs further testing before firm conclusions can be reached about its merit. It is possible that another deduction model will give different derivations for many of our problems and will meet the inventory and additivity requirements as successfully as the present theory. Only further experimentation could then decide between them.[8]

[8] Regarding the possibility of alternative theories, it should be clear that the substance of a theory is the set of derivations it provides for arguments. See Section 21.2.

Part III

FAMILIAR CONTENT AND CLASS INCLUSION

13

The Question of a Qualitative Difference Reexamined

Having found support for a theory of noncausal propositional logic in adolescents, the way is open to determining whether the same or similar mental machinery underlies adolescent judgment of more causally relevant arguments, and of arguments involving classes of objects.

13.1 ESSENTIAL AND NONESSENTIAL DIFFERENCES

In Chapter 1 we argued that the question of a qualitative difference in mental structures between children and adults can best be considered in light of theories of the intellectual organization of each. We have now developed such a theory for a fragment of adolescent logical judgment. Although it is of restricted scope and not well-confirmed even for the data that it does treat, we may attempt to appeal to it to decide the issue of qualitative versus quantitative change. It will be useful to examine the kind of differences in abilities that a deduction model can countenance, that is, we ask which transformations of experimental data leave the theory intact and which force its modification.

1. The additivity requirement. Suppose that the following list of arguments was administered to two groups of subjects (perhaps children and adults):

(I)   (1) $\{o_i, o_j\}$
     (2) $\{o_i\}$
     (3) $\{o_j\}$
     (4) $\{o_k, o_l\}$
     (5) $\{o_k\}$
     (6) $\{o_l\}$

Our theory says nothing about the difficulty of single-operation arguments. The difficulty of Arguments (2), (3), (5), and (6) is thus unspecified. However, given levels of difficulty for these single-operation arguments, the difficulty of the multiple-operation arguments is then specified (up to a linear transformation). It is possible that two groups of subjects equally confirm the additivity property of the theory despite a negligible correlation between their argument difficulties. This will happen if Group 1 finds Arguments (2) and (3) easy and (5) and (6) difficult, whereas this is not true for Group 2. So long as the difficulties of Arguments (1) and (4) are the respective sums of the difficulties of (2) and (3) and of (5) and (6) in each group, the theory is supported. In each group, Arguments (2) and (3) "add up" to Argument (1); (2) and (3) simply add up to a different number for each group; this is also true for (5) and (6).

This analysis presupposes proper labeling of the operations underlying Arguments (1)–(6). A theory of the mental operations involved in these arguments is thus called for. The theory specifies which arguments add up to which other arguments. So long as this additivity property holds, the difficulty of arguments may vary freely between different populations of subjects. Simply correlating the difficulties of arguments administered to different populations is misleading. It is the additivity correlation that is important for deciding whether the same mental derivations are involved in subjects' evaluations of the arguments.

It is also possible for a nontheoretical correlation between argument difficulties to be misleadingly high. Despite a high nontheoretical correlation, the additivity correlation based on a given theory can be high for one group and low for the other, indicating different mental structures. This possibility is illustrated by Table 13.1. The nontheoretical correlation

TABLE   13.1

Argument	Difficulty	
	Group 1	Group 2
$\{o_i, o_j\}$	7	8
$\{o_i\}$	4	4
$\{o_j\}$	3	2
$\{o_k, o_l\}$	9	8
$\{o_k\}$	7	7
$\{o_l\}$	2	3
$\{o_m, o_n\}$	10	9
$\{o_m\}$	5	5
$\{o_n\}$	5	4

between the groups' argument difficulties is .96 ($N = 9$). This is a misleadingly high index of similarity of mental structure, however. The additivity correlation for Group 1, based on the theory describing the arguments' operations, is 1.0 ($N = 3$), whereas it is only .28 ($N = 3$) for Group 2. Thus, nontheoretical correlations of argument difficulty between groups can be misleadingly high as well as misleadingly low.

Notice that we emphasize derivations. The heart of a deduction model is the set of derivations it assigns to arguments. Without supplementation deduction models cannot predict the difficulty of individual steps in a mental derivation. Thus, they shed no light on differences between populations in the difficulty of applying individual operations. Such differences may or may not indicate a qualitative differences in the internal structure of individual logical operations. This question is orthogonal to the question of whether the structure of the mental derivations employing those operations is qualitatively different. Naturally, an explanation for differences between populations in the difficulty of applying individual operations is of interest as well. (See Volume 2, Section 6.3, for discussion of factors influencing the difficulty of individual operations.)

2. The inventory requirement. As with the additivity requirement, the "raw" data for different samples of subjects can vary greatly without jeopardizing the inventory predictions for either group. Consider the six arguments of (I) above. A subject from one population may reject Argument (2), Argument (3), or both, while a subject from the other population may accept them both. The same theory may nonetheless characterize both populations, so long as the first subject rejects Argument (1) while the second accepts it (if he has any intuition about it at all, cf. Section 5.1); the same holds true for Arguments (3)–(6). Again, merely correlating the acceptance rate of arguments between populations can be misleading. It is the pattern of acceptances and rejections that counts in determining whether both sets of subjects employ the same derivations for arguments that they accept. The inventory analysis tests for this pattern.[1]

But an apparent difficulty arises similar to the one discussed in Section 5.3 concerning the soundness of a deduction model. According to the possibility just sketched, Subject 1 from a given population rejects some single-operation arguments honored by Subject 2 who is from another population. Is this not a qualitative difference and should not different theories be used to characterize these subjects? In fact, such a difference may not warrant constructing different theories for the two subjects. Possession of an operation is not an all-or-none affair. An argument not deemed valid one day

[1] In Volume 1, Section 10.3, it was such a difference in pattern that led us to conclude that length concepts are organized differently than class concepts in children.

may be accepted the next due to minor prodding from the environment. Perhaps the wording of the argument is understood differently on different occasions (cf. Section 5.3). The operations for that argument may be present on both occasions, but the range of applicability of the operation might be different due to changes in the operation's input evaluators (cf. Section 16.5). Such factors can prevent an operation from participating in derivations so that arguments are rejected. But the operation may be nascent, ready to appear in the derivations postulated by the theory whenever some minor contingency ceases to block its application.

On this view, the full set of operations, along with the executive, constitutes a theory of potential logical judgment for a population. It specifies the derivations underlying arguments whenever those arguments are accepted. The theory says that no derivation underlies a given argument other than the one the theory provides; but for various reasons subjects may be unable to apply certain operations and will thus reject an argument validated by the theory. The inventory analysis capitalizes on the existence of these inapplicable operations. Thus, the theory may be equally true of two subjects even though they do not accept the same arguments. The inventory (and additivity) analyses may indicate that the theory is true of the structure of each subject's set of potential logical operations.[2]

13.2   THE PROBLEM OF CONTENT IN REASONING

The discussion of the last section applies generally to any set of populations. Determining the difference, if any, in the structure of logical judgment between populations is best attempted in light of theories of logical judgment. The populations can differ in age, natural language, formal training, psychopathology, and so forth.[3]

Populations can differ in another way as well. Two groups of otherwise similar subjects can be asked to evaluate formally analogous sets of arguments. If the same theory holds for the two groups of subjects, then the operations specified by the theory have been shown to be abstract and

[2] A similar argument was made in Volume 1, Section 11.5, regarding the presence in children of axioms (rather than operations) from J. B. Grize's axiomatization of Piaget's grouping structure.

[3] Lakoff (1972) has expressed the view that logical and linguistic judgments may in some cases be mediated by the same processes. Whorf's (1964) analysis of the relation between language and reasoning is well known. See Savin (1972) and Chomsky (1973) for powerful criticism of Whorf's evidence.

Arieti (1955) has expressed the view that the logic of schizophrenics is different than that of normals. Maher (1966) argues otherwise.

broad in their application. If the theory holds for only one kind of problem, then the operations have a more limited scope. In Part III we ask whether our theory applies to arguments with more familiar content and to arguments concerning classes of objects. We have replicated experiments of Part II, using these new but formally analogous arguments. The additivity and inventory analyses were then employed to test the hypothesis that the same operations and executive underlie the subjects' judgments.[4]

Before taking up the experiments, we consider some issues surrounding content in reasoning and the relation between propositional and class inclusion logic.

The effect of the content of an argument on subjects' logical intuitions is well documented. Wason and Johnson-Laird (1972) present an excellent review of this literature. Studies have employed standard deductive reasoning tasks like categorical syllogisms (e.g., Wilkins, 1928) as well as tasks with an inductive component (e.g., Wason, 1968). The results are conflicting, different studies providing different conclusions about the direction and extent of effects due to content variables. In Part II, the theory of the Appendix was tested against arguments with a meager causal framework. The cooccurrence of letters on a blackboard, which was the content of all of the arguments employed so far, suggests little in the way of a causal framework in which to place the argument.[5]

Questions arise in constructing arguments with familiar content. The most important concerns uniformity. Should all the arguments revolve around one causal theme (for example, the interconnections of parts of an automobile)? Or, should the set of arguments have heterogeneous topics? The former strategy has the advantage of comparability with the arguments used in Part II; these were homogeneous. However, the homogeneity of the causal arguments has a disadvantage; it invites the subject to quickly ignore the causal content of the arguments through satiation with their theme, and to treat them in the same formal manner as subjects in Experiments 1–5. Employing a set of heterogeneous arguments mitigates

[4] An additional empirical condition on postulating the same mental mechanisms for the two kinds of arguments can be formulated provided that the same subjects receive both types of arguments. Volume 2, Section 3.4 gives the logic of this requirement. A within-subject procedure of this kind proved unfeasible in the present study, however. Moreover, such a procedure raises delicate questions concerning between-session (or between-argument) contamination of results caused by subjects noticing isomorphisms between arguments. This danger is especially acute for the present experiments since the subjects are older than those described in Volume 2.

[5] It is possible, although we think it unlikely, that subjects were "projecting" causal connections into the arguments. Psychologists have learned that subjects are far from passive receivers of information during an experiment (cf. Prytulak, 1971). Unfortunately, we neglected to question subjects about this possibility during debriefing.

against this danger. But heterogeneous arguments raise problems as well. The scaling part of the experimental procedure relies on delicate judgments of argument difficulty. For the numerical assignments to make theoretical sense they should reflect primarily the "logic" of the argument (i.e., the difficulty in passing from premise to conclusion) rather than extraneous factors surrounding the encoding of statements. The homogeneity and simplicity of the blackboard arguments of Part II facilitate abstracting out logical difficulty. A heterogeneous set of arguments and especially one dealing with different kinds of familiar situations might disrupt a subject's ability to focus on the deduction itself when scaling the arguments for difficulty.

Despite this danger we have elected to employ a moderately heterogeneous set of arguments. Such arguments provide a stronger test of the theory's robustness than a homogeneous set. Other decisions remain. How familiar should the causally relevant content be? What role should tense and time adverbials play in the arguments? Can the cause of events vary as to animacy? These questions and others raise complex issues. In constructing the causal arguments we did not begin with principled answers to these questions. We stipulated only that subjects not have prior opinions about the truth of arguments' premises and conclusions (see Section 6.1). To this end, the arguments were designed to revolve around a set of fictitious persons.

13.3   CLASS INCLUSION AND THE PROBLEM
OF LOGICAL GENERALITY

The theory in the Appendix contains over 20 operations. It is likely that operations will need to be added to account for the full range of propositional arguments about which subjects have intuitions. This many operations for propositional-type arguments is suspiciously large when we remember that propositional logic provides for only a small fraction of the arguments about which we have intuitions. It cannot handle, for example, arguments involving quantifiers or any of the modal notions like possibility, belief, or permissibility. Each of these kinds of arguments requires additional operations.

Two considerations lessen the danger of discovering too many operations. First, a large set of operations might be deducible from a few information-processing schemes in the nervous system. Even assuming that a large number of operations are found to be psychologically primitive in the nonreductionist sense explained in Section 8.6, each operation need not be represented separately in some long-term store. It may be sufficient to store a small set of principles that are not themselves operations, but which enable operations to be specified. As an illustration of this possibility, consider the following four operations from the Appendix:

$A \rightarrow (B \& C)/A \rightarrow B$
$(A \vee B) \rightarrow C/A \rightarrow C$
$A \rightarrow B/(A \& C) \rightarrow B$
$A \rightarrow B/A \rightarrow (B \vee C)$

They may be summarized by the principle that a proposition may be disjoined or conjoined to either side of a conditional so long as the modification does not threaten the truth of the consequent of the conditional more than that of the antecedent. As another example, a model that includes the concepts of *positive* and *negative subformula* could combine the operations $A \vee (B \& C)/A \vee B$, $A \rightarrow (B \& C)/A \rightarrow B$, and $A \& B/A$ into one principle; the same holds for $A \rightarrow B/A \rightarrow (B \vee C)$ and $A/A \vee C$. Use of these concepts also simplifies some of the helping conditions. Other kinds of principles may apply to more of the operations in the Appendix as well as to the operations of other logical domains. To this extent, less needs to be stored in memory and the large number of operations is no cause for alarm.

The second consideration is more relevant to the class inclusion experiments. Our intuitions about arguments in different logical domains sometimes show a common structure. It is possible that there exist mental operations of sufficient abstractness to be recruited for the computations of a variety of isomorphic deductive systems.

To reinforce this possibility, consider the logics of propositions, classes, and "Boolean term schemata" (i.e., one-place predicates like "red" or "friendly"). Formally, these logics are very similar (Quine, 1972a). For example, each of Inferences (1), (2), and (3) has the structure depicted in (4):

(1) $(p \vee q) \rightarrow r/-r \rightarrow -p$
     (For propositions p, q, r: if at least one of p and q is true only if r is true, then if r is false, so is p.)

(2) $(a \cup b) \subseteq c/\bar{c} \subseteq \bar{a}$
     (For sets a, b, c: if the union of a and b is included in c, then the complement of c is included in the complement of a.)

(3) $((F \vee G) \rightarrow H)x/(-H \rightarrow -F)x$
     (For attributes F, G, H: if everything possessing either F or G also possesses H, then anything lacking H does not possess F either.)

(4) $(\alpha * \beta) \supset \gamma$
     $\overline{\quad \neg\gamma \supset \neg\alpha \quad}$

The "∗" in (4) stands ambiguously for disjunction, union, and possession of alternative attributes. " ¬ " stands for denial, complementation, and lack of attribute. "⊃" stands either for a conditional relation or inclusion. If a person had access to the principle represented by (4) and if he could translate the principle into statements in the logic of propositions, classes, and one-place predicates, then he would have access to Principles (1)–(3).[6] The same holds for many other principles based on these logics as well as for other logics (the arithmetic of inequalities concerning "min" and "max," for example). Naturally, the formal isomorphism of these domains does not prove that the psychological processes underlying them are the same. To so believe would constitute the fallacy of logicism.[7] But the isomorphism is suggestive.

The correspondence between the kinds of deductive arguments that we have cited so far has been exact. Partial isomorphisms also exist. Consider the modal operators *necessary*, *obligatory*, and *always*. Each is equivalent to a related "weaker" concept in a similar way. This is shown by the following schemata, where *p*, *a*, and *s* are a proposition, an action, and a situation, respectively, and where, for example, "necessary *p*" is read "it is necessary that proposition *p* is true":

necessary p	$-$ possible $-p$
possible p	$-$ necessary $-p$
obligatory a	$-$ permissible $-a$
permissible a	$-$ obligatory $-a$
always s	$-$ sometimes $-s$
sometimes s	$-$ always $-s$

The schemata

$(\forall x)(Fx)$	$-(\exists x) - Fx$
$(\exists x)(Fx)$	$-(\forall x) - Fx$

show that existence and universality in quantified logic are related the same way.[8]

The point of these examples is to show that our logical judgments manifest certain abstract patterns. A common set of mental operations may

[6] See Volume 2, Section 11.5 for a similar speculation.

[7] However, a formal isomorphism is a necessary condition for the existence of this kind of abstract operation. It is the formal similarity of the arguments that makes them particular cases of the single abstract operation. However, as pointed out earlier (Section 6.5), there are no rigid limits to what aspects of an argument count as part of its formal structure. The distinction between form and content is theory dependent (see Katz, 1972).

[8] Excellent texts in modal logic, from which these examples come, include Snyder (1971) and Hughes and Cresswell (1968).

account for this pattern. However, it is also important to note discrepancies in our intuitions between different modalities. For example, the following two arguments, one intuitively valid, the other invalid, show a difference in the behavior of the necessity and obligation modalities: proposition p is necessary/proposition p is true; act a is obligatory/act a is performed. Determining the levels and connections between abstract operations, if such operations exist, will be nontrivial. Comparison of the operations underlying the logics of classes and propositions is a convenient place to begin the search for inferential generality. The isomorphism between the domains is evident. In addition, there is already evidence suggesting a psychological isomorphism in this case, that is, that the mental operations are the same in both logics. This evidence is reported in Volume 2, Chapters 3 and 9.

The class-inclusion arguments that we prepared refer to a set of blocks that vary in size, color, material, and texture. Naturally, to prevent nondeductive solution of the problems, the blocks themselves were not present.

The interest in inferential generality of operations extends beyond its role in limiting the number of operations that need to be postulated to account for logical judgment. If abstract deductive operations exist in the mind, it is these operations that should serve as grist for speculation about the general nature of human logical ability and its origin.

14

Experiment 6:
Causal Arguments Testing
the Theory of Table 8.1

14.1 AIMS OF THE EXPERIMENT

We wished first to determine the effects of causal content on arguments
from Experiments 1 and 2. Would the theory of Table 8.1 still account
for the 16 multiple-operation arguments of those experiments? The derivations for these arguments are given in Table 8.3.

14.2 METHOD

Two hundred forty-one 9th–11th grade students from Lincoln High School
in San Jose, California and from Burlingame High School in Burlingame,
California participated in Experiments 6–8. These three experiments were
run simultaneously; the envelopes containing arguments for the different
experiments were randomly assigned to students. Subjects were seen in
groups of about 40. After performing the experiments in one of the schools
and before examining the data, it was decided to increase the number of
subjects by addition of another school. The reason was the lack of interest
and cooperation by the first set of students. We hoped to cancel some
"noise" in the data by increasing sample size. Seventy-nine of the 241 students participated in the present experiment.

The instructions to subjects had to be modified in light of the new content of the arguments. All reference to the blackboard and letters was
omitted. Subjects were told that the arguments concerned a fictitious set
of people engaged in various activities. Explanation of the word "and"
(see Section 7.2) was done with the argument

Harry whistles and taps his foot.
_____
Harry whistles.

TABLE 14.1
Single-Operation Arguments for Experiment 6

---

1. $p \rightarrow q, -q/-p$

If Harold is pitching, then the home team is winning.
The home team is not winning.

Harold is not pitching.

2. $p \rightarrow (q \& r), p/q$

If the family goes for a drive, then Sheri brings wine and Virgil brings cheese.
The family goes for a drive.

Sheri brings wine.

3. $(p \lor q) \rightarrow r, p/r$

If either Steve runs the store or June runs the store, then the profits are high.
Steve runs the store.

The profits are high.

4. $p \rightarrow q, p \& r/q$

If Joe does the dishes, then the dishes are sure to be clean.
Joe does the dishes and he wears an apron.

The dishes are sure to be clean.

5. $p \rightarrow q, p/q \lor r$

If Fred gives a speech, then the audience is amused.
Fred gives a speech.

Either the audience is amused or Fred wears a tie.

6. $p \rightarrow q, p \& r/q \& r$

If Claudia does the shopping, then she spends too much money.
Claudia does the shopping and Mike fixes his bicycle.

Claudia spends too much money and Mike fixes his bicycle.

7. $p \rightarrow q, p \lor r/q \lor r$

If Cindy becomes a lawyer, then she specializes in taxes.
Either Cindy becomes a lawyer or Don becomes a dentist.
Either Cindy specializes in taxes or Don becomes a dentist.

TABLE 14.2
Multiple-Operation Arguments for Experiment 6

---

1. $p \rightarrow (q \ \& \ r), \ -q/-p$

    If Steven carves the roast, then the portions are even and there is enough to
    go around.
    The portions are not even.

    Steven does not carve the roast.

2. $(p \lor q) \rightarrow r, \ -r/-p$

    If either the test is multiple choice or the test is true-false, then Kate gets a
    a good grade.
    Kate does not get a good grade.

    The test is not multiple choice.

3. $p \rightarrow q, \ -q \ \& \ r/-p$

    If Ann becomes an astronaut, then she gets her name in the paper.
    Ann does not get her name in the paper and Ann buys a new TV.

    Ann does not become an astronaut.

4. $p \rightarrow q, \ -q/-p \lor r$

    If Jack is the waiter, then service is speedy.
    Service is not speedy.

    Either Jack is not the waiter or Hugh is the busboy.

5. $p \rightarrow q, \ -q \ \& \ r/-p \ \& \ r$

    If Sam is feeling ill, then Mona takes care of the business.
    Mona is not taking care of the business and the hours are 8–5.

    Sam is not feeling ill and the hours are 8–5.

6. $p \rightarrow q, \ -q \lor r/-p \lor r$

    If Gordon teaches the class, then the students learn a lot.
    Either the students do not learn a lot or there is a field trip.

    Either Gordon does not teach the class or there is a field trip.

7. $(p \lor q) \rightarrow (r \ \& \ s), p/s$

    If either Bill grades the test or Mary grades the test, then the results are fair
    and the students get the test back soon.
    Bill grades the test.

    The students get the test back soon.

8. $p \rightarrow (q \ \& \ r), p \ \& \ s/q$

    If Mark smokes, then Maude gets mad and Herman coughs.
    Mark smokes and Barbara drinks a coke.

    Maude gets mad.

(continued)

TABLE 14.2 *(continued)*

9. $p \rightarrow (q \ \& \ r), p/q \lor s$

If Rover learns a trick, then he gets a milk bone and he takes a nap.
Rover learns a trick.

Either Rover gets a milk bone or Rover has fleas.

10. $p \rightarrow (q \ \& \ r), p \ \& \ s/q \ \& \ s$

If Ron serves ice cream, then Harry gets a big scoop and Bob gets none.
Ron serves ice cream and cherry is the flavor of the week.

Harry gets a big scoop and cherry is the flavor of the week.

11. $p \rightarrow (q \ \& \ r), p \lor s/q \lor s$

If the store is open, then Kathy buys an apple and Ken buys meat.
Either the store is open or there is a traffic jam.

Either Kathy buys an apple or there is a traffic jam.

12. $(p \lor q) \rightarrow r, p \ \& \ s/r$

If either Mark is home or Terri is home, then the dog gets walked.
Mark is home and the cat is asleep.

The dog gets walked.

13. $(p \lor q) \rightarrow r, p/r \lor s$

If either it is sunny or he needs exercise, then Jack goes hiking.
It is sunny.

Either Jack goes hiking or he goes swimming.

14. $(p \lor q) \rightarrow r, p \ \& \ s/r \ \& \ s$

If either Herb has enough money or Glen treats, then they eat pizza.
Herb has enough money and George drives.

They eat pizza and George drives.

15. $(p \lor q) \rightarrow r, p \lor s/r \lor s$

If either the grass is brown or fertilizer is on sale, then Fred fertilizes the grass.
Either the grass is brown or Jean is outside.

Either Fred fertilizes the grass or Jean is outside.

16. $p \rightarrow q, p \ \& \ r/q \lor s$

If Penny sleeps on feathers, then she gets congested.
Penny sleeps on feathers and she sets her alarm clock.

Either Penny gets congested or she has a nightmare.

TABLE 14.3
Invalid and Baseline Arguments for Experiment 6

Invalid arguments

1. $p \rightarrow (q \lor r), -r/-p \& s$

    If John goes fishing, then either he gets a sunburn or he falls asleep.
    John does not fall asleep.

    John does not go fishing and the weather is fine.

2. $p \rightarrow (q \lor r), p \lor s/q \lor r$

    If Mary bakes cookies, then either she uses chocolate chips or she uses butterscotch chips.
    Either Mary bakes cookies or Mary bakes a cake.

    Either Mary uses chocolate chips or she uses butterscotch chips.

3. $p \rightarrow q, -p/-q \lor r$

    If Tim visits Carol, then Carol wears perfume.
    Tim does not visit Carol.

    Either Carol does not wear perfume or Carol turns on the stereo.

4. $(p \& q) \rightarrow r, p/q$

    If Greg buys Robin flowers and he takes Robin out to dinner, then Robin will be happy.
    Greg buys Robin flowers.

    Greg takes Robin out to dinner.

5. $p \rightarrow q, p \lor r/q$

    If Jake throws a curve ball, then the batter is sure to strike out.
    Either Jake throws a curve ball or John is catching.

    The batter is sure to strike out.

6. $p \rightarrow q, p/q \& r$

    If Mindy is elected, then she moves to Washington.
    Mindy is elected.

    Mindy moves to Washington and Bill joins the Air Force.

7. $p \rightarrow (q \lor r), p/q$

    If Eve gives a party, then either she serves fondue or she serves hamburgers.
    Eve gives a party.

    Eve serves fondue.

(continued)

TABLE 14.3 *(continued)*

8. $p \rightarrow q, \ p \ \& \ r/q \ \& \ s$

> If Jack becomes manager, then the building is clean.
> Jack becomes manager and Bill moves in.
> ___
> The building is clean and the building is heated by gas.

9. $(p \ \& \ q) \rightarrow r, \ p/r$

> If it is Saturday and it is warm outside, then Bert plays football.
> It is Saturday.
> ___
> Bert plays football.

10. $(p \ \& \ q) \rightarrow r, \ -r/-p$

> If Martha is in New York and Jimmy is in Hawaii, then Steve is upset.
> Steve is not upset.
> ___
> Martha is not in New York.

Baseline argument

> $p \rightarrow q, \ p/q$

> If the radio is on, then Gail is home.
> The radio is on.
> ___
> Gail is home.

Explanation of the word "or" was done with the argument

> Jim paints his car.
> ___
> Either Jim paints his car or he mows the lawn.

Explanation of the asymmetrical nature of the conditional was done with the invalid argument

> If Dave had played football, then he was tired.
> ___
> If Dave was tired, then he had played football.

Subjects were asked not to dwell on any connection between people described in the problems and real people with the same name that they knew; the coincidence in names had no significance.[1] During the ranking and scaling procedures, subjects were warned against letting extraneous

___

[1] Judging from students' reactions, this instruction was unnecessary.

properties of the arguments affect their assessment of argument difficulty. For example, an argument involving tennis should not be judged difficult simply because the subject finds tennis a difficult game.[2] In other respects the instructions were the same as described in Chapter 7.

Each subject in Experiment 6 received seven single-operation arguments, one for each operation in Table 8.1. These arguments are shown in Table 14.1. In addition they received 16 multiple-operation arguments corresponding to those employed in Experiments 1 and 2. These are given in Table 14.2. Finally, each subject received a Modus Ponens baseline argument, and five invalid arguments selected randomly from the ten invalid arguments shown in Table 14.3. In all, each subject received 29 arguments.

14.3   PRELIMINARY ANALYSES OF RESULTS

1. Dropped subjects.   Four subjects were dropped for the following reasons: one subject could not decide about the validity of Modus Ponens; another marked it invalid; a third subject was uncooperative; the fourth did not have time to finish the experiment. Data analyses refer to the 75 remaining subjects.

2. Acceptance rates for arguments.   Table 14.4 shows the number of subjects accepting each valid argument in Experiment 6. The correlation between the acceptance rates of Experiment 1 and the present experiment for the 16 multiple-operation arguments is .64. In this experiment, 80% of the valid arguments were accepted, compared to 77% (excluding word controls) in Experiment 1.

3. Difficulty of the arguments.   Subjects' numerical assignments were normalized in the usual fashion. Table 14.5 shows the mean normalized numerical assignment for each valid argument. The correlation is .84 between the mean normalized numerical assignment of Experiment 1 and the present experiment for the 16 multiple-operation arguments.

14.4   INVENTORY AND ADDITIVITY ANALYSES

1. Inventory analysis.   The derivations of Table 8.3, which conform to the theory of Table 8.1, provide the inventory predictions of the theory. Altogether there are 1161 inventory predictions [(16 multiple-operation arguments) $\times$ (75 subjects) — 39 multiple-operation arguments about which subjects could not decide]. Of these, 885, or 76.2%, were correct. The

---

[2] Again, this precautionary instruction did not appear necessary. The students assured the experimenters that they would never do such a thing.

TABLE 14.4
Acceptance Rates for Valid Arguments
of Experiment 6 ($N = 75$)

	No. accepted	No. rejected	No. cannot decide
Single-operation arguments			
1. $p \rightarrow q, -q/-p$	61	14	0
2. $p \rightarrow (q \& r), p/q$	69	6	0
3. $(p \vee q) \rightarrow r, p/r$	70	5	0
4. $p \rightarrow q, p \& r/q$	71	4	0
5. $p \rightarrow q, p/q \vee r$	45	29	1
6. $p \rightarrow q, p \& r/q \& r$	73	2	0
7. $p \rightarrow q, p \vee r/q \vee r$	66	7	2
Total:	455	67	3
Mean:	65.0		
Multiple-operation arguments			
1. $p \rightarrow (q \& r), -q/-p$	63	11	1
2. $(p \vee q) \rightarrow r, -r/-p$	51	23	1
3. $p \rightarrow q, -q \& r/-p$	63	11	1
4. $p \rightarrow q, -q/-p \vee r$	48	26	1
5. $p \rightarrow q, -q \& r/-p \& r$	58	15	2
6. $p \rightarrow q, -q \vee r/-p \vee r$	60	10	5
7. $(p \vee q) \rightarrow (r \& s), p/s$	69	5	1
8. $p \rightarrow (q \& r), p \& s/q$	63	9	3
9. $p \rightarrow (q \& r), p/q \vee s$	45	27	3
10. $p \rightarrow (q \& r), p \& s/q \& s$	65	8	2
11. $p \rightarrow (q \& r), p \vee s/q \vee s$	51	18	6
12. $(p \vee q) \rightarrow r, p \& s/r$	68	6	1
13. $(p \vee q) \rightarrow r, p/r \vee s$	53	19	3
14. $(p \vee q) \rightarrow r, p \& s/r \& s$	69	5	1
15. $(p \vee q) \rightarrow r, p \vee s/r \vee s$	59	11	5
16. $p \rightarrow q, p \& r/q \vee s$	45	27	3
Total:	930	231	39
Mean:	58.1		
Baseline argument			
$p \rightarrow q, p/q$	75	0	0

TABLE 14.5
Mean Normalized Numerical Assignment for
Valid Arguments of Experiment 6 (N = 75)

	Mean normalized numerical assignments	Standard deviations of mean normalized numerical assignments
Single-operation arguments		
1. $p \rightarrow q$, $-q/-p$	20.97	26.90
2. $p \rightarrow (q \& r)$, p/q	19.00	26.89
3. $(p \vee q) \rightarrow r$, p/r	15.96	21.47
4. $p \rightarrow q$, $p \& r/q$	22.43	23.47
5. $p \rightarrow q$, $p/q \vee r$	46.38	31.06
6. $p \rightarrow q$, $p \& r/q \& r$	32.44	26.82
7. $p \rightarrow q$, $p \vee r/q \vee r$	56.26	33.69
Multiple-operation arguments		
1. $p \rightarrow (q \& r)$, $-q/-p$	27.93	28.66
2. $(p \vee q) \rightarrow r$, $-r/-p$	40.82	33.67
3. $p \rightarrow q$, $-q \& r/-p$	47.20	31.47
4. $p \rightarrow q$, $-q/-p \vee r$	46.23	29.82
5. $p \rightarrow q$, $-q \& r/-p \& r$	43.95	33.02
6. $p \rightarrow q$, $-q \vee r/-p \vee r$	66.14	31.00
7. $(p \vee q) \rightarrow (r \& s)$, p/s	27.60	30.65
8. $p \rightarrow (q \& r)$, $p \& s/q$	35.19	31.55
9. $p \rightarrow (q \& r)$, $p/q \vee s$	48.36	31.66
10. $p \rightarrow (q \& r)$, $p \& s/q \& s$	37.03	30.93
11. $p \rightarrow (q \& r)$, $p \vee s/q \vee s$	66.67	28.13
12. $(p \vee q) \rightarrow r$, $p \& s/r$	27.87	27.76
13. $(p \vee q) \rightarrow r$, $p/r \vee s$	46.85	31.32
14. $(p \vee q) \rightarrow r$, $p \& s/r \& s$	42.88	30.75
15. $(p \vee q) \rightarrow r$, $p \vee s/r \vee s$	67.72	29.86
16. $p \rightarrow q$, $p \& r/q \vee s$	57.41	27.52
Baseline argument		
$p \rightarrow q$, p/q	0.00	0.00

expected number of true predictions, based on Eq. (2) of Section 8.4, is 784.9 or 67.6%. The inventory results are not as strong as in Experiment 1.

   2.   Additivity analysis.   Of the 75 subjects, 68 accepted enough arguments to make the within-subject analysis possible, producing at least five

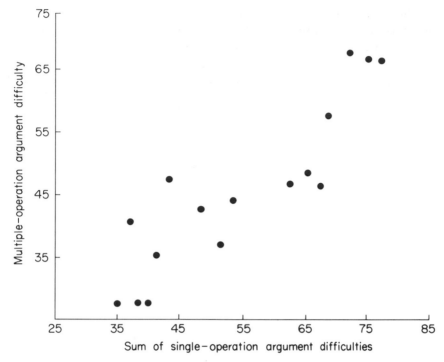

FIG. 14.1.   Scatter plot for the additivity analysis of Experiment 6, based on the theory of Table 8.1.

correlatable observations. The average number of degrees of freedom for these correlations is 11.0. Twenty-four of the 68 correlations were significant beyond the 5% level. An additional seven subjects produced correlations significant beyond the 10% level. Over all 68 subjects, the mean additivity correlation is .34. These results are somewhat weaker than those of Experiment 1. The between-subjects test of the additivity requirement gives an additivity correlation of .89 ($N = 16$). Figure 14.1 shows the scatter plot for this correlation.

14.5   CONCLUSIONS OF EXPERIMENT 6

The results of Experiment 6, especially the between-subjects additivity correlation, support the idea that the theory of the Appendix applies both to arguments with artificial content and to arguments with more familiar content. Note that the additivity correlation is higher in both Experiment 1 and the present experiment than the correlation of either acceptance rate or difficulty of arguments between the two experiments for multiple-operation arguments (cf. Section 13.1). The additivity correlation can be considered a measure of the ability to predict the difficulty of multiple-operation arguments from the difficulty of single-operation arguments. The relevant comparison is between the nontheoretical correlation of multiple-operation argument difficulty between Experiments 1 and 6 and the additivity correlations within each experiment. All three of these correlations have the same number of degrees of freedom.

15

Experiment 7:
Causal Arguments Testing
the Theory of Table 11.1

15.1 AIMS OF THE EXPERIMENT

Experiments 7 and 8 tested the model of Table 11.1. In the present experiment, the arguments from Experiment 4 were employed. They were given the causally relevant content used in Experiment 6. The model's derivations for the 12 multiple-operation arguments are shown in Table 11.3.

15.2 METHOD

The 83 subjects who participated in Experiment 7 were drawn from the pool of 241 9th–11th-grade students described in Section 14.2. The instructions are described in Section 14.2.

Each subject in Experiment 7 received 14 single-operation arguments, one for each operation in Table 11.1. These arguments are shown in Table 15.1. They also received 12 multiple-operation arguments corresponding to those used in Experiment 4. These are given in Table 15.2. Finally, each subject received a baseline argument $p \rightarrow q/p \rightarrow q$, and five invalid arguments selected randomly from the ten invalid arguments shown in Table 15.3. In all, each subject received 32 arguments.

15.3 PRELIMINARY ANALYSES OF RESULTS

1. Dropped subjects. Three subjects were dropped for the following reasons: one subject was uncooperative; one did not finish; one found the baseline argument to be comparatively difficult. Data analyses refer to the remaining 80 subjects.

TABLE 15.1
Single-Operation Arguments for Experiments 7 and 8

1. $p \rightarrow (q \& r)/p \rightarrow q$

    If John is playing music, then the music is loud and he is staying up late.
    If John is playing music, then the music is loud.

2. $(p \lor q) \rightarrow r/p \rightarrow r$

    If Pete wears his red shirt or his blue suspenders, then he is in a good mood.
    If Pete wears his red shirt, then he is in a good mood.

3. $p \rightarrow q/-q \rightarrow -p$

    If Martha is the apartment manager, then the tenants are satisfied.
    If the tenants are not satisfied, then Martha is not the apartment manager.

4. $p \rightarrow q/(p \& r) \rightarrow (q \& r)$

    If Al prunes the roses, then they are sure to be beautiful.
    If Al prunes the roses and the yard is large, then the roses are sure to be beautiful
       and the yard is large.

5. $p \rightarrow q/(p \lor r) \rightarrow (q \lor r)$

    If Brad wears leather shoes, then he gets blisters on his feet.
    If Brad wears leather shoes or he wears a hat, then he gets blisters on his feet or he
       wears a hat.

6. $p \rightarrow q/(p \& r) \rightarrow q$

    If Harold serves ice cream, then the scoops are big.
    If Harold serves ice cream and rocky road is the flavor of the week, then the scoops
       are big.

7. $p \rightarrow q/p \rightarrow (q \lor r)$

    If Paul cooks the dinner, then the guests are pleased.
    If Paul cooks the dinner, then either the guests are pleased or there is a linen table-
       cloth.

8. $-(p \lor q)/-p \& -q$

    It is not true that Bill either mows the lawn or rakes the leaves.
    Bill does not mow the lawn and Bill does not rake the leaves.

(continued)

TABLE 15.1 (*continued*)

---

9. $-(p \& q)/-p \vee -q$

It is not true that both Fred is a lawyer and his brother is a lawyer.
Either Fred is not a lawyer or his brother is not a lawyer.

10. $p \& (q \vee r)/(p \& q) \vee (p \& r)$

Pam is in school and either she is learning physics or she is learning math.
Either Pam is in school and she is learning physics or Pam is in school and she is
   learning math.

11. $p \vee (q \& r)/p \vee q$

Bart either makes a casserole or he packs a lunch and he has a picnic.
Bart either makes a casserole or he packs a lunch.

12. $p \vee q/-p \rightarrow q$

Either Fido is barking or he is playing.
If Fido is not barking, then Fido is playing.

13. $-p \rightarrow q/p \vee q$

If the faucet does not leak, then Jerry can sleep.
Either the faucet leaks or Jerry can sleep.

14. $p \rightarrow q/-(p \& -q)$

If Marty drives to work, then he eats breakfast downtown.
It is not true that both Marty drives to work and he does not eat breakfast downtown.

---

2. Acceptance rates for arguments. Table 15.4 shows the number
of subjects accepting each valid argument in Experiment 7. The correlation
in acceptance rate between Experiment 4 and the present experiment for
the 12 multiple-operation arguments is .85. For the 14 (simple) single-
operation arguments, it is .78. In both the present experiment and in
Experiment 4, 68% of the valid arguments (excluding complex, single-
operation arguments in Experiment 4) were accepted.

3. Difficulty of the arguments. Subjects' numerical assignments were
normalized in the usual fashion. Table 15.5 shows the mean normalized

TABLE 15.2
Multiple-Operation Arguments for Experiment 7

---

1. $-(p \& q) \to r/-p \to r$

   If it is not true that both Doug eats cake and he eats pie, then he feels comfortable.

   If Doug does not eat cake, then he feels comfortable.

2. $p \to (q \lor r)/(-q \& -r) \to -p$

   If Peter is ice skating, then Martha either goes to a movie or she visits a museum.

   If Martha does not go to a movie and she does not visit a museum, then Peter is not ice skating.

3. $(p \& q) \to r/-r \to (-p \lor -q)$

   If both Jim is playing and Steve is playing, the home team is ahead.

   If the home team is not ahead, then either Jim is not playing or Steve is not playing.

4. $(p \lor q) \to r/-(p \& -r)$

   If either Mark runs the store or Sarah runs the store, then profits increase.

   It is not true that both Mark runs the store and profits do not increase.

5. $(p \lor q) \to (r \& s)/-(p \& -r)$

   If either Father paints the house or Mother mows the lawn, then the family has a picnic and the neighbors stop complaining.

   It is not true that both Father paints the house and the family does not have a picnic.

6. $p \lor q/(-p \& r) \to q$

   Either Carl is drinking or he is watching the late show.

   If Carl is not drinking and the baby is crying, then Carl is watching the late show.

7. $p \lor q/(-p \& r) \to (q \& r)$

   Either it rains Sunday or Harry goes golfing.

   If it does not rain Sunday and the newspaper is late, then Harry goes golfing and the newspaper is late.

8. $(p \& q) \lor r/-p \to r$

   Either Daryl wears a work shirt and jeans or he wears blue overalls.

   If Daryl does not wear a work shirt, then he wears blue overalls.

(continued)

TABLE 15.2 (*continued*)

---

9. $p \vee (q \,\&\, r)/-p \rightarrow (q \vee s)$

Either Barry eats oatmeal or he eats eggs and bacon.

If Barry does not eat oatmeal, then he eats either eggs or toast.

10. $p \vee (q \,\&\, r)/(-p \vee s) \rightarrow (q \vee s)$

Either Professor Hall takes a vacation or he both teaches and does research.

If either Professor Hall does not take a vacation or he makes a discovery, then either Professor Hall teaches or he makes a discovery.

11. $(-p \vee -q) \rightarrow r/p \vee r$

If Eleanor is not home or Art is not home, then Paul leaves a note.

Either Eleanor is home or Paul leaves a note.

12. $[p \,\&\, (q \vee r)] \rightarrow s/(p \,\&\, q) \rightarrow s$

If Harvey takes pottery lessons and he takes either music lessons or art classes, then he will be too busy.

If Harvey takes pottery lessons and he takes music lessons, then he will be too busy.

---

numerical assignment for each valid argument. The correlation in mean normalized numerical assignment between Experiment 4 and the present experiment for the multiple-operation arguments is .76 ($N = 12$). For the (simple) single-operation arguments, the correlation is .62 ($N = 12$).

15.4 INVENTORY AND ADDITIVITY ANALYSES

1. Inventory analysis. The derivations of Table 11.3, which conform to the theory of Table 11.1, provide the inventory and additivity predictions of the theory. Altogether, there are 928 inventory predictions [(12 multiple-operation arguments) $\times$ (80 subjects) $-$ 32 multiple-operation arguments about which subjects could not decide]. Of these predictions, 581 or 62.2% were correct. The expected number of true predictions, based on Eq. 2 of Section 8.4, is 500.9 or 65.0%. This inventory result is somewhat weak, but no worse than that reported for Experiment 4.

2. Additivity analysis. The within-subject analysis is impractical because few subjects provided enough observations to make a correlation

TABLE 15.3
Invalid and Baseline Arguments for Experiments 7 and 8

Invalid arguments

1. $p \rightarrow q/-p \rightarrow (-q \vee r)$

If Betsy listens to the stereo, then she listens to classical music.

If Betsy does not listen to the stereo, then either she does not listen to classical music or she feeds the cat.

2. $p \rightarrow q/p \rightarrow (q \& r)$

If Art buys a motorcycle, then he buys a Honda.

If Art buys a motorcycle, then he buys a Honda and he drives to Florida.

3. $-(p \& q)/-p \& -q$

It is not true that both George goes to a party and Sally goes to a party.

George does not go to a party and Sally does not go to a party.

4. $(p \& q) \rightarrow r/p \rightarrow r$

If Sarah makes the poster and she uses colored paints, then the poster is beautiful.

If Sarah makes the poster, then the poster is beautiful.

5. $p \rightarrow (q \vee r)/-p \rightarrow q$

If Debbie goes for a drive Saturday, then either she visits a friend or she goes shopping.

If Debbie does not go for a drive Saturday, then she visits a friend.

6. $-(p \vee q)/p \& -q$

It is not true that Andy either makes his bed or cleans his room.

Andy makes his bed and he does not clean his room.

7. $-p \& q/-q \& p$

Betty does not get out of bed and she reads a book.

Betty does not read a book and she gets out of bed.

8. $p \vee -q/-q \vee -p$

Either the sun is shining or Willie does not go skiing.

Either Willie does not go skiing or the sun is not shining.

(*continued*)

TOTAL 15.3 (*continued*)

---

9. $p \vee (q \ \& \ r)/p \ \& \ q$

Either John wears a turtleneck or he wears both a coat and a tie.

John wears a turtleneck and he wears a coat.

10. $p \vee q/(-q \ \& \ r) \rightarrow -p$

Either Ed smokes a pipe or Ed smokes a cigar.

If Ed does not smoke a cigar and he reads the newspaper, then Ed does not smoke a pipe.

Baseline argument
  $p \rightarrow q/p \rightarrow q$

If the radio is on, then Gail is home.

If the radio is on, then Gail is home.

---

meaningful. The between-subject additivity correlation is only .57 ($N = 12$). Figure 15.1 shows the scatter plot for this correlation.

15.5 CONCLUSIONS OF EXPERIMENT 7

The additivity correlation is disappointingly low. Two explanations come to mind. First, the heterogeneity in the content of the arguments may have disrupted subjects' ability to make accurate judgments of argument difficulty. This was a danger discussed in Section 13.2. Even the large sample size cannot protect us against the possibility that these disturbances are partly systematic, running counter to the additivity of the model. Against this possibility, the results of Experiment 6 were quite different, giving an additivity correlation of .89. Perhaps there was something unfortunate about the particular causal arguments used in Experiment 7, a factor not present in Experiment 6. This is possible, but would need demonstration.

A second possibility is that changing the content of the arguments changes the order of the operations. In particular, perhaps noncausal content is governed by the theory of Table 11.1, whereas causal content of the present variety is governed by the theory of Table 11.2. This switch would leave the predictions for Experiment 6 untouched, since the order of the operations in Table 8.1 is preserved within both models. This conjecture is refuted, however, by the fact that for the present experiment the additivity correlation based on the theory of Table 11.2 is appreciably lower than the correlation based on the "official" model of Table 11.1.

TABLE 15.4
Acceptance Rates for Valid Arguments
of Experiment 7 (N = 80)

	No. accepted	No. rejected	No. cannot decide
Single-operation arguments			
1. $p \rightarrow (q \ \& \ r)/p \rightarrow q$	68	11	1
2. $(p \lor q) \rightarrow r/p \rightarrow r$	73	6	1
3. $p \rightarrow q/-q \rightarrow -p$	58	21	1
4. $p \rightarrow q/(p \ \& \ r) \rightarrow (q \ \& \ r)$	62	15	3
5. $p \rightarrow q/(p \lor r) \rightarrow (q \lor r)$	51	27	2
6. $p \rightarrow q/(p \ \& \ r) \rightarrow q$	70	9	1
7. $p \rightarrow q/p \rightarrow (q \lor r)$	40	35	5
8. $-(p \lor q)/-p \ \& \ -q$	49	28	3
9. $-(p \ \& \ q)/-p \lor -q$	60	16	4
10. $p \ \& \ (q \lor r)/(p \ \& \ q) \lor (p \ \& \ r)$	74	4	2
11. $p \lor (q \ \& \ r)/p \lor q$	67	13	0
12. $p \lor q/-p \rightarrow q$	71	8	1
13. $-p \rightarrow q/p \lor q$	57	22	1
14. $p \rightarrow q/-(p \ \& \ -q)$	39	38	3
Total:	839	253	28
Mean:	59.9		
Multiple-operation arguments			
1. $-(p \ \& \ q) \rightarrow r/-p \rightarrow r$	37	37	6
2. $p \rightarrow (q \lor r)/(-q \ \& \ -r) \rightarrow -p$	62	18	0
3. $(p \ \& \ q) \rightarrow r/-r \rightarrow (-p \lor -q)$	58	22	0
4. $(p \lor q) \rightarrow r/-(p \ \& \ -r)$	48	27	5
5. $(p \lor q) \rightarrow (r \ \& \ s)/-(p \ \& \ -r)$	41	34	5
6. $p \lor q/(-p \ \& \ r) \rightarrow q$	48	29	3
7. $p \lor q/(-p \ \& \ r) \rightarrow (q \ \& \ r)$	61	19	0
8. $(p \ \& \ q) \lor r/-p \rightarrow r$	63	13	4
9. $p \lor (q \ \& \ r)/-p \rightarrow (q \lor s)$	32	46	2
10. $p \lor (q \ \& \ r)/(-p \lor s) \rightarrow (q \lor s)$	37	37	6
11. $(-p \lor -q) \rightarrow r/p \lor r$	32	48	0
12. $[p \ \& \ (q \lor r)] \rightarrow s/(p \ \& \ q) \rightarrow s$	66	13	1
Total:	585	343	32
Mean:	48.8		
Baseline argument			
$p \rightarrow q/p \rightarrow q$	80	0	0

TABLE 15.5
Mean Normalized Numerical Assignments for
Valid Arguments of Experiment 7 ($N = 80$)

	Mean normalized numerical assignments	Standard deviations for mean normalized numerical assignments
Single-operation arguments		
1. $p \to (q \,\&\, r)/p \to q$	23.23	24.49
2. $(p \lor q) \to r/p \to r$	26.08	25.70
3. $p \to q/-q \to -p$	26.01	26.29
4. $p \to q/(p \,\&\, r) \to (q \,\&\, r)$	41.49	32.06
5. $p \to q/(p \lor r) \to (q \lor r)$	55.95	33.91
6. $p \to q/(p \,\&\, r) \to q$	27.25	28.86
7. $p \to q/p \to (q \lor r)$	43.09	31.25
8. $-(p \lor q)/-p \,\&\, -q$	43.61	32.93
9. $-(p \,\&\, q)/-p \lor -q$	32.67	28.30
10. $p \,\&\, (q \lor r)/(p \,\&\, q) \lor (p \,\&\, r)$	32.03	27.27
11. $p \lor (q \,\&\, r)/p \lor q$	32.25	26.82
12. $p \lor q/-p \to q$	13.97	20.28
13. $-p \to q/p \lor q$	34.79	30.06
14. $p \to q/-(p \,\&\, -q)$	41.38	31.31
Multiple-operation arguments		
1. $-(p \,\&\, q) \to r/-p \to r$	65.21	30.60
2. $p \to (q \lor r)/(-q \,\&\, -r) \to -p$	39.41	30.20
3. $(p \,\&\, q) \to r/-r \to (-p \lor -q)$	34.94	30.43
4. $(p \lor q) \to r/-(p \,\&\, -r)$	50.03	34.34
5. $(p \lor q) \to (r \,\&\, s)/-(p \,\&\, -r)$	71.79	30.68
6. $p \lor q/(-p \,\&\, r) \to q$	46.88	29.75
7. $p \lor q/(-p \,\&\, r) \to (q \,\&\, r)$	49.19	32.12
8. $(p \,\&\, q) \lor r/-p \to r$	33.81	31.48
9. $p \lor (q \,\&\, r)/-p \to (q \lor s)$	33.21	27.35
10. $p \lor (q \,\&\, r)/(-p \lor s) \to (q \lor s)$	86.45	23.34
11. $(-p \lor -q) \to r/p \lor r$	35.99	28.99
12. $[p \,\&\, (q \lor r)] \to s/(p \,\&\, q) \to s$	37.03	27.59
Baseline argument		
$\quad p \to q/p \to q$	0.00	0.00

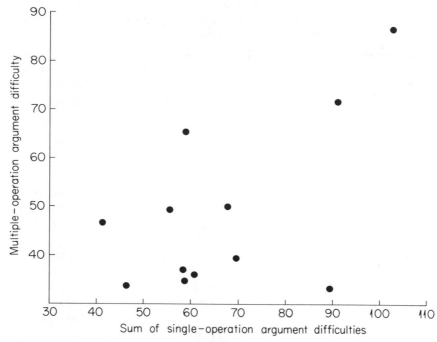

FIG. 15.1.   Scatter plot for the additivity analysis of Experiment 7, based on the theory of Table 11.1.

A third explanation for the low additivity correlation of the present experiment is that the theory of the Appendix simply does not apply to arguments with familiar content. Before discussing that possibility, we examine the results of the third causality experiment.

16

Experiment 8:
More Causal Arguments
Testing the Theory of Table 11.1

16.1 AIMS OF THE EXPERIMENT

In the present experiment, the arguments from Experiment 5 were employed. They were given the causally relevant content used in Experiments 6 and 7. The model's derivations for the 12 multiple-operation arguments are shown in Table 12.3.

16.2 METHOD

The 79 subjects who participated in Experiment 8 were drawn from the pool of 241 9th–11th grade students described in Section 14.2. The instructions are described in Section 14.2. Each subject in Experiment 8 received the same 14 single-operation arguments employed in Experiment 7. These arguments are shown in Table 15.1. In addition, subjects received 12 multiple-operation arguments corresponding to those used in Experiment 5. These are given in Table 16.1. Finally, each subject received a baseline argument $p \rightarrow q/p \rightarrow q$, and five invalid arguments selected randomly from the ten invalid arguments shown in Table 15.3. In all, each subject received 32 arguments.

16.3 PRELIMINARY ANALYSES OF RESULTS

1. Dropped subjects. Five subjects were dropped for the following reasons: three subjects were uncooperative; one subject did not finish; one subject sorted the baseline argument as invalid. Data analyses pertain to the 74 remaining subjects.

TABLE 16.1
Multiple-Operation Arguments for Experiment 8

---

1. $p \rightarrow -(q \vee r)/p \rightarrow -q$

If it is windy, then it is not true either that Hank goes camping or that Hank goes to the football game.

If it is windy, then Hank does not go camping.

2. $-(p \ \& \ q) \rightarrow r/p \vee r$

If it is not true that both Martha is violin teacher and classes are once a week, then Ken learns slowly.

Either Martha is violin teacher or Ken learns slowly.

3. $(p \vee q) \rightarrow r/-r \rightarrow (-p \ \& -q)$

If Doug leads the tour or Julie leads the tour, then the tour is interesting.

If the tour is not interesting, then Doug is not leading it and Julie is not leading it.

4. $p \rightarrow (q \ \& \ r)/(-q \vee -r) \rightarrow -p$

If Al drives the sports car, then both the car goes fast and it squeals on corners.

If either the sports car does not go fast or it does not squeal on corners, then Al is not driving it.

5. $p \rightarrow (q \ \& \ r)/-(p \ \& -q)$

If Milt rides his motorcycle, then the baby cries and the dog howls.

It is not true that both Milt rides his motorcycle and the baby does not cry.

6. $p \vee q/(-p \vee r) \rightarrow (q \vee r)$

Either Tom sees a movie or he goes to a concert.

If either Tom does not see a movie or he visits Janet, then either Tom goes to a concert or he visits Janet.

7. $p \vee q/-p \rightarrow (q \vee r)$

Either Jamie goes to school or she reads her history book.

If Jamie does not go to school, then either she reads her history book or she writes a paper.

(continued)

TABLE 16.1 (*continued*)

---

8. $p \vee (q \& r)/-p \to q$

   Either the car starts or both Todd takes a bus to work and he calls a tow truck.

   If the car does not start, then Todd takes a bus to work.

9. $p \vee (q \& r)/(-p \& s) \to (q \& s)$

   Either Susan fixes her bicycle or she builds some shelves and paints the bathroom.

   If Susan does not fix her bicycle and she wears sneakers, then Susan builds some
   shelves and she wears sneakers.

10. $p \vee (q \& r)/(-p \& s) \to q$

    Either Tammy learns to play flute or she sells her flute and learns to play violin.

    If Tammy does not learn to play flute and her sister sings, then Tammy sells her
    flute.

11. $-p \to (q \& r)/p \vee q$

    If Dan is not home, then both his mother and his sister are home.

    Either Dan is home or his mother is home.

12. $p \& (q \vee r)/-(p \& q) \to (p \& r)$

    Jack goes to Hawaii and either Jack learns to surf or he learns to sail.

    If it is not true that Jack goes to Hawaii and learns to surf, then Jack goes to
    Hawaii and learns to sail.

---

2. *Acceptance rates for arguments.* Table 16.2 shows the number
of subjects accepting each valid argument in Experiment 8. The correlation
in acceptance rate of single-operation arguments between Experiment 7 and
the present experiment is .86 ($N = 14$). This high correlation indicates,
again, the freedom from context effects that subjects enjoy during sorting
(see Section 12.3 for a similar correlation). The correlation in acceptance
rate between Experiment 5 and the present experiment for the 12 multiple-
operation arguments is .70 ($N = 12$). For the (simple) single-operation
arguments, it is .66 ($N = 14$). Of the valid arguments in this experiment,
65% were accepted, compared to 67% of the valid arguments (excluding
complex arguments) in Experiment 5.

3. *Difficulty of the arguments.* Subjects' numerical assignments were
normalized in the usual fashion. Table 16.3 shows the mean normalized

TABLE 16.2
Acceptance Rates for Valid Arguments
of Experiment 8 (N = 74)

	No. accepted	No. rejected	No. cannot decide
Single-operation arguments			
1. $p \to (q \ \& \ r)/p \to q$	63	11	0
2. $(p \lor q) \to r/p \to r$	63	11	0
3. $p \to q/-q \to -p$	56	18	0
4. $p \to q/(p \ \& \ r) \to (q \ \& \ r)$	47	25	2
5. $p \to q/(p \lor r) \to (q \lor r)$	45	26	3
6. $p \to q/(p \ \& \ r) \to q$	45	28	1
7. $p \to q/p \to (q \lor r)$	32	40	2
8. $-(p \lor q)/-p \ \& \ -q$	43	29	2
9. $-(p \ \& \ q)/-p \lor -q$	56	18	0
10. $p \ \& \ (q \lor r)/(p \ \& \ q) \lor (p \ \& \ r)$	66	6	2
11. $p \lor (q \ \& \ r)/p \lor q$	63	11	0
12. $p \lor q/-p \to q$	57	17	0
13. $-p \to q/p \lor q$	52	19	3
14. $p \to q/-(p \ \& \ -q)$	34	38	2
Total:	722	297	17
Mean:	51.6		
Multiple-operation arguments			
1. $p \to -(q \lor r)/p \to -q$	50	22	2
2. $-(p \ \& \ q) \to r/p \lor r$	25	42	7
3. $(p \lor q) \to r/-r \to (-p \ \& \ -q)$	61	12	1
4. $p \to (q \ \& \ r)/(-q \lor -r) \to -p$	46	27	1
5. $p \to (q \ \& \ r)/-(p \ \& \ -q)$	38	34	2
6. $p \lor q/(-p \lor r) \to (q \lor r)$	39	31	4
7. $p \lor q/-p \to (q \lor r)$	34	38	2
8. $p \lor (q \ \& \ r)/-p \to q$	63	11	0
9. $p \lor (q \ \& \ r)/(-p \ \& \ s) \to (q \ \& \ s)$	27	43	4
10. $p \lor (q \ \& \ r)/(-p \ \& \ s) \to q$	31	41	2
11. $-p \to (q \ \& \ r)/p \lor q$	55	17	2
12. $p \ \& \ (q \lor r)/-(p \ \& \ q) \to (p \ \& \ r)$	61	10	3
Total:	530	328	30
Mean:	44.2		
Baseline argument			
$p \to q/p \to q$	74	0	0

TABLE 16.3
Mean Normalized Numerical Assignments for
Valid Arguments of Experiment 8 (N = 74)

	Mean normalized numerical assignments	Standard deviations for mean normalized numerical assignments
Single-operation arguments		
1. $p \rightarrow (q \ \& \ r)/p \rightarrow q$	28.76	27.69
2. $(p \vee q) \rightarrow r/p \rightarrow r$	26.45	25.76
3. $p \rightarrow q/-q \rightarrow -p$	30.51	25.58
4. $p \rightarrow q/(p \ \& \ r) \rightarrow (q \ \& \ r)$	43.49	27.09
5. $p \rightarrow q/(p \vee r) \rightarrow (q \vee r)$	63.32	29.72
6. $p \rightarrow q/(p \ \& \ r) \rightarrow q$	36.88	33.41
7. $p \rightarrow q/p \rightarrow (q \vee r)$	42.73	30.09
8. $-(p \vee q)/-p \ \& \ -q$	45.98	35.50
9. $-(p \ \& \ q)/-p \vee -q$	53.19	31.44
10. $p \ \& \ (q \vee r)/(p \ \& \ q) \vee (p \ \& \ r)$	35.08	30.67
11. $p \vee (q \ \& \ r)/p \vee q$	32.58	28.08
12. $p \vee q/-p \rightarrow q$	22.04	25.62
13. $-p \rightarrow q/p \vee q$	27.40	28.03
14. $p \rightarrow q/-(p \ \& \ -q)$	72.61	26.01
Multiple-operation arguments		
1. $p \rightarrow -(q \vee r)/p \rightarrow -q$	62.18	33.74
2. $-(p \ \& \ q) \rightarrow r/p \vee r$	63.01	35.14
3. $(p \vee q) \rightarrow r/-r \rightarrow (-p \ \& \ -q)$	30.92	26.38
4. $p \rightarrow (q \ \& \ r)/(-q \vee -r) \rightarrow -p$	58.70	32.55
5. $p \rightarrow (q \ \& \ r)/-(p \ \& \ -q)$	54.07	32.06
6. $p \vee q/(-p \vee r) \rightarrow (q \vee r)$	66.59	30.25
7. $p \vee q/-p \rightarrow (q \vee r)$	47.58	28.41
8. $p \vee (q \ \& \ r)/-p \rightarrow q$	46.90	31.85
9. $p \vee (q \ \& \ r)/(-p \ \& \ s) \rightarrow (q \ \& \ s)$	65.15	32.16
10. $p \vee (q \ \& \ r)/(-p \ \& \ s) \rightarrow q$	61.33	32.07
11. $-p \rightarrow (q \ \& \ r)/p \vee q$	39.34	27.85
12. $p \ \& \ (q \vee r)/-(p \ \& \ q) \rightarrow (p \ \& \ r)$	57.31	32.76
Baseline argument		
$p \rightarrow q/p \rightarrow q$	0.00	0.00

numerical assignment for each valid argument. The correlation in mean normalized numerical assignment between the single-operation arguments of Experiments 7 and 8 is .76 ($N = 14$). This correlation indicates the relative freedom from context effects that subjects enjoy during scaling (see Section 12.3). The correlation in mean normalized numerical assignment between Experiment 5 and the present experiment for the 12 multiple-operation arguments is .68. For the 14 (simple) single-operation arguments, it is .83.

16.4 INVENTORY AND ADDITIVITY ANALYSES

1. Inventory analysis.   The derivations of Table 12.3, which conform to the theory of Table 11.1, provide the inventory and additivity predictions of the theory. Altogether there are 858 inventory predictions [(12 multiple-operation arguments) $\times$ (74 subjects) $-$ 30 multiple-operation arguments about which subjects could not decide]. Of these predictions, 524 or 61.1% are correct. The expected number of true predictions based on Eq. (2) of Section 8.4 is 454.5 or 53.0.% This inventory result is comparable to that reported for Experiment 5, but it is not overly impressive.

2. Additivity analysis.   The within-subject analysis is again impractical for the same reasons as before. The between-subject additivity correlation is only .54 ($N = 12$). Figure 16.1 shows the scatter plot for this correlation.

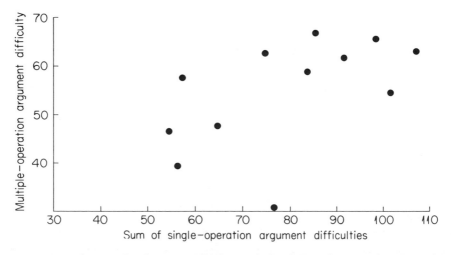

FIG. 16.1.   Scatter plot for the additivity analysis of Experiment 8, based on the theory of Table 11.1.

16.5   CONCLUSIONS OF EXPERIMENT 8

The low additivity correlation of the present experiment shows that the poor results for Experiment 7 were no accident. The theory of the Appendix seems not to apply as well to arguments with causal content as to the arguments with artificial content used in Part 2. At least, this can be said for that part of the theory not contained in Table 8.1; the fragment of the theory dealing with conditionals performs well for both artificial and causal content. It is when the operations of Tables 8.1 and 10.1 are combined to form Table 11.1 that the theory falters. Apparently, for causal content the operations dealing with DeMorgan laws, distributivity, and so forth, are organized differently for causally relevant arguments than for others.

Before accepting this conclusion, we should note the following three facts: First, at least one plausible alternative to the theory of Table 11.1, namely, the theory of Table 11.2, gives worse results than those obtained. The theory of Table 11.2, discredited by the data of Experiment 4, gives additivity correlations of .49 and .36 for Experiments 7 and 8, respectively. Second, if we combine the results of the three causality experiments, the resulting additivity correlation is .68 ($N = 40$). The scatter plot for this correlation is given in Fig. 16.2. As indicated in Section 12.5, there are dangers in combining different subjects' normalized numerical assignments in this way. But these problems can only be expected to spuriously lower the overall correlation, not raise it. Thus, the causality correlation of .68, only 6 points lower than the combined correlation for the experiments of Part 2, is rather impressive. Third, the inventory results for Experiments 7 and 8 are comparable to those for Experiments 4 and 5. It must be added, however, that none of the inventory results for those four experiments are strong.

We believe (tentatively, needless to say) that the theory of the Appendix describes the mental derivations underlying adolescents' evaluations of arguments with causal content. Or, more conservatively, our conviction in this regard is only a little less strong than our conviction that the Appendix describes adolescents' mental derivations for arguments with artificial content. Why, then, are the additivity correlations so weak in Experiments 7 and 8? As suggested earlier, the answer might be that varying the causal content of an argument varies the difficulty subjects have, not only in applying an operation, but also in recognizing that a given operation is legal and helpful. Since the content of the causal problems is heterogeneous, these difficulty factors are idiosyncratic. Thus, the additivity property of the derivations is weakened.

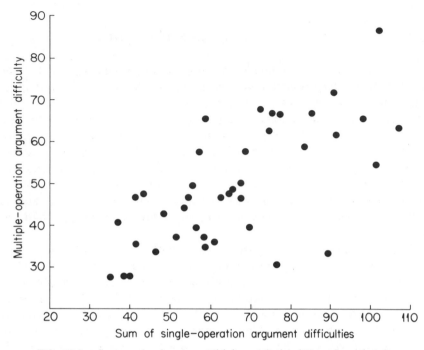

FIG. 16.2.   Scatter plot for the additivity analysis of Experiments 6–8.

If this explanation of the results is correct, then we might expect that as subjects mature intellectually, the additivity correlations for experiments like 7 and 8 would improve, for intellectual maturity can be expected to bring an increased ability to recognize the underlying logical structure of arguments. The older subject might be better able to cut through the varying causal content of arguments to reach the operational requirements of their derivations. In that case, the disturbance to subjects' numerical assignments would diminish. Apparently, with respect to the derivations of Experiment 6, this state of affairs is already true for adolescents. This may be due to the comparatively short derivations for those arguments. Thus, if the model of the Appendix applies to the mental derivations of causal as well as noncausal arguments, we would expect to find that it fulfills the additivity requirement better for adults than for adolescents.

This explanation of the causality results is a special case of a position enunciated by Fodor (1972). He suggests that

> . . .the young child differs from the adult not in the *kinds* of conceptual integrations it can effect, but rather *in the areas in which it can effect them.* Adults can bring their thinking to bear on a wide area of what we

call, in our ignorance, "general" problem solving. Children seem to have available comparably powerful computational apparatus, but it is special purpose equipment [p. 93].

Fodor's appeal to "kinds of conceptual integration" calls for theoretical elucidation. But, in general terms, his suggestion about young children seems extendable to the limitations on the scope of adolescents' computational apparatus for logical judgment. With maturity, the adolescent's logical operations will apply indifferently to arguments of varying content.

17

Experiment 9:
Class-Inclusion Arguments
Testing the Theory of Table 8.1

17.1 AIMS OF THE EXPERIMENT

Experiments 9–11 were designed to assess the logical generality of the theory of the Appendix. We wished first to determine whether the fragment of the theory of the Appendix that is presented in Table 8.1 holds for class-inclusion as well as propositional arguments.

Throughout the experiments we shall be matching class-inclusion arguments with their propositional counterparts. The isomorphism between the two types of arguments works this way: with each propositional logic formula we associate the Boolean term of which it is an instance. Each such term, T, is identified with the formula $T = 1$, where 1 is the largest term of the Boolean algebra. The identity $T = 1$ is then interpreted within the model for Boolean algebra that consists of all subsets of a given set. This amounts chiefly to substituting classes of objects, a, b, c for propositions p, q, r in a formula; substituting the class operations of complementation ( ), union ($\cup$), and intersection ($\cap$), respectively, for the propositional connectives negation ($-$), disjunction (v), and conjunction (&); substituting the class-inclusion relation, $\subseteq$, for the propositional operation of material implication, $\rightarrow$ ($\rightarrow$ always being the main connective of the formula in which it occurs). The results of this translation procedure are exemplified by the arguments enumerated in each experiment; in tables we omit the "$=1$" from class-inclusion formulas.

The passage from propositional to class-inclusion problems can be effected differently, using an isomorphism that logicians might consider more natural. To illustrate, instead of converting the propositional argument

(i) $p \vee q/(-p \mathbin{\&} s) \rightarrow q$

into the class-inclusion argument

   (ii) $(a \cup b) = 1/(\bar{a} \cap c) \subseteq b$

as we have done, (i) goes into the class-inclusion formula

   (iii) $\{x : x \in a \vee x \in b\} \subseteq \{x : (x \notin a \& x \in c) \rightarrow x \in b\}.$

Formula (iii) may be read "the class of objects x, such that either x is a member of a or x is a member of b is included in the class of objects x, such that if both x is not a member of a, and x is a member of c, then x is a member of b. Equivalently, for our purposes, (iii) could be written

   (iv) $\{x : Fx \vee Gx\} \subseteq \{x : (-Fx \& Hx) \rightarrow Gx\},$

substituting open sentences like "Fx" for membership constructions like $x \in a$. We have chosen our way (ii) of transforming propositional arguments like (i) into the logic of class inclusion because we wish to preserve the premise–conclusion form of the problems. Neither (iii) nor (iv) are arguments, since the formulas flanking the inclusion sign are not statements, as in (ii), but classes.

    The operations of the theory are transformed in the same way as the arguments. Table 17.1 restates the model of Table 8.1 in class-inclusion notation. Rather than standing for propositional formulas, we now let A, B, and C stand for class terms. Notice that Operations (4)–(7) in Table 17.1 are commutative variants of Operations (4)–(7) in Table 8.1. A number of class-inclusion arguments proved easier to formulate with this change.

    In the present experiment, we use the class-inclusion version of the 16 arguments figuring in Experiments 1 and 2. The derivations of these arguments can be constructed from Table 8.3.

17.2 METHOD

One hundred thirty-one 9th–11th-grade students from Hillsdale High School in San Mateo, California participated in Experiments 9–11. These experiments were run simultaneously; the envelopes containing arguments for the three different experiments were randomly assigned to students. Subjects were seen in groups of about 40. Of the 131 students, 46 participated in the present experiment.

    The instructions to subjects were modified in light of the new content of the arguments. All reference to the blackboard and letters was omitted. Instead, subjects were told that the arguments concerned a set of wooden blocks that they could imagine was elsewhere in the school. The blocks

TABLE 17.1
Class-Inclusion Version of the Model of Table 8.1

---

1. $A \subseteq (B \cap C)/A \subseteq B$

No subclass of C occurs intersecting B in the conclusion.

2. $(A \cup B) \subseteq C/A \subseteq C$

No subclass of B occurs in union with A in the conclusion.

3. $A \subseteq B/\bar{B} \subseteq \bar{A}$

A subclass of A and a subclass of B occur in the conclusion, each with a changed sign.

4. $A \subseteq B/(C \cap A) \subseteq (C \cap B)$

$(F \cap A)$ and $(F \cap B)$ occur in the conclusion, for some class F. Then C equals F in line l_{i+1}.

5. $A \subseteq B/(C \cup A) \subseteq (C \cup B)$

$(F \cup A)$ and $(F \cup B)$ occur in the conclusion, for some class F. Then C equals F in line l_{i+1}.

6. $A \subseteq B/(C \cap A) \subseteq B$

$(F \cap A)$ occurs in the conclusion, for some class F. Then C equals F in line l_{i+1}.

7. $A \subseteq B/A \subseteq (C \cup B)$

$(F \cup B)$ occurs in the conclusion, for some class F. Then C equals F in line l_{i+1}.

---

were of various shapes, sizes, colors, textures, and thicknesses. The instructions concerning use of logical words in the experiment were modified to suit the class-inclusion content of the problems. The argument

All the blocks are both red and square.
All the blocks are red.

was used to illustrate the properties of "and" (class intersection). The argument

All the blocks are thin.
All the blocks are either thin or blue.

(*Text continued on page 211*)

TABLE 17.2
Single-Operation Arguments for Experiment 9

---

1. $a \subseteq b / \bar{b} \subseteq \bar{a}$

   All the round blocks are pine.

   All the blocks that are not pine are not round.

2. $a \subseteq (b \cap c)/a \subseteq b$

   All the green blocks are both striped and square.

   All the green blocks are striped.

3. $(a \cup b) \subseteq c/a \subseteq c$

   All the oak blocks and thin blocks are yellow.

   All the oak blocks are yellow.

4. $a \subseteq b/(c \cap a) \subseteq b$

   All the blue blocks are thick.

   All the smooth blocks that are blue are thick.

5. $a \subseteq b/a \subseteq (c \cup b)$

   All the striped blocks are redwood.

   All the striped blocks are either square or redwood.

6. $a \subseteq b/(c \cap a) \subseteq (c \cap b)$

   All the brown blocks are spotted.

   All the rough blocks that are brown are both rough and spotted.

7. $a \subseteq b/(c \cup a) \subseteq (c \cup b)$

   All the maple blocks are green.

   All the round blocks and maple blocks are either round or green.

TABLE 17.3
Multiple-Operation Arguments for Experiment 9

1. $a \subseteq (b \cap c)/\bar{b} \subseteq \bar{a}$

   All the red blocks are both striped and thick.
   All the blocks that are not striped are not red.

2. $(a \cup b) \subseteq c/\bar{c} \subseteq \bar{a}$

   All the thick blocks and green blocks are spotted.
   All the blocks that are not spotted are not thick.

3. $a \subseteq b/(c \cap \bar{b}) \subseteq \bar{a}$

   All the round blocks are striped.
   All the blue blocks that are not striped are not round.

4. $a \subseteq b/\bar{b} \subseteq (c \cup \bar{a})$

   All the maple blocks are blue.
   All the blocks that are not blue are either square or not maple.

5. $a \subseteq b/(c \cap \bar{b}) \subseteq (c \cap \bar{a})$

   All the round blocks are thick.
   All the brown blocks that are not thick are both brown and not round.

6. $a \subseteq b/(c \cup \bar{b}) \subseteq (c \cup \bar{a})$

   All the spotted blocks are green.
   All the pine blocks and blocks that are not green are either pine or not spotted.

7. $(a \cup b) \subseteq (c \cap d)/a \subseteq d$

   All the square blocks and thin blocks are both spotted and blue.
   All the square blocks are blue.

8. $a \subseteq (b \cap c)/(d \cap a) \subseteq b$

   All the smooth blocks are both round and spotted.
   All the yellow blocks that are smooth are round.

9. $a \subseteq (b \cap c)/a \subseteq (d \cup b)$

   All the red blocks are both maple and striped.
   All the red blocks are either thick or maple.

(*continued*)

TABLE 17.3 (*continued*)

10. $a \subseteq (b \cap c)/(d \cap a) \subseteq (d \cap b)$

All the square blocks are both pine and spotted.

All the thin blocks that are square are both thin and pine.

11. $a \subseteq (b \cap c)/(d \cup a) \subseteq (d \cup b)$

All the oak blocks are both thick and round.

All the green blocks and oak blocks are either green or thick.

12. $(a \cup b) \subseteq c/(d \cap a) \subseteq c$

All the spotted blocks and pine blocks are blue.

All the rough blocks that are spotted are blue.

13. $(a \cup b) \subseteq c/a \subseteq (d \cup c)$

All the maple blocks and round blocks are striped.

All the maple blocks are either red or striped.

14. $(a \cup b) \subseteq c/(d \cap a) \subseteq (d \cap c)$

All the yellow blocks and thick blocks are redwood.

All the spotted blocks that are yellow are both spotted and redwood.

15. $(a \cup b) \subseteq c/(d \cup a) \subseteq (d \cup c)$

All the thin blocks and oak blocks are green.

All the striped blocks and thin blocks are either striped or green.

16. $a \subseteq b/(c \cap a) \subseteq (d \cup b)$

All the red blocks are smooth.

All the thin blocks that are red are either pine or smooth.

TABLE 17.4
Invalid and Baseline Arguments for Experiment 9

Invalid arguments

1. $a \subseteq (b \cup c)/\overline{c} \subseteq (d \cap \overline{a})$

All the square blocks are either thick or yellow.

All the blocks that are not yellow are both striped and not square.

2. $a \subseteq (b \cup c)/(d \cup a) \subseteq (b \cup c)$

All the thin blocks are either spotted or round.

All the green blocks and thin blocks are either spotted or round.

3. $a \subseteq b/\overline{a} \subseteq (c \cup \overline{b})$

All the rough blocks are red.

All the blocks that are not rough are either spotted or not red.

4. $(a \cap b) \subseteq c/a \subseteq b$

All the square blocks that are striped are thick.

All the square blocks are striped.

5. $a \subseteq b/(c \cup a) \subseteq b$

All the red blocks are spotted.

All the round blocks and red blocks are spotted.

6. $a \subseteq b/a \subseteq (c \cap b)$

All the thin blocks are blue.

All the thin blocks are both spotted and blue.

7. $a \subseteq (b \cup c)/a \subseteq b$

All the striped blocks are either green or thick.

All the striped blocks are green.

8. $a \subseteq b/(c \cap a) \subseteq (d \cap b)$

All the thick blocks are striped.

All the green blocks that are thick are both round and striped.

9. $(a \cap b) \subseteq c/a \subseteq c$

All the red blocks that are spotted are thick.

All the red blocks are thick.

(*continued*)

TABLE 17.4 (*continued*)

---

10. $(a \cap b) \subseteq c/\bar{c} \subseteq \bar{a}$

All the thin blocks that are yellow are striped.

All the blocks that are not striped are not thin.

Baseline argument

$a \subseteq b/a \subseteq b$

All the thick blocks are round.

All the thick blocks are round.

---

was used to illustrate the properties of "or" (class union).[1] The invalid argument

All the smooth blocks are square.

All the square blocks are smooth.

was used to stress the asymmetrical nature of class inclusion. In all other respects, the instructions were the same as detailed in Chapter 7.

Each subject in Experiment 9 received seven single-operation arguments, one for each operation in Table 17.1. These arguments are shown in Table 17.2.[2] In addition, they received 16 multiple operation arguments, corresponding to those employed in Experiments 1, 2, and 6. These are given in Table 17.3. Finally, each subject received a baseline argument $a \subseteq b/a \subseteq b$, and five invalid arguments selected randomly from the ten invalid arguments shown in Table 17.4. In all, each subject received 29 arguments.

---

[1] In some dialects, the sentence "all the blocks are either thin or red" is ambiguous, having one of the following two meanings in the notation of predicate logic:

(1) $(\forall x)(Bx \rightarrow (Tx \vee Rx))$

(2) $(\forall x)(Bx \rightarrow Tx) \vee (\forall x)(Bx) \rightarrow Rx$

Interpretation (1) is the intended meaning, and postexperimental discussions with the subjects indicated that interpretation (2) did not occur to them.

In general, a deduction is none the worse if a subject interprets a locution differently than the experimenter intended so long as the subject is consistent in giving that locution the same interpretation in every problem containing it. If the subject is inconsistent, the inventory or additivity results may suffer, for, if the inconsistency spans a multiple-operation argument and one of the relevant single-operation arguments, prediction of the multiple-operation argument's acceptance and difficulty will be based on single-operation arguments involving the wrong operations.

[2] For class inclusion, the two-premise version of arguments is impossible.

TABLE 17.5
Acceptance Rates for Valid Arguments of Experiment 9 ($N = 43$)

	No accepted	No. rejected	No. cannot decide
Single-operation arguments			
1. $a \subseteq b / \overline{b} \subseteq \overline{a}$	25	18	0
2. $a \subseteq (b \cap c) / a \subseteq b$	38	5	0
3. $(a \cup b) \subseteq c / a \subseteq c$	38	5	0
4. $a \subseteq b / (c \cap a) \subseteq b$	34	9	0
5. $a \subseteq b / a \subseteq (c \cup b)$	28	14	1
6. $a \subseteq b / (c \cap a) \subseteq (c \cap b)$	36	6	1
7. $a \subseteq b / (c \cup a) \subseteq (c \cup b)$	36	7	0
Total:	235	64	2
Mean:	33.6		
Multiple-operation arguments			
1. $a \subseteq (b \cap c) / \overline{b} \subseteq \overline{a}$	30	13	0
2. $(a \cup b) \subseteq c / \overline{c} \subseteq \overline{a}$	28	15	0
3. $a \subseteq b / (c \cap \overline{b}) \subseteq \overline{a}$	32	11	0
4. $a \subseteq b / \overline{b} \subseteq (c \cup \overline{a})$	26	16	1
5. $a \subseteq b / (c \cap \overline{b}) \subseteq (c \cap \overline{a})$	30	13	0
6. $a \subseteq b / (c \cup \overline{b}) \subseteq (c \cup \overline{a})$	27	15	1
7. $(a \cup b) \subseteq (c \cap d) / a \subseteq d$	33	10	0
8. $a \subseteq (b \cap c) / (d \cap a) \subseteq b$	29	14	0
9. $a \subseteq (b \cap c) / a \subseteq (d \cup b)$	21	21	1
10. $a \subseteq (b \cap c) / (d \cap a) \subseteq (d \cap b)$	31	12	0
11. $a \subseteq (b \cap c) / (d \cup a) \subseteq (d \cup b)$	31	12	0
12. $(a \cup b) \subseteq c / (d \cap a) \subseteq c$	30	12	1
13. $(a \cup b) \subseteq c / a \subseteq (d \cup c)$	24	18	1
14. $(a \cup b) \subseteq c / (d \cap a) \subseteq (d \cap c)$	32	10	1
15. $(a \cup b) \subseteq c / (d \cup a) \subseteq (d \cup c)$	34	9	0
16. $a \subseteq b / (c \cap a) \subseteq (d \cup b)$	24	19	0
Total:	462	220	6
Mean:	28.9		
Baseline argument			
$a \subseteq b / a \subseteq b$	43	0	0

TABLE 17.6
Mean Normalized Numerical Assignments for
Valid Arguments of Experiment 9 (N = 43)

	Mean normalized numerical assignments	Standard deviations of mean normalized numerical assignments
Single-operation arguments		
1. $a \subseteq b/\overline{b} \subseteq \overline{a}$	39.55	23.88
2. $a \subseteq (b \cap c)/a \subseteq b$	19.50	22.17
3. $(a \cup b) \subseteq c/a \subseteq c$	21.64	21.88
4. $a \subseteq b/(c \cap a) \subseteq b$	38.72	26.53
5. $a \subseteq b/a \subseteq (c \cup b)$	40.49	25.96
6. $a \subseteq b/(c \cap a) \subseteq (c \cap b)$	52.26	23.69
7. $a \subseteq b/(c \cup a) \subseteq (c \cup b)$	51.82	27.63
Multiple-operation arguments		
1. $a \subseteq (b \cap c)/\overline{b} \subseteq \overline{a}$	57.93	26.39
2. $(a \cup b) \subseteq c/\overline{c} \subseteq \overline{a}$	54.20	27.84
3. $a \subseteq b/(c \cap \overline{b}) \subseteq \overline{a}$	52.04	25.94
4. $a \subseteq b/\overline{b} \subseteq (c \cup \overline{a})$	70.47	28.46
5. $a \subseteq b/(c \cap \overline{b}) \subseteq (c \cap \overline{a})$	73.16	26.65
6. $a \subseteq b/(c \cup \overline{b}) \subseteq (c \cup \overline{a})$	75.04	21.72
7. $(a \cup b) \subseteq (c \cap d)/a \subseteq d$	29.70	20.46
8. $a \subseteq (b \cap c)/(d \cap a) \subseteq b$	52.01	27.89
9. $a \subseteq (b \cap c)/a \subseteq (d \cup b)$	43.16	21.10
10. $a \subseteq (b \cap c)/(d \cap a) \subseteq (d \cap b)$	61.20	26.46
11. $a \subseteq (b \cap c)/(d \cup a) \subseteq (d \cup b)$	59.21	24.47
12. $(a \cup b) \subseteq c/(d \cap a) \subseteq c$	43.30	27.47
13. $(a \cup b) \subseteq c/a \subseteq (d \cup c)$	45.24	27.75
14. $(a \cup b) \subseteq c/(d \cap a) \subseteq (d \cap c)$	66.22	22.95
15. $(a \cup b) \subseteq c/(d \cup a) \subseteq (d \cup c)$	63.08	23.80
16. $a \subseteq b/(c \cap a) \subseteq (d \cup b)$	50.30	27.54
Baseline argument		
$a \subseteq b/a \subseteq b$	0.00	0.00

17.3   PRELIMINARY ANALYSES OF RESULTS

1. Dropped subjects. Three subjects were dropped. Two found the baseline argument to be of considerable difficulty; the other subject was uncooperative. Data analyses refer to the 43 remaining subjects.

2. Acceptance rate for arguments. Table 17.5 shows the number of subjects accepting each valid argument in Experiment 9. The correlation in acceptance rate between Experiment 1 and the present experiment for the multiple-operation arguments is .53 ($N = 16$). With respect to the first causality experiment, this correlation is .75 ($N = 16$).

3. Difficulty of the arguments. Subjects' numerical assignments were normalized in the usual fashion. Table 17.6 shows the mean normalized numerical assignment for each valid argument. The correlation in mean normalized numerical assignment between Experiment 1 and the present experiment for the multiple-operation arguments is .57 ($N = 16$). With respect to the first causality experiment, this correlation is .45 ($N = 16$).

17.4   INVENTORY AND ADDITIVITY ANALYSES

1. Inventory analysis. The derivations of Table 8.3, which correspond to the theory of Table 17.1, provide the inventory and additivity predictions of the theory. Altogether, there are 682 inventory predictions [(16 multiple-operation arguments) $\times$ (43 subjects) — 6 multiple-operation arguments about which subjects could not decide]. Of these predictions, 440 or 64.5% were correct. The expected number of true predictions, based on Eq. 2 of Section 8.4, is 373.5 or 54.8%.

2. Additivity analysis. Of the 43 subjects, 33 accepted enough arguments to make the within-subject additivity analysis possible. These 33 subjects produced at least 5 correlatable observations. The average number of degrees of freedom for these correlations is 9.2. Fourteen of the 33 correlations reach significance beyond the 5% level; an additional subject yields a correlation significant at the 10% level. Over all 33 subjects, the average additivity correlation is .45. The between-subject additivity correlation, relying on mean normalized numerical assignments, is .84 ($N = 16$). Figure 17.1 shows the scatter plot for this correlation.

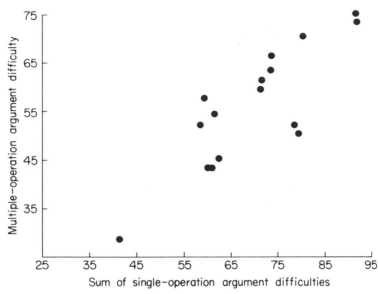

FIG. 17.1. Scatter plot for the additivity analysis of Experiment 9, based on the theory of Table 17.1.

17.5 CONCLUSIONS OF EXPERIMENT 9

The results of Experiment 9 support the idea that the theory of the Appendix applies both to propositional and class-inclusion arguments. They also serve as indirect confirmation of results reported in Volume 2, Chapter 3, and Section 9.1. In Volume 2 we used a different kind of evidence to argue for the similarity of the mental derivations underlying certain class-inclusion arguments. These arguments are very similar to those employed in the present experiment.

The results also bear out the proposal of Section 13.1 that the best dependent variable for assessing the similarity of two populations' mental derivations is based on theories of each population separately. We have been using the following dependent variable: degree of conformity to the inventory and especially additivity requirements of the theory. The additivity correlations from Experiments 1, 6, and 9, all testing versions of the theory of Table 8.1, are .88, .89, and .84, respectively. In contrast, the nontheoretical correlations between the mean normalized numerical assignments for multiple-operation arguments of the three experiments are as follows:

Experiment 1–Experiment 6: .84 $(N = 16)$
Experiment 1–Experiment 9: .57 $(N = 16)$
Experiment 6–Experiment 9: .45 $(N = 16)$

Thus, reliance on nontheoretical correlations leads to an underestimation of the similarity of the mental processes involved in these three experiments.[3]

[3] When the seven single-operation arguments based on Table 8.1 (or Table 17.1) are added in, these correlations are as follows:

Experiment 1–Experiment 6: .91 $(N = 16)$
Experiment 1–Experiment 9: .73 $(N = 16)$
Experiment 6–Experiment 9: .66 $(N = 16)$

As argued earlier, however, the most revealing comparison is between the additivity correlations and the nontheoretical correlations between multiple-operation arguments.

18

Experiment 10: Class-Inclusion Arguments Testing The Theory of Table 11.1

18.1 AIMS OF THE EXPERIMENT

Experiments 10 and 11 tested the class-inclusion version of the model of Table 11.1. Table 18.1 restates that model in the notation of class-inclusion. The structure of the arguments from Experiment 4 was employed in the present experiment. They were given the class-inclusion interpretation used in Experiment 9. The model's derivations for the 12 class-inclusion multiple-operation arguments can be constructed from Table 11.3.

18.2 METHOD

The 43 subjects who participated in Experiment 10 were drawn from the pool of 131 9th–11th-grade students seen at Hillsdale High School. The instructions are described in Section 17.2. Each subject received 14 single-operation arguments, one for each operation in Table 18.1. These arguments are shown in Table 18.2. They also received 12 multiple-operation arguments corresponding to those used in Experiment 4. These are given in Table 18.3. Finally, each subject received a baseline argument $a \subseteq b/a \subseteq b$, and five invalid arguments selected randomly from the ten invalid arguments shown in Table 18.4. In all, each subject received 32 arguments.

18.3 PRELIMINARY ANALYSIS OF RESULTS

1. Dropped subjects. One subject was dropped for failing to complete the experiment. Data analyses refer to the remaining 42 subjects.

(*Text continued on page 223*)

TABLE 18.1
Class-Inclusion Version of the Theory of Table 11.1

---

1. $A \cap (B \cup C)/(A \cap B) \cup (A \cap C)$

Either $(A \cap B)$ or $(A \cap C)$ occurs in the conclusion. Applies to subformulas.

2. $A \cup (B \cap C)/A \cup B$

No subclass of C occurs intersecting B in the conclusion.

2' (variant of 2). $(A \cap B) \cup C/A \cup C$

No subclass of B occurs intersecting A in the conclusion.

3. $(\overline{A \cup B})/\overline{A} \cap \overline{B}$

A subclass of $A[B]$ occurs in the conclusion, not in union with $B[A]$. (Bracketed material provides an alternative helping condition.) Applies to subformulas.

4. $(\overline{A \cap B})/\overline{A} \cup \overline{B}$

A subclass of $A[B]$ occurs in the conclusion, not intersecting $B[A]$. (Bracketed material provides an alternative helping condition.) Applies to subformulas.

5. $A \subseteq (B \cap C)/A \subseteq B$

No subclass of C occurs intersecting B in the conclusion, and no subclass of C' occurs in union with B' in the conclusion, where B' equals B with changed sign, and C' equals C with changed sign.

6. $(A \cup B) \subseteq C/A \subseteq C$

No subclass of B occurs in union with A in the conclusion, and no subclass of B' occurs intersecting A' in the conclusion, where A' equals A with changed sign, and B' equals B with changed sign.

7. $A \subseteq B/\overline{B} \subseteq \overline{A}$

A subclass of A and a subclass of B occur in the conclusion, each with a changed sign.

8. $A \subseteq B/(C \cap A) \subseteq (C \cap B)$

$(F \cap A)$ and $(F \cap B)$ occur in the conclusion, for some class F. Then C equals F in line l_{i+1}.

(continued)

TABLE 18.1 (*continued*)

---

9. $A \subseteq B/(C \cup A) \subseteq (C \cup B)$

$(F \cup A)$ and $(F \cup B)$ occur in the conclusion, for some class F. Then C equals F in line l_{i+1}.

10. $A \subseteq B/(C \cap A) \subseteq B$

$(F \cap A)$ occurs in the conclusion, for some class F. Then C equals F in line l_{i+1}.

11. $A \subseteq B/A \subseteq (C \cup B)$

$(F \cup B)$ occurs in the conclusion, for some class F. Then C equals F in line l_{i+1}.

12. $A \cup B/\overline{A} \subseteq B$

A subclass of A occurs in the conclusion under the scope of a changed sign, this occurrence being within the antecedent of an inclusion whose consequent contains a subclass of B. Applies to subformulas.

13. $\overline{A} \subseteq B/A \cup B$

A subclass of A and a subclass of B occur in union with each other in the conclusion. Applies to subformulas.

14. $A \subseteq B/\overline{(A \cap \overline{B})}$

A and B occur in the conclusion intersecting each other, the intersection occuring under the scope of a negation. Applies to subformulas.

TABLE 18.2
Single-Operation Arguments for Experiments 10 and 11

---

1. $a \subseteq (b \cap c)/a \subseteq b$

All the green blocks are both striped and square.
All the green blocks are striped.

2. $(a \cup b) \subseteq c/a \subseteq c$

All the oak blocks and thin blocks are yellow.
All the oak blocks are yellow.

3. $a \subseteq b/\bar{b} \subseteq \bar{a}$

All the round blocks are pine.
All the blocks that are not pine are not round.

4. $a \subseteq b/(c \cap a) \subseteq (c \cap b)$

All the brown blocks are spotted.
All the rough blocks that are brown are both rough and spotted.

5. $a \subseteq b/(c \cup a) \subseteq (c \cup b)$

All the maple blocks are green.
All the round blocks and maple blocks are either round or green.

6. $a \subseteq b/(c \cap a) \subseteq b$

All the blue blocks are thick.
All the smooth blocks that are blue are thick.

7. $a \subseteq b/a \subseteq (c \cup b)$

All the striped blocks are redwood.
All the striped blocks are either square or redwood.

8. $\overline{a \cup b}/\bar{a} \cap \bar{b}$

None of the blocks are either blue or smooth.
All of the blocks are both not blue and not smooth.

(*continued*)

TABLE 18.2 (*continued*)

9. $\overline{a \cap b}/\overline{a} \cup \overline{b}$

None of the blocks are both pine and round.

All the blocks are either not pine or not round.

10. $a \cap (b \cup c)/(a \cap b) \cup (a \cap c)$

All the blocks are thick and either green or square.

All the blocks are either thick and green or thick and square.

11. $a \cup (b \cap c)/a \cup b$

All the blocks are either striped or both yellow and thin.

All the blocks are either striped or yellow.

12. $a \cup b/\overline{a} \subseteq b$

All the blocks are either rough or maple.

All the blocks that are not rough are maple.

13. $\overline{a} \subseteq b/a \cup b$

All the blocks that are not redwood are thick.

All the blocks are either redwood or thick.

14. $a \subseteq b/\overline{a \cap \overline{b}}$

All the green blocks are oak.

None of the blocks is both green and not oak.

TABLE 18.3
Multiple-Operation Arguments for Experiment 10

---

1. $(\overline{a \cap b}) \subseteq c / \overline{a} \subseteq c$

    All the blocks that are not both blue and striped are thin.
    All the blocks that are not blue are thin.

2. $a \subseteq (b \cup a)/(\overline{b} \cap \overline{c}) \subseteq \overline{a}$

    All the square blocks are either smooth or red.
    All the blocks that are both not smooth and not red are not square.

3. $(a \cap b) \subseteq c / \overline{c} \subseteq (\overline{a} \cup \overline{b})$

    All the thick blocks that are yellow are pine.
    All the blocks that are not pine are either not thick or not yellow.

4. $(a \cup b) \subseteq c / \overline{a \cap \overline{c}}$

    All the oak blocks and rough blocks are round.
    None of the blocks are both oak and not round.

5. $(a \cup b) \subseteq (c \cap d) / \overline{a \cap \overline{c}}$

    All the brown blocks and square blocks are both pine and smooth.
    None of the blocks are both brown and not pine.

6. $a \cup b / (c \cap \overline{a}) \subseteq b$

    All the blocks are either thick or redwood.
    All the blue blocks that are not thick are redwood.

7. $a \cup b / (c \cap \overline{a}) \subseteq (c \cap b)$

    All the blocks are either thin or square.
    All the red blocks that are not thin are both red and square.

8. $(a \cap b) \cup c / \overline{a} \subseteq c$

    All the blocks are either both rough and yellow or oak.
    All the blocks that are not rough are oak.

9. $a \cup (b \cap c) / \overline{a} \subseteq (b \cup d)$

    All the blocks are either smooth or both pine and striped.
    All the blocks that are not smooth are either pine or green.

(*continued*)

TABLE 18.3 (*continued*)

10. $a \cup (b \cap c)/(d \cup \overline{a}) \subseteq (d \cup b)$

All the blocks are either maple or both spotted and round.

All the rough blocks and blocks that are not maple are either rough or spotted.

11. $(\overline{a} \cup \overline{b}) \subseteq c/a \cup c$

All the blocks that are either not thick or not square are green.

All the blocks are either thick or green.

12. $[a \cap (b \cup c)] \subseteq d/(a \cap b) \subseteq d$

All the rough blocks that are either spotted or thin are redwood.

All the rough blocks that are spotted are redwood.

---

2. Acceptance rates for arguments. Table 18.5 shows the number of subjects accepting each valid argument in Experiment 10. The correlation in acceptance rate for the 12 multiple-operation arguments between the present experiment and Experiment 5 is .90. For the 14 (simple) single-operation arguments, the correlation is .25. The correlation for multiple-operation arguments between the present experiment and the causal Experiment 7 is .84 ($N = 12$). For the 14 single-operation arguments, the correlation is .56.

3. Difficulty of the arguments. Table 18.6 shows the mean normalized numerical assignment for each valid argument. The correlations in difficulty between Experiment 4 and the present experiment for multiple-operation and single-operation arguments are .63 ($N = 12$) and .70 ($N = 14$), respectively. With respect to Experiment 7, these correlations are .32 ($N = 12$) and .61 ($N = 14$), respectively.

18.4 INVENTORY AND ADDITIVITY ANALYSES

1. Inventory analysis. The derivations of Table 11.3 provide the inventory and additivity predictions of the theory. Altogether, there are 497 inventory predictions [(12 multiple-operation arguments) × (42 subjects) — 7 multiple-operation arguments about which subjects could not decide]. Of these predictions, 299 or 60.2% were correct. The expected number of true predictions is 262.8 or 52.9%.

TABLE 18.4
Invalid and Baseline Arguments for
Experiments 10 and 11

Invalid arguments

1. $a \subseteq b/\overline{a} \subseteq (c \cup \overline{b})$

All the square blocks are redwood.

All the blocks that are not square are either striped or not redwood.

2. $a \subseteq b/a \subseteq (b \cap c)$

All the oak blocks are spotted.

All the oak blocks are both spotted and green.

3. $\overline{a \cap b}/\overline{a} \cap \overline{b}$

None of the blocks are both round and pine.

All the blocks are both not round and not pine.

4. $(a \cap b) \subseteq c/a \subseteq c$

All the thick blocks that are yellow are square.

All the thick blocks are square.

5. $a \subseteq (b \cup c)/\overline{a} \subseteq \overline{b}$

All the maple blocks are either rough or brown.

All the blocks that are not maple are rough.

6. $\overline{a \cup b}/a \cap \overline{b}$

None of the blocks are either red or thin.

All the blocks are both red and not thin.

7. $a \cap \overline{b}/b \cap \overline{a}$

All the blocks are both square and not rough.

All the blocks are both rough and not square.

8. $a \cup \overline{b}/\overline{b} \cup \overline{a}$

All the blocks are either pine or not thick.

All the blocks are either not thick or not pine.

9. $a \cup (b \cap c)/a \cap b$

All the blocks are either blue or both oak and square.

All the blocks are both blue and oak.

(continued)

TABLE 18.4 (*continued*)

---

10. $a \cup b/(c \cap \overline{b}) \subseteq \overline{a}$

All the blocks are either round or maple.

All the green blocks that are not maple are not round.

Baseline argument
   $a \subseteq b/a \subseteq b$

All the square blocks are oak.

All the square blocks are oak.

---

2. Additivity analysis. The within-subject additivity analysis was again impractical. The between-subject additivity correlation is only .63 ($N = 12$). Figure 18.1 shows the scatter plot for this correlation.

18.5 CONCLUSIONS OF EXPERIMENT 10

The additivity correlation is disappointingly low. This result cannot be attributed to peculiarities of the subjects, since in this experiment subjects were quite cooperative and interested. Nor can it be attributed to heterogeneity of the arguments as in the causal experiments (see Sections 13.2 and 16.5). The class-inclusion arguments, dealing exclusively with blocks,

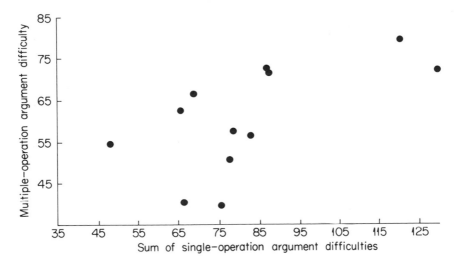

FIG. 18.1. Scatter plot for the additivity analysis of Experiment 10, based on the theory of Table 18.1.

TABLE 18.5
Acceptance Rates for Valid Arguments of
Experiment 10 ($N = 42$)

	No. accepted	No. rejected	No. cannot decide
Single-operation arguments			
1. $a \subseteq (b \cap c)/a \subseteq b$	37	5	0
2. $(a \cup b) \subseteq c/a \subseteq c$	40	2	0
3. $a \subseteq b/\overline{b} \subseteq \overline{a}$	20	22	0
4. $a \subseteq b/(c \cap a) \subseteq (c \cap b)$	31	11	0
5. $a \subseteq b/(c \cup a) \subseteq (c \cup b)$	32	9	1
6. $a \subseteq b/(c \cap a) \subseteq b$	34	8	0
7. $a \subseteq b/a \subseteq (c \cup b)$	21	21	0
8. $\overline{a \cup b}/\overline{a} \cap \overline{b}$	34	7	1
9. $\overline{a \cap b}/\overline{a} \cup \overline{b}$	33	9	0
10. $a \cap (b \cup c)/(a \cap b) \cup (a \cap c)$	36	6	0
11. $a \cup (b \cap c)/a \cup b$	31	10	1
12. $a \cup b/\overline{a} \subseteq b$	31	11	0
13. $\overline{a} \subseteq b/a \cup b$	32	10	0
14. $a \subseteq b/a \cap \overline{b}$	30	12	0
Total:	442	143	3
Mean:	31.6		
Multiple-operation arguments			
1. $\overline{a \cap b} \subseteq c/\overline{a} \subseteq c$	18	23	1
2. $a \subseteq (b \cup c)/(\overline{b} \cap \overline{c}) \subseteq \overline{a}$	31	11	0
3. $(a \cap b) \subseteq c/\overline{c} \subseteq (\overline{a} \cup \overline{b})$	26	14	2
4. $(a \cup b) \subseteq c/a \cap \overline{c}$	30	12	0
5. $(a \cup b) \subseteq (c \cap d)/\overline{a \cap \overline{c}}$	29	13	0
6. $a \cup b/(c \cap \overline{a}) \subseteq b$	33	9	0
7. $a \cup b/(c \cap \overline{a}) \subseteq (c \cap b)$	31	11	0
8. $(a \cap b) \cup c/\overline{a} \subseteq c$	29	12	1
9. $a \cup (b \cap c)/\overline{a} \subseteq (b \cup d)$	14	27	1
10. $a \cup (b \cap c)/(d \cup \overline{a}) \subseteq (d \cup b)$	17	23	2
11. $(\overline{a} \cup \overline{b}) \subseteq c/a \cup c$	14	28	0
12. $[a \cap (b \cup c)] \subseteq d/(a \cap b) \subseteq d$	37	5	0
Total:	309	188	7
Mean:	25.8		
Baseline argument			
$a \subseteq b/a \subseteq b$	42	0	0

TABLE 18.6
Mean Normalized Numerical Assignments for Valid Arguments
of Experiment 10 ($N = 42$)

	Mean normalized numerical assignments	Standard deviations of mean normalized numerical assignments
Single-operation arguments		
1. $a \subseteq (b \cap c)/a \subseteq b$	21.57	21.26
2. $(a \cup b) \subseteq c/a \subseteq c$	19.77	21.34
3. $a \subseteq b/\bar{b} \subseteq \bar{a}$	37.57	27.20
4. $a \subseteq b/(c \cap a) \subseteq (c \cap b)$	46.36	29.24
5. $a \subseteq b/(c \cup a) \subseteq (c \cup b)$	51.53	28.46
6. $a \subseteq b/(c \cap a) \subseteq b$	35.24	22.69
7. $a \subseteq b/a \subseteq (c \cup b)$	42.08	30.48
8. $\overline{a \cup b}/\bar{a} \cap \bar{b}$	45.36	24.54
9. $\overline{a \cap b}/\bar{a} \cup \bar{b}$	49.14	30.07
10. $a \cap (b \cup c)/(a \cap b) \cup (a \cap c)$	55.50	32.03
11. $a \cup (b \cap c)/a \cup b$	47.51	28.58
12. $a \cup b/\bar{a} \subseteq b$	30.83	22.92
13. $\bar{a} \subseteq b/a \cup b$	28.16	24.87
14. $a \subseteq b/a \cap \bar{b}$	45.80	30.35
Multiple-operation arguments		
1. $a \cap b \subseteq \bar{c}/\bar{a} \subseteq c$	66.34	22.62
2. $a \subseteq (b \cup c)/(\bar{b} \cap \bar{c}) \subseteq \bar{a}$	56.53	22.27
3. $(a \cap b) \subseteq c/\bar{c} \subseteq (\bar{a} \cup \bar{b})$	72.46	25.73
4. $(a \cup b) \subseteq c/\bar{a} \cap \bar{c}$	62.17	29.47
5. $(a \cup b) \subseteq (c \cap d)/\overline{a \cap \bar{c}}$	71.76	22.10
6. $a \cup b/(c \cap \bar{a}) \subseteq b$	41.29	25.92
7. $a \cup b/(c \cap \bar{a}) \subseteq (c \cap b)$	50.77	27.74
8. $(a \cap b) \cup c/\bar{a} \subseteq c$	57.37	29.81
9. $a \cup (b \cap c)/\bar{a} \subseteq (b \cup d)$	79.05	31.41
10. $a \cup (b \cap c)/(d \cup \bar{a}) \subseteq (d \cup b)$	72.02	27.36
11. $(\bar{a} \cup \bar{b}) \subseteq c/a \cup c$	54.45	30.44
12. $[a \cap (b \cup c)] \subseteq d/(a \cap b) \subseteq d$	39.90	26.16
Baseline argument		
$a \subseteq b/a \subseteq b$	0.00	0.00

have as homogeneous a content as the propositional arguments of Part 2. The low additivity correlation may indicate that the theory of the Appendix is not generalizable to class inclusion, that the mental derivations for these two kinds of arguments are not the same. Against this possibility is the fact that the additivity correlation for the alternative theory of Table 11.2 (the theory discredited for propositional arguments by Experiment 4) is appreciably lower than the correlation based on the theory of the Appendix.

We pursue this question in light of the results of Experiment 11.

19

Experiment 11:
More Class-Inclusion Arguments
Testing the Theory of Table 18.1

19.1 AIMS OF THE EXPERIMENT

The present experiment supplements Experiment 10 in testing the theory of Table 18.1. The arguments from Experiment 5 were employed. They were given the class-inclusion content used in Experiments 9 and 10. The model's derivations for these 12 multiple-operation arguments can be constructed from Table 12.1.

19.2 METHOD

The 42 subjects who participated in Experiment 11 were drawn from the 131 9th–11th graders seen at Hillsdale High School. The instructions are described in Section 17.2. Each subject received the same 14 single-operation arguments employed in Experiment 10. These arguments are shown in Table 18.2. In addition, subjects received 12 multiple-operation arguments corresponding to those used in Experiment 5. These are given in Table 19.1. Finally, each subject received a baseline argument $a \subseteq b/a \subseteq b$ and five invalid arguments selected randomly from the ten invalid arguments shown in Table 18.4. In all, each subject received 32 arguments.

19.3 PRELIMINARY ANALYSES OF RESULTS

1. Dropped subjects. One subject was dropped for failing to complete the experiment. Data analyses pertain to the 41 remaining subjects.

2. Acceptance rates for arguments. Table 19.2 shows the number of subjects accepting each valid argument in Experiment 11. The correlation

TABLE 19.1
Multiple-Operation Arguments for Experiment 11

---

1. $a \subseteq \overline{(b \cup c)}/a \subseteq \overline{b}$

All the round blocks are not either smooth or pine.
All the round blocks are not smooth.

2. $\overline{(a \cap b)} \subseteq c/a \cup c$

All the blocks that are not both spotted and thin are blue.
All the blocks are either spotted or blue.

3. $(a \cup b) \subseteq c/\overline{c} \subseteq (\overline{a} \cap \overline{b})$

All the green blocks and square blocks are striped.
All the blocks that are not striped are both not green and not square.

4. $a \subseteq (b \cap c)/(\overline{b} \cup \overline{c}) \subseteq \overline{a}$

All the oak blocks are both red and smooth.
All the blocks that are either not red or not smooth are not oak.

5. $a \subseteq (b \cap c)/\overline{a \cap \overline{b}}$

All the round blocks are both maple and yellow.
None of the blocks are both round and not maple.

6. $a \cup b/(c \cup \overline{a}) \subseteq (c \cup b)$

All the blocks are either rough or pine.
All the thin blocks and blocks that are not rough are either thin or pine.

7. $a \cup b/\overline{a} \subseteq (b \cup c)$

All the blocks are either redwood or thick.
All the blocks that are not redwood are either thick or striped.

8. $a \cup (b \cap c)/\overline{a} \subseteq b$

All the blocks are either maple or both spotted and red.
All the blocks that are not maple are spotted.

9. $a \cup (b \cap c)/(d \cap \overline{a}) \subseteq (d \cap b)$

All the blocks are either smooth or both oak and thin.
All the red blocks that are not smooth are both red and oak.

(continued)

TABLE 19.1 (continued)

---

10. $a \cup (b \cap c)/(d \cap \overline{a}) \subseteq b$

All the blocks are either rough or both thick and brown.
All the striped blocks that are not rough are thick.

11. $\overline{a} \subseteq (b \cap c)/a \cup b$

All the blocks that are not blue are both round and spotted.
All the blocks are either blue or round.

12. $a \cap (b \cup c)/\overline{(a \cap b)} \subseteq (a \cap c)$

All the blocks are square and either thick or pine.
All the blocks that are not both square and thick are both square and pine.

---

in acceptance rate of single-operation arguments between Experiment 10 and the present experiment is .81 ($N = 14$). Context effects are thus small for the class-inclusion arguments (see Sections 16.3 and 12.3). The correlations in acceptance rate between Experiment 5 and the present experiment for single- and multiple-operation arguments are, respectively, .64 ($N = 14$) and .65 ($N = 12$). In this regard, the correlations between the causal Experiment 8 and the present experiment are, respectively, .49 ($N = 14$), and .74 ($N = 12$).

3. *Difficulty of the arguments.*   Table 19.3 shows the mean normalized numerical assignment for each valid argument. The correlation in difficulty between the single-operation arguments of Experiments 10 and 11 is .87 ($N = 14$), indicating relatively little effect of context on scaling (see Sections 16.3 and 12.3). The correlations in difficulty for the single- and multiple-operation arguments between Experiment 5 and the present experiment are, respectively, .74 ($N = 14$) and .46 ($N = 12$). The comparable correlations between the present experiment and the causal Experiment 8 are .71 ($N = 14$) and .36 ($N = 12$).

19.4   INVENTORY AND ADDITIVITY ANALYSES

1. *Inventory analysis.*   The derivations of Table 12.1 provide the inventory and additivity predictions of the theory. Altogether, there are 482 inventory predictions [(12 multiple-operation arguments) $\times$ (41 subjects) — 10 multiple-operation arguments about which subjects could not

TABLE 19.2
Acceptance Rates for Valid Arguments of
Experiment 11 (N = 41)

	No. accepted	No. rejected	No. cannot decide
Single-operation arguments			
1. $a \subseteq (b \cap c)/a \subseteq b$	34	7	0
2. $(a \cup b) \subseteq c/a \subseteq c$	38	3	0
3. $a \subseteq b/\bar{b} \subseteq \bar{a}$	18	23	0
4. $a \subseteq b/(c \cap a) \subseteq (c \cap b)$	27	14	0
5. $a \subseteq b/(c \cup a) \subseteq (c \cup b)$	22	19	0
6. $a \subseteq b/(c \cap a) \subseteq b$	38	2	1
7. $a \subseteq b/a \subseteq (c \cup b)$	19	22	0
8. $\overline{a \cup b}/\bar{a} \cap \bar{b}$	35	6	0
9. $\overline{a \cap b}/\bar{a} \cup \bar{b}$	32	9	0
10. $a \cap (b \cup c)/(a \cap b) \cup (a \cap c)$	36	5	0
11. $a \cup (b \cap c)/a \cup b$	31	9	1
12. $a \cup b/\bar{a} \subseteq b$	38	3	0
13. $\bar{a} \subseteq b/a \cup b$	36	5	0
14. $a \subseteq b/a \cap \bar{b}$	26	12	3
Total:	430	139	5
Mean:	30.7		
Multiple-operation arguments			
1. $a \subseteq (\bar{b} \cup c)/\bar{a} \subseteq \bar{b}$	23	18	0
2. $(\overline{a \cap b}) \subseteq c/a \cup c$	24	17	0
3. $(a \cup b) \subseteq c/\bar{c} \subseteq (\bar{a} \cap \bar{b})$	24	16	1
4. $a \subseteq (b \cap c)/(\bar{b} \cup \bar{c}) \subseteq \bar{a}$	30	9	2
5. $a \subseteq (b \cap c)/\bar{a} \cap \bar{b}$	22	19	0
6. $a \cup b/(c \cup \bar{a}) \subseteq (c \cup b)$	18	20	3
7. $a \cup b/\bar{a} \subseteq (b \cup c)$	17	24	0
8. $a \cup (b \cap c)/\bar{a} \subseteq b$	32	9	0
9. $a \cup (b \cap c)/(d \cap \bar{a}) \subseteq (d \cap b)$	13	27	1
10. $a \cup (b \cap c)/(d \cap \bar{a}) \subseteq b$	20	20	1
11. $\bar{a} \subseteq (b \cap c)/a \cup b$	32	9	0
12. $a \cap (b \cup c)/(\overline{a \cap b}) \subseteq (a \cap c)$	29	10	2
Total:	284	198	10
Mean:	23.7		
Baseline argument			
$a \subseteq b/a \subseteq b$	41	0	0

TABLE 19.3
Mean Normalized Numerical Assignments for Valid Arguments
of Experiment 11 ($N = 41$)

	Mean normalized numerical assignments	Standard deviations for mean normalized numerical assignments
Single-operation arguments		
1. $a \subseteq (b \cap c)/a \subseteq b$	23.23	21.05
2. $(a \cup b) \subseteq c/a \subseteq c$	22.72	26.10
3. $a \subseteq b/\overline{b} \subseteq \overline{a}$	32.94	30.84
4. $a \subseteq b/(c \cap a) \subseteq (c \cap b)$	50.03	29.16
5. $a \subseteq b/(c \cup a) \subseteq (c \cup b)$	53.04	27.90
6. $a \subseteq b/ (c \cap a) \subseteq b$	26.93	22.41
7. $a \subseteq b/a \subseteq (c \cup b)$	32.36	19.38
8. $\overline{a \cup b}/\overline{a} \cap \overline{b}$	45.99	32.27
9. $\overline{a \cap b}/\overline{a} \cup \overline{b}$	44.16	33.53
10. $a \cap (b \cup c)/(a \cap b) \cup (a \cap c)$	45.10	30.32
11. $a \cup (b \cap c)/a \cup b$	42.87	26.42
12. $a \cup b/\overline{a} \subseteq b$	25.99	25.84
13. $\overline{a} \subseteq b/a \cup b$	36.31	27.45
14. $a \subseteq b/a \cap \overline{b}$	46.58	31.50
Multiple-operation arguments		
1. $a \subseteq (\overline{b} \cup c)/a \subseteq \overline{b}$	31.30	26.28
2. $(\overline{a \cap b}) \subseteq c/a \cup c$	42.78	22.42
3. $(a \cup b) \subseteq c/\overline{c} \subseteq (\overline{a} \cap \overline{b})$	68.13	29.87
4. $a \subseteq (b \cap c)/(\overline{b} \cup \overline{c}) \subseteq \overline{a}$	54.99	29.04
5. $a \subseteq (b \cap c)/\overline{a \cap \overline{b}}$	59.72	27.60
6. $a \cup b/(c \cup \overline{a}) \subseteq (c \cup b)$	76.85	24.78
7. $a \cup b/\overline{a} \subseteq (b \cup c)$	59.31	21.42
8. $a \cup (b \cap c)/\overline{a} \subseteq b$	52.30	30.18
9. $a \cup (b \cap c)/(d \cap \overline{a}) \subseteq (d \cap b)$	69.93	26.15
10. $a \cup (b \cap c)/(d \cap \overline{a}) \subseteq b$	63.89	25.31
11. $\overline{a} \subseteq (b \cap c)/a \cup b$	41.56	23.02
12. $a \cap (b \cup c)/(\overline{a \cap b}) \subseteq (a \cap c)$	59.11	33.98
Baseline argument		
$a \subseteq b/a \subseteq b$	0.00	0.00

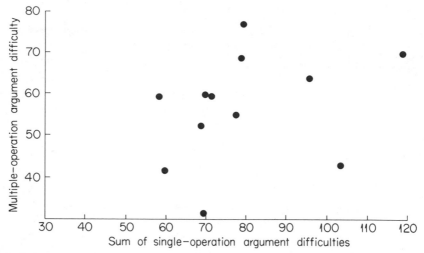

FIG. 19.1. Scatter plot for the additivity analysis of Experiment 11, based on the theory of Table 18.1.

decide]. Of these predictions, 288 or 59.8% are correct. The expected number of true predictions is 265.1 or 53.1%.

2. Additivity analysis.   The within-subject additivity analysis is impractical. The between-subject additivity correlation is only .31 ($N = 12$). Figure 19.1 shows the scatter plot. If we employ derivations based on the alternative theory of Table 11.2, the correlation is slightly lower.

19.5 CONCLUSIONS OF EXPERIMENT 11

The additivity analysis indicates that the mental derivations for the class-inclusion arguments are not isomorphic to the mental derivations for the arguments of Part 2. The results of the inventory analyses are too weak in Experiments 9–11 to alter this conclusion. Thus, the theory of the Appendix is not a special case of a more general mental schematism germane to both propositional and class-inclusion arguments.

Despite strong intuitions about the mental isomorphism of propositional and class-inclusion arguments, our results are difficult to interpret any other way. The arguments were homogeneous in content, and subjects were quite cooperative. Pooling the results of the three class-inclusion experiments gives a correlation of only .58 ($N = 40$). Figure 19.2 shows the scatter plot. One might wish to argue that the mental derivations provided by the theory are correct, but that the class-inclusion content has unpredictable effects on subjects' judgments of argument difficulty. However, besides

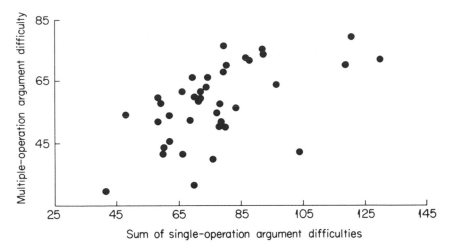

FIG. 19.2.   Scatter plot for the additivity analysis of Experiments 9–11.

being ad hoc, this hypothesis must explain why the additivity correlation of Experiment 9, based on the fragment of the theory in Table 17.1, is so high.

Rather than attempt to rescue the theory for class inclusion in this way, it is more reasonable to conclude that there is only partial overlap in the set of derivations for propositional and class-inclusion arguments. As the results of Volume 2 also showed, the operations in Table 8.1 seem comparable for both logical realms. When further operations are added involving formulas with main connectives other than implication or inclusion, the sets of mental derivations for the two kinds of arguments diverge.

This pattern of results coincides with an interesting difference in the arguments used in the three class-inclusion experiments. Both the premise and conclusion of every argument in Experiment 9 have inclusion as their main connective. This is not true for most of the arguments in the other experiments. Now the inclusion connective has a property not shared by the other class connectives. In translating an argument of the form $(A \subseteq B) = 1$ into English, reference to the universal class, denoted by "1," is unnecessary; it is implicit in the inclusion locution. This is not the case for the other connectives. When something other than inclusion is the main connective of a formula, reference must be made to either the universal class or its negation; otherwise, the expression is not a statement, but a complex term representing a class. In short, inclusion locutions can serve as relations, whereas the other connectives serve only as operations. This difference is apparent from inspection of the arguments used in the three experiments. As we have seen, it was the arguments of Experiment 9 that conformed most closely to the theory of the Appendix (additivity correlation of .84). These arguments had inclusion for the main connective of every premise and conclusion. The two experiments with poor additivity results frequently had main connectives requiring mention of the universal class, 1, or its complement. None of the propositional arguments, of course, included an analog to a universal class or its complement. This difference might be the basis of an explanation for the results of the three class-inclusion experiments. But the details of such an explanation are beyond us at present.

Finally, we wish to stress the utility of theoretical analyses in deciding whether the same or different mental processes underlay evaluation of these two kinds of arguments. The correlation of normalized mean numerical assignments between the valid arguments of Experiment 5 and the present experiment is .75. Had we relied on this rather substantial correlation to decide whether the mental processes are the same, we would have seriously overestimated the extent of commonality. Instead of this nontheoretical correlation, the important correlations stem from the additivity analysis: an additivity correlation of .71 in Experiment 5, and only .31 in the present experiment.

Part IV
FURTHER ISSUES

20

Other Properties of Argument Difficulty and Acceptance Rate

20.1 BETWEEN-SUBJECT CONSISTENCY

Our proposed deduction model attributes a pattern of results to each subject. The pattern specifies the relationship between argument difficulties and between argument acceptances. There are no predictions about individual arguments per se. Thus, subjects can differ in their responses to arguments, even though each conforms to the pattern. This would be another reflection of the fact that superficial differences can obscure deeper similarities (Sections 1.3 and 13.1).

Nonetheless, it is of interest to examine between-subject consistency in the arguments. We consider argument difficulty first. Since different subjects accepted and rejected different arguments (and thus assigned numbers to different arguments), a coefficient of concordance cannot be computed. Instead, we selected five subjects at random from each experiment and intercorrelated their numerical assignments for the valid arguments that they accepted. For each of the ten resulting correlations between pairs of subjects, the number of degrees of freedom is determined by the number of arguments both subjects accepted. This analysis was performed twice for each experiment. There were thus two sets of five randomly selected subjects. Table 20.1 provides the mean correlations for each experiment. Between-subject consistency in scaling is low.

To determine the extent of consistency between subjects with respect to acceptance and rejection of arguments, we also computed phi coefficients for each group of five subjects. The phi coefficient was sometimes meaningless due to empty cells. Excluding these latter coefficients, Table 20.2 shows the median phi correlations for each experiment. Between-subject consistency in the acceptance and rejection of arguments is also low.

TABLE 20.1
Between-Subject Consistency in Argument Difficulty

Experiment	Mean product—moment correlation	
	Group 1	Group 2
1	.52	.51
2 (Session 1)	.51	.59
3	.47	.44
4	.39	.38
5	.50	.29
6	.16	.47
7	.28	.24
8	.30	.48
9	.56	.27
10	.38	.41
11	.39	.13

TABLE 20.2
Between-Subject Consistency in Argument Acceptance

Experiment	Median phi correlation	
	Group 1	Group 2
1	.63	−.11
2 (Session 1)	.03	−.14
3	.25	.09
4	.19	.17
5	.12	.15
6	−.09	−.10
7	.22	.04
8	.11	.20
9	.30	.02
10	.11	.08
11	.21	.05

TABLE 20.3
Correlation of Mean Normalized Numerical Assignment
with Number of Words and with Unsigned Difference
between Number of Words in Premise and
Conclusion for Multiple-Operation Arguments

Experiment	N	Correlation with number of words	Correlation with unsigned difference between number of words in premise and conclusion
1	16	.73	−.49
2 (Session 1)	16	.72	−.62
3	17	.67	.09
4	12	.63	−.02
5	12	.64	.36
6	16	.33	−.33
7	12	.49	.56
8	12	.42	.47
9	16	.73	.50
10	12	.62	−.15
11	12	.70	.19

20.2 NUMBER OF WORDS IN AN ARGUMENT RELATED TO DIFFICULTY

Section 8.3 presented evidence infirming the hypothesis that subjects relied on the number of words in an argument to judge argument difficulty. In addition, argument difficulty does not consistently correlate highly with the length of an argument in words. Table 20.3 shows the correlation in each experiment between the number of words in a multiple-operation argument and its mean normalized numerical assignment.[1] The low correlation for some of the experiments, along with the data of Section 8.3, rules out a causal connection between word length and argument difficulty. That all the correlations in Table 20.3 are positive is likely due to the fact that complicated arguments, that is, those with numerous and difficult operations,

[1] We use only the multiple-operation arguments in these correlations in order to make them comparable to the additivity correlation. The additivity analysis can be thought of as an attempt to predict the difficulty of the multiple-operation arguments from the difficulty of combinations of single-operation arguments theoretically related to them. The correlations reported in the present section and in the next attempt to predict the difficulty of multiple-operation arguments by other means.

are expressed in natural language with more words. Finally, if the length in words of the multiple-operation arguments are substituted for their mean normalized numerical assignment, the additivity correlations based on the theory of the Appendix are invariably lower, sometimes by more than 65 points.

The difficulty of arguments also cannot be predicted by the difference in the number of words between premise and conclusion. Table 20.3 shows the correlation for each experiment between the mean normalized numerical assignment of each multiple-operation argument and the unsigned difference in number of words between the arguments' premise(s) and conclusion. Using the signed difference weakens these correlations further.

Suppose we represent each argument with the notation of propositional logic or the logic of classes (as in the tables enumerating experimental arguments). The number of symbols in the schema associated with an argument does not predict its difficulty, nor does the unsigned (or signed) difference in number of symbols between premise(s) and conclusion predict argument difficulty. Table 20.4 documents this by providing the relevant correlations for each experiment with respect to the multiple-operation arguments.

TABLE 20.4

Correlation of Mean Normalized Numerical Assignment
with Number of Symbols and with Unsigned Difference
between Number of Symbols in Premise and
Conclusion for Multiple-Operation Arguments

Experiment	N	Correlation with number of symbols	Correlation with unsigned difference between number of symbols in premise and conclusion
1	16	.52	−.56
2 (Session 1)	16	.50	−.66
3	17	.55	−.26
4	12	.44	−.06
5	12	.40	.21
6	16	.51	−.48
7	12	.24	.06
8	12	.11	.12
9	16	.67	.45
10	12	.35	−.31
11	12	.54	.27

20.3 TRUTH TABLES

It is of some interest to determine whether the size of an argument's truth table is related to its difficulty (cf. Section 3.3). Results reported in Volume 2 (Chapter 4) cast doubt on that possibility.

We shall employ the following method for constructing truth tables.[2] All of the propositional arguments have either the form A/B or $A,C/B$, where A, B, and C are formulas. For the former kind of argument we construct the formula $A \rightarrow B$; for the latter kind of argument we construct the formula $A \rightarrow (C \rightarrow B)$. In either case, each symbol, except parentheses, dominate a column of the truth table. For example, the argument

$$(p \lor q) \rightarrow r$$
$$\frac{-r}{-p}$$

is transformed into the formula $((p \lor q) \rightarrow r) \rightarrow (-r \rightarrow -p)$, whose truth table is:

$$((p \lor q) \rightarrow r) \rightarrow (-r \rightarrow -p)$$

t t t	t t	t	f t t	f t
t t t	f f	t	t f f	f t
t t f	t t	t	f t t	f t
t t f	f f	t	t f f	f t
f t t	t t	t	f t t	t f
f t t	f f	t	t f t	t f
f f f	t t	t	f t t	t f
f f f	t f	t	t f t	t f

This table has 88 entries. Tables for the other arguments are constructed similarly.

Table 20.5 shows the correlation between the number of truth table entries of a multiple-operation argument and the argument's mean normalized numerical assignment in Experiments 1–8. There is little relationship. Other kinds of truth tables can be constructed, but they are unlikely to yield much better results.

20.4 THE RELATIONSHIP BETWEEN ACCEPTANCE RATE AND DIFFICULTY OF ARGUMENTS

Table 20.6 shows the correlation in each experiment between the acceptance rate of multiple-operation arguments and their mean normalized

[2] The class-inclusion arguments are excluded from the present analysis.

TABLE 20.5

Correlation of Mean Normalized Numerical Assignment
with Number of Entries in Truth Table for
Multiple-Operation Arguments

Experiment	N	Correlation with number of entries in truth table
1	16	−.09
2 (Session 1)	16	−.02
3	17	.64
4	12	.61
5	12	.45
6	16	.15
7	12	.41
8	12	.36

numerical assignment. These two variables are largely unrelated. This supports the idea that subjects' judgments in the sorting procedure were "principled": They were not labeling an argument invalid simply because they found it too complex to judge. If they were using the latter criterion, then we would expect that arguments generally considered difficult would be most often rejected. Consistent with the idea that rejections were principled is the low rate of CANNOT DECIDE responses during the sorting procedure. Arguments rejected on grounds of overwhelming complexity would be sorted into the CANNOT DECIDE category. But there were many more rejected arguments than arguments about which subjects could not decide.

TABLE 20.6

Correlation between Mean Normalized Numerical Assignment
and Accept Rate for Multiple-Operation Arguments

Experiment	Correlation	Experiment	Correlation
1	−.09	6	−.51
2 (Session 1)	−.46	7	−.41
2 (Session 2)	−.31	8	−.61
3	−.16	9	.12
4	−.67	10	−.64
5	.02	11	−.51

We are thus led to different conclusions than those reached in Volume 2 (Sections 6.5, 11.4). In Volume 2 we decided that subjects' decisions not to accept an argument were due to information overload rather than to an absence of required operations. This is still possible, given that the subjects in Volume 2 were younger than subjects dealt with here. But the present results suggest otherwise.

21

Some Remaining Theoretical Issues

21.1   WHY DO SUBJECTS REJECT ARGUMENTS?

We return to the question posed in Section 5.3. How shall subjects' rejections of arguments that are given derivations by the theory be interpreted? Only principled rejections are at issue. Responses of CANNOT DECIDE are best ascribed to computational overload of some nature. One possible reason for a principled rejection of an argument is that one or more of the operations required for that argument do not exist in the subjects' logical competence. We now explore the empirical consequences of this hypothesis. For the moment, it is not important whether the reason for the missing operation is the one proposed in Section 5.3. The latter proposal is taken up again at the end of the present section.

Let $\langle \mathbf{o}_1, \ldots, \mathbf{o}_n \rangle$ be the ordered set of operations of a deduction model. Each operation is associated with a helping condition. Suppose that operation $\mathbf{o}_i$ constitutes an invalid logical transformation from the point of view of a given subject. Operation $\mathbf{o}_i$ thus does not appear in the mental derivation of any argument accepted by this subject. Instead of representing his logical abilities by the full model $\langle \mathbf{o}_1, \ldots, \mathbf{o}_n \rangle$, we are led to the truncated model $\langle \mathbf{o}_1, \ldots, \mathbf{o}_{i-1}, \mathbf{o}_{i+1}, \ldots, \mathbf{o}_n \rangle$, on the hypothesis that $\mathbf{o}_i$ simply does not exist in this subject's logical competence. The truncated model represents our hypothetical subject's logical competence as well as does the full model; it will provide derivations for no fewer arguments that he accepts than does the complete model, for our subject will reject the single-operation argument $\{\mathbf{o}_i\}$ as well as any multiple-operation argument that requires $\mathbf{o}_i$.

Now let us ask which multiple-operation arguments require operation $\mathbf{o}_i$. We must not be misled by our notation into the answer "Any argument of the form $\{\mathbf{o}_{\alpha_1}, \ldots, \mathbf{o}_i, \ldots, \mathbf{o}_{\alpha_m}\}$." This answer is based on an equivocation.

246

According to the conventions of Section 5.1, the complex symbol $\{o_{\alpha_1}, \ldots,$ $o_i, \ldots, o_{\alpha_m}\}$ refers to the argument given the derivation $o_{\alpha_1}, \ldots, o_i, \ldots,$ o_{α_m} by the full model $\langle o_1, \ldots, o_n \rangle$.[1] For neutrality, call this argument: Argument A. Since derivations are unique within any deduction model (see Remark 4 of Section 4.2), operation o_i is required, in a trivial sense, for the derivation of Argument A within the model $\langle o_1, \ldots, o_n \rangle$. But this does not imply that operation o_i is required for the derivation of Argument A within any deduction model. In particular, it would be misleading to designate Argument A by $\{o_{\alpha_1}, \ldots, o_i, \ldots, o_{\alpha_m}\}$ when considering the deductive power of the truncated model $\langle o_1, \ldots, o_{i-1}, o_{i+1}, \ldots, o_n \rangle$: Argument A may have a derivation within the truncated model, and thus not require the presence of o_i in order to be accepted.

Given the existence of a derivation for Argument A within the theory $\langle o_1, \ldots, o_{i-1}, o_{i+1}, \ldots, o_n \rangle$, we have a different empirical prediction than before concerning subjects' acceptance of A. Our former inventory prediction was that subjects accept Argument A if and only if they accept each of the single-operation arguments $\{o_{\alpha_1}\}, \ldots, \{o_{\alpha_m}\}$, where the derivation of A within the theory $\langle o_1, \ldots, o_n \rangle$ is based on $o_{\alpha_1}, \ldots, o_{\alpha_m}$. Our revised inventory requirement is more general. It says that a subject who accepts single-operation arguments $\{o_{\beta_1}\}, \ldots, \{o_{\beta_k}\}$ from the theory $\langle o_1, \ldots, o_n \rangle$ will accept Argument A if and only if a derivation for Argument A is provided by the theory $\langle o_{\beta_1}, \ldots, o_{\beta_k} \rangle$, where the o_{β_i}'s are ordered relative to one another the same as in $\langle o_1, \ldots, o_n \rangle$. For example, if the theory $\langle o_{\beta_1}, \ldots, o_{\beta_k} \rangle$ is the same as $\langle o_1, \ldots, o_n \rangle$ except for the absence of o_i, then a subject will accept Argument A in light of our assumption that the theory $\langle o_1, \ldots, o_{i-1}, o_{i+1}, \ldots,$ $o_n \rangle$ provides a derivation for Argument A. Of course, by the same reasoning as before, possession of the operations $o_{\beta_1}, \ldots, o_{\beta_k}$ may not be a necessary condition for accepting Argument A, since yet another derivation may be possible without some of the o_{β_i}'s. Similar considerations apply to the additivity requirement.

The new inventory prediction is false, as we shall shortly argue. So it is important to see how we came to it. The crucial assumption was this: An operation that does not occur in any of a subject's mental derivations has no functional existence for that subject. Given a true deduction model $\langle o_1, \ldots,$ $o_n \rangle$ for a population of subjects, the assumption is that a subject who gives evidence of missing operation o_i (by dint of rejecting $\{o_i\}$), is fully characterized by the model $\langle o_1, \ldots, o_{i-1}, o_{i+1}, \ldots, o_n \rangle$.

The evidence leading to the rejection of this assumption comes from Experiments 4 and 5. Assume that the theory of Table 11.1 is correct, as the data of these experiments indicate. In Experiment 4, the derivation

---

[1] We ignore the complication mentioned in Footnote 1 of Chapter 5 that there is a many-to-one mapping of arguments into sets of operations that are involved in their derivation.

TABLE 21.1

Operations Underlying the Derivations of Six Multiple-Operation
Arguments from Experiments 4 and 5, According to the Theory of
Table 11.1, and According to Truncated Versions of that Theory

Argument	Original derivation	Missing operation	New derivation
$p \vee (q \& r)/$			
$-p \rightarrow (q \vee s)$	2, 12, 11	2	12, 5, 11
$p \vee (q \& r)/$			
$(-p \vee s) \rightarrow (q \vee s)$	2, 12, 9	2	12, 5, 9
$p \vee (q \& r)/$			
$-p \rightarrow q$	2, 12	2	12, 5
$p \vee (q \& r)/$			
$(-p \& s) \rightarrow (q \& s)$	2, 12, 8	2	12, 5, 8
$p \vee (q \& r)/$			
$(-p \& s) \rightarrow r$	2, 12, 10	2	12, 5, 10
$-p \rightarrow (q \& r)/$			
$p \vee q$	5, 13	5	13, 2

of multiple-operation Argument (10) makes use of Operations (2), (12),
and (9) from the theory of Table 11.1. However, if Operation (2) were
missing, the truncated theory would still provide a derivation for Argument
(10) by means of Operations (12), (5), and (9), in that order.[2] The
reader may verify this by examining the ordering and helping conditions
of the operations of Table 11.1 when Operation (2) is expunged. The
same situation obtains for five other multiple-operation arguments in Experiments 4 and 5. The relevant information is given in Table 21.1. Now
consider those subjects in Experiment 4 who rejected the single-operation
argument based on Operation (2), but accepted those based on Operations
(12), (5), and (9). There are nine such subjects. According to the original
formulation of the inventory prediction, we expect these nine subjects to
reject the multiple-operation Argument (10), for want of Operation (2);
this, in spite of the sufficiency of Operations (12), (5), and (9). According
to the revised inventory prediction, we expect these nine subjects to accept
multiple-operation Argument (10), despite the lack of Operation (2),
since Operations (12), (5), and (9) produce a derivation for Argument
(10) within the truncated model that lacks Operation (2). In fact, all nine

[2] In fact, this is just the derivation given for this argument by the theory of Table
11.2.

subjects rejected Argument (10), disconfirming the revised inventory prediction.

The same analysis was carried out for the remaining five arguments of Table 21.1. The results are the same as for Argument (10) of Experiment 4, although not always as striking. Overall, the revised inventory predictions are fulfilled only 25% of the time (hence, the original inventory predictions are fulfilled 75% of the time). In each case, the number of true, revised, inventory predictions is less than the number to be expected on the basis of the acceptance rate for the multiple-operation argument in question over all subjects in those experiments. On the basis of this evidence, we reaffirm our inventory (and additivity) predictions: The derivations provided by the deduction model proposed in this volume are both necessary and sufficient for accepting arguments they underlie, not just sufficient.

So, an operation that does not appear in any argument accepted by a given subject has not simply vanished. Rather, it is better thought of as "defective": It applies during a mental derivation that normally calls for it, but it applies in such a way as to send the derivation irretrievably down the wrong path. As explained in Chapter 4, a derivation that ends in a blind alley is labeled invalid by the subject. To be more specific, one way to account for the data reported in this section is to assume that a defective operation has the same left-hand formula and the same helping condition as its nondefective counterpart. It is the right-hand formula of the defective operation that differs. For example, the defective version of the operation $-(A \vee B)/-A \mathbin{\&} -B$ with the helping condition as given in Table 11.1 might be $-(A \vee B)/-A \vee -B$, with the same helping condition. Since the left-hand sides and the helping conditions of the defective and nondefective operations are identical to each other, the defective operation will be brought to bear in a mental derivation whenever the nondefective operation would have applied. The nature of the right-hand side of the defective operation, however, makes it unlikely that the resulting derivation will terminate in the desired conclusion.[3] The executive routine exits with a decision of invalid, as is the normal procedure when no further operations are both legal and helpful, and the question of alternative derivations within a truncated list of operations never arises.[4]

---

[3] It is unlikely that the derivation will find its way to the desired conclusion once the defective operation has applied, but it is not logically impossible that it will do so. Much depends on (a) what other operations, defective and nondefective, are available, (b) the helping conditions of other operations, and (c) the form of the right-hand side of the defective operation. Our proposal is not precise enough to determine when, if ever, a derivation for a given argument will be constructed despite a defective operation.

[4] The terms "defective" and "wrong" are not to be taken normatively. To say that an operation is defective is to say no more than that it does not occur in our "official" deduction model.

The defective-operation hypothesis is compatible with the conceptual analysis of the soundness requirement given in Section 5.3. In Section 5.3 we argued that principled rejections of arguments validated by the theory result from a difference between subject and model in the interpretation given to logical words in the argument; that is, for at least one logical connective, the subject has in mind a meaning that is inconsistent with the behavior of that connective within the "official" model's operations. To ascribe to a subject an operation that employs a logical connective, *, in a manner incompatible with the behavior of * in the official model (i.e., to ascribe to a subject a "defective" operation) is tantamount to crediting the subject with a different meaning for the natural language counterpart of *.

The claims of Section 5.3 thus receive further support. However, potentially troublesome questions immediately arise. Are there defective operations whose right sides are identical to nondefective counterparts, but whose left sides differ (rather than vice versa)? Can a defective operation exist without supplanting a nondefective one? If a defective operation has a different right-hand side than before, what prevents it from having an appropriately reformulated helping condition as well? Do defective operations lead to the acceptance of arguments labeled invalid by the standard model? Can a subject possess a meaning for a logical connective such that certain operations would in fact vanish without a trace? What, in general, are the limitations on the way that subjects construe logical vocabulary?[5] To these questions, we have no convincing answers.

21.2   THE PROBLEM OF EQUIVALENT
DEDUCTION MODELS

Every scientific theory is underdetermined by the data that supports it. The derivations generated by our model conform to the additivity and inventory requirements, but other derivations for the same arguments may do as well or better. Further test of the proposed model with new arguments may lead to its abandonment even without the existence of a superior one to replace it. This much uncertainty is intrinsic to an empirical enterprise.

As developed in this volume, however, deduction models like ours are open to a more pernicious kind of underdetermination than the garden variety just mentioned. All of the empirical constraint on theory construction is focused on the model's derivations; the operations and executive are tested only through the derivations they produce. The formulation of the additivity and

---

[5] That there must be some limits is evident from an argument attributed to Prior (1967). See Section 21.3.

inventory requirements in Chapter 5 make this clear. Consequently, two deduction models that produce the same derivations for the same arguments, no matter how distinct otherwise, are empirically indistinguishable from the viewpoint of the additivity and inventory requirements. Moreover, it is easy to construct new deduction models that are equivalent in this sense to the model summarized in the Appendix. For example, there are pairs of operations that may be interchanged in the ordering with minimal affect on the resulting derivations. The commutativity operations A & B/B & A and $A \vee B/B \vee A$ are such a pair. At most, it seems, this change will affect the substitution instances of transformations that apply in a derivation. But we saw in Chapter 9 that the data do not allow us to determine which substitution instance of an operation has applied in a derivation, but only whether some substitution instance of that operation has applied. Less trivially than the commutativity example, it is clear that complementary changes in the ordering and helping conditions of our operations will result in alternative deduction models that produce the same derivations as the original model. More radical changes are also possible without disturbing the derivations. These alternatives are empirically indistinguishable so far as the additivity and inventory requirements are concerned.[6]

What makes this kind of underdetermination irksome is that it reduces a deduction model to a mere time-saver: the content of the theory is the set of derivations it provides, and it is simply easier to present a deduction model from which the derivations can be deduced than to present them in a list. Since the number of propositional logic arguments that can be evaluated intuitively is for all intents and purposes finite, the set of required derivations is also finite, and hence the deduction model is in principle eliminable. It will not suffice to reply that the deduction model is more "elegant" or "simple" than a list of derivations. The elegance of a deduction model is small consolation for abandoning the goal we have set ourselves, namely, to determine the order and nature of the decisions a person makes in evaluating an inference. A system that gives correct derivations by means of a set of decisions that is indifferent to the real-time mental events that it mimics is likely to be of restricted psychological interest. What distinguishes present-day psychology from much of philosophy, linguistics, and artificial intelligence is its concern for mental processes. Systems that are simply coextensive with human intuition are of intrinsic value and demand the attention of psychologists for a variety of reasons. But such

---

[6] Needless to say, the more arguments for which a model can provide psychologically accurate derivations, the more highly valued is that model, other things being equal. Thus, we prefer a model M_1 to a model M_2 if all the derivations provided by M_2 are provided by M_1, and there are psychologically accurate derivations that M_1 provides that are not forthcoming from M_2.

systems are not yet psychological theories, in one good sense of the word "psychological."[7]

What are wanted, then, are empirical criteria for choosing between equivalent deduction models so that the preferred model is likely to have greater fidelity to the processes by which people construct derivations. It is difficult to give such criteria, however. Introspective evidence seems to be unavailable (introspection about mental derivations is uncertain enough). On the other hand, the following kind of experiment may be envisioned. Suppose a deduction model posits three operations, o_i, o_j, o_k, ordered as given. Then, application of o_j in a mental derivation requires that o_i be examined for legality and helpfulness (and rejected), whereas o_k undergoes no such examination. This asymmetry between o_i and o_k might be reflected in "transfer" from the argument $\{o_j\}$ to the argument $\{o_i\}$ and no such transfer from argument $\{o_j\}$ to argument $\{o_k\}$. (A few obvious control experiments would be required.) Such experiments have not been performed, but it is difficult to be optimistic about the information one might gain from them.

In lieu of empirical criteria linked directly to psychological processes, we may hope to distinguish equivalent deduction models by criteria that are concerned with "simplicity," but from a psychological perspective. The mental mechanism responsible for logical judgment conforms to the limitations of a finite nervous system. We may be justly suspicious of a deduction model whose formulation is long and cumbersome, especially when a simpler equivalent is available (cf. Section 13.3). Within certain limits, our best guess about the actual device for constructing mental derivations is that it is not needlessly complex. For example, given equivalent deduction models, we should value more highly the one with fewer operations. Again, other things equal, we should prefer a deduction model whose helping conditions are short and general, for example, for a given operation, we should prefer the helping condition "C occurs in the conclusion," to "either $C \& D$ or $-C \vee -D$ occurs in the conclusion." How to make such requirements explicit, as well as how seriously to take them altogether, must remain open questions at present.

21.3   LIMITATIONS ON THE EXPLANATORY ADEQUACY OF DEDUCTION MODELS

Even putting aside the difficulty discussed in the last section, it is important to see that the present approach to logical judgment is drastically incomplete. As indicated in Section 8.6, deduction models provide a nonreductionist

---

[7] It should be evident that the argument of Chapter 13 regarding cognitive development, content of arguments, inferential generality, and so forth, is untouched by the question of the psychological reality of our deduction model. The inventory and additivity analyses provide evidence for the psychological reality of the model's derivations, and this is all that is required for the purposes of Chapter 13.

account of logical intuition. This approach might be termed *synthetic;* the reductionist approach, *analytic.* These approaches are complementary. The model of the Appendix, if true, places conditions on any reductionist explanation of the operations and executive. The explanation must allow, and hopefully require, the mental derivations specified by our model. Similarly, a true reductionist account of the properties of the operations and executive conditions the set of derivations generated by a proposed deduction model.

In another terminology, our model at best provides a "syntactic" account of logical judgment. We need also to investigate the psychological "semantics" of our operations and executive that determine the role they play in generating derivations. To see the importance of the semantic side of a theory of logical judgment, consider a question that is related, once again, to the problem of soundness. What distinguishes operations that reflect inferences that subjects honor from operations that reflect inferences that subjects reject? The answer can be found, it seems, only in the meaning of the logical connectives contained in the operations (cf. Sections 5.3 and 21.1). This explanation is true regardless of whether the meanings of these connectives are represented in subjects' spontaneous vocabularies, or whether the meanings are partially determined by instructions from the experimenter (see Sections 5.3 and 6.2). Yet, the present syntactic approach has little to contribute to the problem of representing and explaining the meaning of logical connectives. We believe that it is incorrect to maintain that the operations that are discovered in a subject's logical competence *constitute* the meaning of the connectives they contain; that is, we believe that it is insufficient to characterize the meaning of a connective by describing its role in the premises and conclusions of simple deduction rules, as logical "and" is sometimes characterized by the inference rules

$A, B/A$ and $B,$
A and $B/A,$

and

A and B/B

The argument against the sufficiency of such a characterization is given by Prior (1967). Prior points out that if this were all to giving the meaning of a connective, then nothing prevents a logician from defining a connective "tonk" by the rules

(i) A/A tonk B
(ii) A tonk B/B

The unfortunate result of such a definition is that any proposition, p, implies any other, q, since p implies p tonk q by (i), p tonk q implies q by (ii), so by transitivity of inference, p implies q. Since this result is untenable, there must not be such a connective as "tonk," with the properties (i) and (ii). Consequently, it will not suffice to define a connective purely in terms of the inferences in which it has a role. As Prior (1967) suggests, "an expression must have some independently determined meaning before we can discover whether inferences involving it are valid or invalid [pp. 129–130]."[8] Deduction models, per se, do not specify the meaning of logical connectives independently of the operations that include them; hence the need for a complementary semantic approach.[9] But what will this complementary approach look like?[10]

[8] Belnap (1967) replies to Prior. Belnap relies on the notion of conservative extension to legitimate the definition of "and" given above while ruling Prior's definition of "tonk" out of bounds. However, the notion of conservative extension presupposes the set of all valid deductions. But it is the latter set that needs explanation in the first place.

It might be suggested that A & B differs from A tonk B in that only the former can be given a truth-table characterization that is consistent with its deductive properties. This suggestion comes as no surprise, since the notion of a truth-table characterization presupposes the concepts of *and*, *or*, and *not*, but not *tonk*. For example, we say of the truth table for p & q that "&" dominates a "t" in all but only those rows in which p *and* q dominate "t's." (It will not help to reply that we need not say anything, but only point to the relevant rows of the truth table, for this leaves unanswered the question of how to interpret the information.) The difficulty is that if we had this kind of antecedent understanding of *tonk*, we might similarly be able to construct tables that would express the truth conditions of p tonk q in terms of the truth of its constituent propositions. To understand this point more clearly, note that in a standard truth table, if v and v' are truth-values in the same row, and p dominates v and q dominates v', then for that row p is assigned the truth-value v, *and q* is assigned the truth-value v'. In a tonkish truth table, under the same conditions, for that row p is assigned the truth-value v, *tonk q* is assigned the truth-value v'. In addition, we may state a condition parallel to that for "&" stated above: in the truth table for p tonk q, "tonk" dominates a "t" in all but only those rows in which p tonk q dominate "t's." That such conditions are not translatable into the vocabulary of "and," "or," and "not" does not argue for the illegitimacy of "tonk" any more than it argues for the illegitimacy of "and," "or," and "not."

[9] If the model of the Appendix is correct, then one constraint on the semantics of its conditional is that it does conform to some of the "paradoxes" of implication. The present model generates the arguments $p \rightarrow q/-(p \& -q)$, $-(p \& -q)/p \rightarrow q$, and $-p \vee q/p \rightarrow q$. With a slight adjustment, it will also generate $p \rightarrow q/-p \vee q$. If some of these arguments do not seem intuitively valid, we suggest that they often do not seem intuitively invalid either. Rather, their derivations may be too long for the limitations of logical intuition. Indeed, the model assigns comparatively long derivations to some of them. Hence, some of the remarks in Osherson (1975) appear now to be incorrect.

[10] Katz's (1972) theory offers a comprehensive framework for investigating the structure of concepts that give them their logical properties. Despite its importance to psychologists (see Savin, 1973), however, Katz's theory is a formal reconstruction of competence only. It may not bear a direct connection to the psychological processes underlying logical judgment.

21.4 THE RANGE OF LOGICAL INTUITION

A person engages in inference when he takes the truth of one or more statements to sustain the truth of another. People recognize a broad range of inferential connections. The following is a sample:

(a) If equal length sticks are concatenated to the ends of unequal length sticks, the inequality is preserved.

(b) If there exists someone who is either tall or polite, then either there exists someone who is tall or there exists someone who is polite.

(c) If someone is a bachelor, then he is unmarried.

(d) If the law of gravitation necessarily holds, then it is not possible for the law of gravitation not to hold.

(e) If either Harry will arrive or Bill will arrive, then if Harry does not arrive, then Bill will.

(f) If a number x is less than a number y, and z is a positive number, then x is less than $y + z$.

(g) If situation S_1 implies that situation S_2 obtains, and situation S_1 always obtains, then so does situation S_2.

(h) If one class is included in another, then the complement of the latter is included in the complement of the former.

(i) If it is obligatory to show your ticket to the conductor, then it is permissible to do so.

These arguments represent different kinds of deductive inference. Within each kind, there are very many arguments whose validity we can judge. Not represented are the various forms of inductive inference, as well as other kinds of deductive arguments.

The model of the Appendix applies to only a fragment of the arguments whose validity rests on simple propositions [like Inference (e)]. We saw in Chapters 17–19 that it cannot be easily extended into the logic of classes. Our model is therefore of extremely restricted scope. Still, it may allow us to begin to answer the developmental questions that motivate our inquiry.

Appendix:

A Full Statement of the Theory

The operations discussed in Part II are brought together and ordered in this Appendix. The 59 multiple-operation arguments used to test the theory are given derivations within this system. Due to considerations of Sections 8.6 and 11.1, Footnote 2, some of these derivations do not precisely match those given earlier, since earlier derivations did not always include psychologically primitive operations. The derivations given herein are "official."

Two of the multiple-operation arguments derived here served as single-operation arguments for the theory of Table 8.1. Recall that this latter theory was found to contain two operations that are not psychologically primitive (see Chapter 8). Also, Operations (15) and (16) are given more complete helping conditions than before, as indicated in Section 4.2, Footnote 4. Yet even these are not fully adequate.

As we have stressed throughout, the theory is neither logically nor psychologically complete. The reader can best understand the theory's limitations by using it to construct new derivations. Remember that the helping conditions should be interpreted strictly.

1. $A \& B/A$

A subformula of A occurs in the conclusion, with no subformula of B conjoined to it.

2. $A \& B/B$

A subformula of B occurs in the conclusion, with no subformula of A conjoined to it.

3. $A \& B / B \& A$

A and B occur in reverse order in the conclusion (not necessarily conjoined or disjoined to each other), or, if only one appears, B [A] occurs to the immediate right [left] of a connective that A [B] occurred to the immediate right [left] of in l_i. (Bracketed material provides an alternative helping condition.) Applies to subformulas.

4. $A \vee B / B \vee A$

A and B occur in reverse order in the conclusion (not necessarily conjoined or disjoined to each other), or, if only one appears, B [A] occurs to the immediate right [left] of a connective that A [B] occurred to the immediate right [left] of in l_i. (Bracketed material provides an alternative helping condition.) Applies to subformulas.

5. $A \& (B \vee C) / (A \& B) \vee (A \& C)$

Either $(A \& B)$ or $(A \& C)$ occurs in the conclusion. Applies to subformulas.

6. $A \vee (B \& C) / A \vee B$

No subformula of C occurs conjoined to B in the conclusion.

7. $(A \& B) \vee C / A \vee C$

No subformula of B occurs conjoined to A in the conclusion.

8. $--A / A$

A occurs in the conclusion, under the scopes of two fewer negations than in line l_i. Applies to subformulas.

9. $-A \vee -C / -(A \& C)$

$-(A \& C)$ occurs in the conclusion. Applies to subformulas.

10. $-(A \vee B) / -A \& -B$

A subformula of A [B] occurs in the conclusion, not disjoined to B [A]. (Bracketed material provides an alternative helping condition.) Applies to subformulas.

11. $-(A \& B) / -A \vee -B$

A subformula of A [B] occurs in the conclusion, not conjoined to B [A]. (Bracketed material provides an alternative helping condition.) Applies to subformulas.

12. $A \rightarrow (B \& C)/A \rightarrow B$

No subformula of C occurs conjoined to B in the conclusion, and no subformula of C' occurs disjoined to B' in the conclusion, where B' equals B with changed sign, and C' equals C with changed sign.

13. $(A \vee B) \rightarrow C/A \rightarrow C$

No subformula of B occurs disjoined to A in the conclusion, and no subformula of B' occurs conjoined to A' in the conclusion, where A' equals A with changed sign, and B' equals B with changed sign.

14. $A \rightarrow B/-B \rightarrow -A$

A subformula of A and a subformula of B occur in the conclusion, each with a changed sign.

15. $A \rightarrow B/(A \& C) \rightarrow B$

Either of the following holds:
(a) $(A \& F)$ occurs in the conclusion, for some formula F. Then C equals F in line l_{i+1}.
(b) $-(A' \vee F)$ occurs in the conclusion, for some formula F, where A' equals A with changed sign. Then C equals $-F$ in line l_{i+1}.

16. $A \rightarrow B/A \rightarrow (B \vee C)$

Either of the following holds:
(a) $(B \vee F)$ occurs in the conclusion, for some formula F. Then C equals F in line l_{i+1}.
(b) $-(B' \& F)$ occurs in the conclusion, for some formula F, where B' equals B with changed sign. Then C equals $-F$ in line l_{i+1}.

17. $(A \& B) \rightarrow C/(A \& B) \rightarrow (C \& B)$

$(C \& B)$ occurs in the conclusion.

18. $A \rightarrow (B \vee C)/(A \vee C) \rightarrow (B \vee C)$

$(A \vee C)$ occurs in the conclusion.

19. $A/A \vee B$

Any of the following holds:
(a) The conclusion has the form $A \vee F$, for some formula F. Then B equals F in line l_{i+1}.

(b) The conclusion has the form $-A \rightarrow F$, for some formula F. Then B equals F in line l_{i+1}.

(c) The conclusion has the form $-F \rightarrow A$, for some formula F. Then B equals F in line l_{i+1}.

(d) The conclusion has the form $-(A' \& F)$, for some formula F, where A' equals A with changed sign. Then B equals $-F$ in line l_{i+1}.

20. $A \lor B / -A \rightarrow B$

A subformula of A occurs in the conclusion under the scope of a changed sign, this occurrence being within the antecedent of a conditional whose consequent contains a subformula of B. Applies to subformulas.

21. $-A \rightarrow B / A \lor B$

A subformula of A and a subformula of B occur disjoined to each other in the conclusion. Applies to subformulas.

22. $A \rightarrow B / -(A \& -B)$

A and $-B$ occur in the conclusion conjoined to each other, the conjunction occurring under the scope of a negation. Applies to subformulas.

MULTIPLE-OPERATION ARGUMENTS APPEARING IN THE EXPERIMENTS

$p \& -(q \lor r)$		$-(p \lor -q)$	
$-(q \lor r)$	2	$-p \& --q$	10
$-q \& -r$	10	$--q$	2
$-r$	2	q	8
$p \lor (q \& r)$			
$p \lor q$	6	$-(p \lor q)$	
$-p \rightarrow q$	20	$-p \& -q$	10
		$-p$	1
$-(p \lor -q)$		$-p \lor r$	19
$-p \& --q$	10		
$-p \& q$	8	$-(p \lor q)$	
		$-p \& -q$	10
$-(p \& -q)$		$-p$	1
$-p \lor --q$	11	$-p \lor -r$	19
$-p \lor q$	8	$-(p \& r)$	9

$p \,\&\, q$	
p	1
$p \lor r$	19
$-(p \lor q)$	
$-(q \lor p)$	4
$-q \,\&\, -p$	10
$-(p \,\&\, q)$	
$-(q \,\&\, p)$	3
$-q \lor -p$	11
$-(p \,\&\, q)$	
$-p \lor -q$	11
$--p \to -q$	20
$p \to -q$	8
$-p \lor q$	
$--p \to q$	20
$p \to q$	8
$p \,\&\, (q \lor r)$	
$p \,\&\, (r \lor q)$	4
$(p \,\&\, r) \lor (p \,\&\, q)$	5
$-[p \lor (q \,\&\, r)]$	
$-p \,\&\, -(q \,\&\, r)$	10
$-(q \,\&\, r)$	2
$-q \lor -r$	11
$-[p \,\&\, (q \lor r)]$	
$-p \lor -(q \lor r)$	11
$-p \lor (-q \,\&\, -r)$	10
$-p \lor -q$	6
$p \lor (q \,\&\, r)$	
$p \lor (r \,\&\, q)$	3
$p \lor r$	6
$-(p \lor q)$	
$-p \,\&\, -q$	10
$-q$	2

$p \to (q \,\&\, r)$	
$p \to q$	12
$-q \to -p$	14
$(p \lor q) \to r$	
$p \to r$	13
$-r \to -p$	14
$p \to q$	
$-q \to -p$	14
$(-q \,\&\, r) \to -p$	15
$p \to q$	
$-q \to -p$	14
$-q \to (-p \lor r)$	16
$p \to q$	
$-q \to -p$	14
$(-q \,\&\, r) \to -p$	15
$(-q \,\&\, r) \to (-p \,\&\, r)$	17
$p \to q$	
$-q \to -p$	14
$-q \to (-p \lor r)$	16
$(-q \lor r) \to (-p \lor r)$	18
$(p \lor q) \to (r \,\&\, s)$	
$(p \lor q) \to r$	12
$p \to r$	13
$p \to (q \,\&\, r)$	
$p \to q$	12
$(p \,\&\, s) \to q$	15
$p \to (q \,\&\, r)$	
$p \to q$	12
$p \to (q \lor s)$	16
$p \to (q \,\&\, r)$	
$p \to q$	12
$(p \,\&\, s) \to q$	15
$(p \,\&\, s) \to (q \,\&\, s)$	17

$p \to (q \,\&\, r)$	
$p \to q$	12
$p \to (q \lor s)$	16
$(p \lor s) \to (q \lor s)$	18
$(p \lor q) \to r$	
$p \to r$	13
$(p \,\&\, s) \to r$	15
$(p \lor q) \to r$	
$p \to r$	13
$p \to (r \lor s)$	16
$(p \lor q) \to r$	
$p \to r$	13
$(p \,\&\, s) \to r$	15
$(p \,\&\, s) \to (r \,\&\, s)$	17
$(p \lor q) \to r$	
$p \to r$	13
$p \to (r \lor s)$	16
$(p \lor s) \to (r \lor s)$	18
$p \to q$	
$(p \,\&\, r) \to q$	15
$(p \,\&\, r) \to (q \lor s)$	16
$p \to q$	
$(p \,\&\, r) \to q$	15
$(p \,\&\, r) \to (q \,\&\, r)$	17
$p \to q$	
$p \to (q \lor s)$	16
$(p \lor s) \to (q \lor s)$	18
$p \to -(q \lor r)$	
$p \to (-q \,\&\, -r)$	10
$p \to -q$	12
$-(p \,\&\, q) \to r$	
$(-p \lor -q) \to r$	11
$-p \to r$	13
$p \lor r$	21

$(p \lor q) \to r$	
$-r \to -(p \lor q)$	14
$-r \to (-p \,\&\, -q)$	10
$p \to (q \,\&\, r)$	
$-(q \,\&\, r) \to -p$	14
$(-q \lor -r) \to -p$	11
$p \to (q \,\&\, r)$	
$p \to q$	12
$-(p \,\&\, -q)$	22
$p \lor q$	
$-p \to q$	20
$-p \to (q \lor r)$	16
$(-p \lor r) \to (q \lor r)$	18
$p \lor q$	
$-p \to q$	20
$-p \to (q \lor r)$	16
$p \lor (q \,\&\, r)$	
$p \lor q$	6
$-p \to q$	20
$p \lor (q \,\&\, r)$	
$p \lor q$	6
$-p \to q$	20
$(-p \,\&\, s) \to q$	15
$(-p \,\&\, s) \to (q \,\&\, s)$	17
$p \lor (q \,\&\, r)$	
$p \lor q$	6
$-p \to q$	20
$(-p \,\&\, s) \to q$	15
$-p \to (q \,\&\, r)$	
$-p \to q$	12
$p \lor q$	21
$p \,\&\, (q \lor r)$	
$(p \,\&\, q) \lor (p \,\&\, r)$	5
$-(p \,\&\, q) \to (p \,\&\, r)$	20

$-(p \ \& \ q) \rightarrow r$	
$(-p \lor -q) \rightarrow r$	11
$-p \rightarrow r$	13

$p \rightarrow (q \lor r)$	
$-(q \lor r) \rightarrow -p$	14
$(-q \ \& \ -r) \rightarrow -p$	10

$(p \ \& \ q) \rightarrow r$	
$-r \rightarrow -(p \ \& \ q)$	14
$-r \rightarrow (-p \lor -q)$	11

$(p \lor q) \rightarrow r$	
$p \rightarrow r$	13
$-(p \ \& \ -r)$	22

$(p \lor q) \rightarrow (r \ \& \ s)$	
$(p \lor q) \rightarrow r$	12
$p \rightarrow r$	13
$-(p \ \& \ -r)$	22

$p \lor q$	
$-p \rightarrow q$	20
$(-p \ \& \ r) \rightarrow q$	15

$p \lor q$	
$-p \rightarrow q$	20
$(-p \ \& \ r) \rightarrow q$	15
$(-p \ \& \ r) \rightarrow (q \ \& \ r)$	17

$(p \ \& \ q) \lor r$	
$p \lor r$	7
$-p \rightarrow r$	20

$p \lor (q \ \& \ r)$	
$p \lor q$	6
$-p \rightarrow q$	20
$-p \rightarrow (q \lor s)$	16

$p \lor (q \ \& \ r)$	
$p \lor q$	6
$-p \rightarrow q$	20
$-p \rightarrow (q \lor s)$	16
$(-p \lor s) \rightarrow (q \lor s)$	18

$(-p \lor -q) \rightarrow r$	
$-p \rightarrow r$	13
$p \lor r$	21

$[p \ \& \ (q \lor r)] \rightarrow s$	
$[(p \ \& \ q) \lor (p \ \& \ r)] \rightarrow s$	5
$(p \ \& \ q) \rightarrow s$	13

References

Anderson, J., & Johnstone, H. *Natural deduction*. Belmont: Wadsworth, 1962.

Arieti, S. *Interpretation of schizophrenia*. New York: Bruner, 1955.

Banks, W., & Hill, D. The apparent magnitude of number scaled by random production. *Journal of Experimental Psychology Monograph*, 1974, **102**, 353–376.

Belnap, N. D. Tonk, plonk, and plink. *Analysis*, 1962, **22**, 130–134. Reprinted in P. F. Strawson (Ed.), *Philosophical logic*. New York: Oxford University Press, 1967.

Bourne, L. *Human conceptual behavior*. Boston: Allyn and Bacon, 1966.

Bruner, J. S., Goodnow, J., & Austin, G. *A study of thinking*. New York: Wiley, 1956.

Burks, A. W. The logic of causal propositions. *Mind*, 1951, **60**, 363–382.

Bynum, T. W., Thomas, J. A., & Weitz, L. J. Truth-functional logic in formal operational thinking: Inhelder and Piaget's evidence. *Developmental Psychology*, 1972, **7**(2), 129–132.

Ceraso, J., & Provitera, A. Sources of error in syllogistic reasoning. *Cognitive Psychology*, 1971, **2**, 400–410.

Chapman, L., & Chapman, J. Atmosphere effect reexamined. *Journal of Experimental Psychology*, 1959, **58**(3), 220–226.

Chomsky, N. *Aspects of the theory of syntax*. Cambridge, Massachusetts: MIT Press, 1965.

Chomsky, N., Introduction to Schaff, A. *Language and cognition*. New York: McGraw-Hill, 1973.

Clark, H., & Chase, W. On the process of comparing sentences against pictures. *Cognitive Psychology*, 1972, **3**, 472–517.

Copi, I. *Symbolic logic*. London: Macmillan, 1967.

Flavell, J. *The developmental psychology of Jean Piaget*. Princeton, New Jersey: Van Nostrand-Rheinhold, 1963.

Fodor, J. D. Some reflections on L. S. Vygotsky's *Thought and Language*. *Cognition*, 1972, **1**(1), 83–96.

Fodor, J. D. Formal linguistics and formal logic. In J. Lyons (Ed.), *New horizons in linguistics*. London: Penguin Books, 1970.

Fodor, J. D., & Garrett, M. Some reflections on competence and performance. In J. Lyons & R. J. Wales (Eds.), *Psycholinguistic papers*. Edinburgh: Edinburgh University Press, 1966.

263

Frase, L. T. Validity judgments of syllogisms in relation to two sets of terms. *Journal of Educational Psychology,* 1966, **57,** 239–244.

Geiss, J., & Zwicky, A. On invited inferences. *Linguistic Inquiry,* 1971, **2,** 561–566.

Gentzen, G. *Recherches sur la deduction logique.* Paris: Presses Universitaires de France, 1955.

Grize, J. B. Du groupemerrt au nombre: Essai de formalisation. In P. Greco, J. Grize, S. Papert, & J. Piaget. (Eds.), *Études d'épistemologie génétique.* Vol. II. *Problemes de la construction du nombre.* Paris: Presses Universitaires de France, 1960.

Grize, J. B. Du groupement au nombre. In L. Apostel *et al. La filiation des structures.* Paris: Universitaires de France, 1963.

Hall, V., & Kingsley, R. Conservation and equilibration theory. *The Journal of Genetic Psychology,* 1968, **113,** 195–213.

Henle, M. On the relation between logic and thinking. *Psychological Review,* 1962, **69,** 366–378.

Hintikka, J. *Knowledge and belief.* Ithaca, New York: Cornell University Press, 1962.

Hughes, G., & Cresswell, M. *An introduction to modal logic.* London: Methuen, 1968.

Hunter, I. The solving of three term series problems. *British Journal of Psychology,* 1957, **48,** 286–298.

Inhelder, B., & Piaget, J. *The growth of logical thinking.* New York: Basic Books, 1958.

Jacobs, R., & Rosenbaum, P. *English transformational grammar.* Waltham: Blaisdell, 1968.

Jeffrey, R. *Formal logic.* New York: McGraw-Hill, 1967.

Johnson-Laird, P. N. Models of deduction. In R. J. Falmagne (Ed.), *Reasoning: Representation and process in children and adults.* Hillsdale, New Jersey: Lawrence Erlbaum Associates, 1975.

Katz, J. Some remarks on Quine on analyticity. *Journal of Philosophy,* 1967, **64,** 36–52.

Katz, J. *The underlying reality of language.* New York: Harper & Row, 1971.

Katz, J. *Semantic theory.* New York: Harper & Row, 1972.

Katz, J., & Bever, T. *The fall and rise of empiricism.* Indiana University Linguistics Club, 1974.

Keyser, S., & Halle, M. What we do when we speak. In P. Kolers & M. Eden (Eds.), *Recognizing patterns.* Cambridge, Massachusetts: MIT Press, 1968.

Lakoff, G. Linguistics and natural logic. In D. Davidson & G. Harman (Eds.), *Semantics of natural language.* Dordrecht: Reidel, 1972.

Lenneberg, E. *Biological foundations of language.* New York: Wiley, 1967.

Maher, B. A. *Principles of psychopathology.* New York: McGraw-Hill, 1966.

Mates, B. *Elementary logic.* New York: Oxford University Press, 1972.

Miller, G., & Isard, S. Free recall of self-embedded English sentences. *Information & Control,* 1964, **7,** 292–303.

Neimark, E. Development of comprehension of logical connectives. *Psychonomic Science,* 1970, **21,** 217–219.

Neimark, E., & Slotnick, N. Development of the understanding of logical connectives. *Journal of Educational Psychology,* 1970, **61**(6), 451–460.

Newell, A., & Simon, H. GPS, a program that simulates human thought. In E. Feigenbaum & J. Feldman (Eds.), *Computers and thought.* New York: McGraw-Hill, 1963. (a)

Newell, A., & Simon, H. Computers in psychology. In R. Luce, R. Bush, & E. Galanter

(Eds.), *Handbook of mathematical psychology.* Vol. 1. New York: Wiley, 1963. (b)

Newell, A., & Simon, H. *Human problem solving.* Englewood Cliffs, New Jersey: Prentice-Hall, 1972.

Nilsson, N. *Problem-solving methods in artificial intelligence.* New York: McGraw-Hill, 1971.

Olson, D. R. *Cognitive development.* New York: Academic Press, 1970.

Osherson, D. N. *Logical abilities in children.* Vol 1: *Organization of length and class concepts: Empirical consequences of a piagetian formalism.* Hillsdale, New Jersey: Lawrence Erlbaum associates, 1974. (a)

Osherson, D. N. *Logical abilities in children.* Vol. 2: *Logical inference: Underlying operations.* Hillsdale, New Jersey: Lawrence Erlbaum Associates, 1974. (b)

Osherson, D. N. Models of logical thinking. In R. J. Falmagne (Ed.), *Reasoning: Representation and process in children and adults.* Hillsdale, New Jersey: Lawrence Erlbaum Associates, 1975.

Papert, S. Sur la logique Piagetienne. In Apostel, *et al. La filiation des structures.* Paris: Universitaires de France, 1963.

Parsons, C. Inhelder and Piaget's *The growth of logical thinking. British Journal of Psychology,* 1960, **51**(1), 75–84.

Pascual-Leone, J. A mathematical model for the transition rule in Piaget's developmental stages. *Acta psychologica,* 1970, **32**, 301–345.

Piaget, J. *Classes, relations et nombres.* Paris: Vrin, 1942.

Piaget, J. *Traite de logique.* Paris: Colin, 1949.

Piaget, J. *The psychology of intelligence.* London: Routledge, 1950.

Piaget, J. *Logic and psychology.* New York: Basic Books, 1957.

Piaget, J. *The child's conception of number.* New York: Norton, 1965.

Piaget, J. *Genetic epistemology.* New York: Columbia University Press, 1970. (a)

Piaget, J. *Structuralism* New York: Basic Books, 1970. (b)

Piaget, J. *The child and reality.* New York: Grossman, 1973.

Piaget, J., & Inhelder, B. *The psychology of the child.* New York: Basic Books, 1969.

Pinard, A., & Laurendeau, M. "Stage" in Piaget's cognitive-developmental theory: Exegesis of a concept. In D. Elkind & H. Flavell (Eds.), *Studies in cognitive development.* New York: Oxford University Press, 1969.

Prawitz, D. *Natural Deduction: A proof-theoretical study,* Stockholm: Almqvist & Wiksell, 1965.

Prior, A. N. The runabout inference-ticket. *Analysis,* 1960, **21**, 38–39. Reprinted in Strawson P. F. (Ed.), *Philosophical logic.* New York: Oxford, University Press, 1967.

Prytulak, L. S. Natural language mediation. *Cognitive Psychology,* 1971, **2**(1), 1–56.

Putnam, H. Reductionism and the nature of psychology. *Cognition,* 1973, **2**(1), 131–146.

Quine, W. V. *Philosophy of logic.* Englewood Cliffs, New Jersey: Prentice-Hall, 1970.

Quine, W. V. *Methods of logic.* New York: Holt, Rinehart & Winston, 1972. (a)

Quine, W. V. Methodological reflections on current linguistic theory. In D. Davidson & G. Harman (Eds.), *Semantics of natural language.* Dordrecht: Reidel, 1972. (b)

Revlis, R. Two models of syllogistic reasoning: Feature selection and conversion. Unpublished manuscript, 1974.

Revlis, R. Syllogistic reasoning: Logical deductions from a complex data base. In R. J. Falmagne (Ed.), *Reasoning: Representation and process in children and adults.* New Jersey: Lawrence Erlbaum Associates, 1975.

Savin, H. Language, thought, and the English-speaker's conception of reality. Unpublished manuscript, University of Pennsylvania, 1972.

Savin, H. Meaning and concepts: A review of Jerrold J. Katz' *Semantic theory*. *Cognition*, 1973, **2**(2), 213–238.

Shapiro, B., & O'Brien, T. Logical thinking in children ages six through thirteen. *Child Development*, 1970, **41**, 823–829.

Sinclair, H. Some comments on Fodor's "Reflections on L. S. Vygotsky's *Thought and language.*" *Cognition*, 1972, **1**(2), 317–318.

Skyrms, B. *Choice and chance*. Belmont: Dickenson, 1966.

Snyder, D. P. *Modal logic and its applications*. Princeton, New Jersey: Van Nostrand-Rheinhold, 1971.

Springston, F., & Clark, J. *And* and *or*, or the comprehension of pseudo-imperatives. *Journal of Verbal Learning and Verbal Behavior*, in press.

Stoll, R. *Set theory and logic*. San Francisco: W. H. Freeman, 1963.

Strawson, P. F. (Ed.) *Philosophical logic*. New York: Oxford University Press, 1967.

Suppes, P. *Introduction to logic*. New York: Van Nostrand, 1957.

Suppes, P. On the behavioral foundations of mathematical concepts. *Monographs of the Society for Research in Child Development*, 1965, **30**(1),

Taplin, J. E., & Staudenmayer, H. Interpretation of abstract conditional sentences in deductive reasoning. *Journal of Verbal Learning and Verbal Behavior*, 1973, **12**, 530–542.

Toulmin, S. The concept of "stages" in psychological development. In T. Mischel (Ed.), *Cognitive development and epistemology*. New York: Academic Press, 1971.

Trabasso, T., Riley, C. A., & Wilson, E. G. The representation of linear order and spatial strategies in reasoning: A developmental study. In R. J. Falmagne (Ed.), *Reasoning: Representation and process in children and adults*. Lawrence Hillsdale, New Jersey: Lawrence Erlbaum Associates, 1975.

Wason, P. Reasoning about a rule. *Quarterly Journal of Experimental Psychology*, 1968, **20**, 273–281.

Wason, P., & Johnson-Laird, P. N. *Psychology of reasoning*. Cambridge, Massachusetts: Harvard University Press, 1972.

Whitehead, A., & Russell, B. *Principia mathematica*. Cambridge, England: Cambridge University Press, 1970.

Whorf, B. *Language, thought and reality*. Cambridge, Massachusetts: MIT Press, 1964.

Wilkins, M. The effect of changed material on the ability to do formal syllogistic reasoning. *Archives of psychology*, 1928, **16**(102).

Author Index

The numbers in *italics* refer to the pages on which the complete references are listed.

Subject Index